SURVIVAL RUSSIAN

an insider's guide to the
words, phrases, idioms and customs
you need to survive, and thrive, in Russia

enlarged second edition

mikhail ivanov

© 2007, Russian Information Services, Inc.

All rights reserved. No part of this guide may be reproduced or transmitted in any form, by any means mechanical or electronic, including photocopying, recording, or any information storage retrieval system now known or to be invented, without the expressed written permission of the publisher.

Published by:

Russian Information Services, Inc.
PO Box 567
Montpelier, VT 05601

802-223-4955 phone
802-223-6105 fax
orders@russianlife.net
www.russianlife.net

Printed and bound in the U.S.

Russian Information Services, Montpelier, VT USA

Library of Congress Control Number: 2007923339

ISBN: 978-1-880100-56-1

Cover photograph:
Minin, Pozharsky and Spassky.
Red Square, Moscow
by Paul E. Richardson

Table of Contents

Compliments & Insults
"You Look Like a Cucumber" and Other Compliments. 10
What's in a Name? 12
Russian You'd Rather Not Hear 14
Insults That Taste Russian. 15
Open Sesame, Russian-style 16

Fathers & Sons
No Longer a Comrade, Not Yet a Mister. 20
You Say You Want a Revolution?. 21
From *Devushka* to *Babushka*, Non-Stop 23
The *Babushka* Factor 25
The Flowers of Life on Their Parents' Grave 27
No Sweat, Dude, Really!. 28

Out & About
Why Going Dutch is not Russian 32
Ending Telephone Hangups. 34
Of Tickets, Hares and Dozing Fathers 36
Beware the Teapots and Snowdrops. 38
To Queue or Not to Queue 40

Euphemisms & Expletives
Show Your Colors. 44
Of Despicable Metal and Easy Behavior 46
Invoking Heaven and Hell 49
Walking A Verst in Russia's *Lapti* 51

Russlish & Beyond
A Few "False Friends". 54
Khalyava: All Play and No Work 55
Excuse My Russian 57
Survival German. 58
When P.R. Sounds Like Samovar. 60
Excuse My English 61
Linguistic Escapades in *Lingua Russe* 63

War & Competition
Russia, Widen Your Step! 68
War-Torn Language 70
It's the Participation That Counts! 71
Setting the Bar High 73

Weather & Seasons
Don't Ask Me for Snow in Winter. 76
It's Spring, Say "Thank You" to the Party!. 77
The General Zima Factor 79

Power & Glory
Dear Demosthenes 82
Tsar Struck. 84
Pulling the Blanket to One's Side 85
Crisis Russian 87
Tsar Boris' Firm Handshake 89
Lost in Translation 91
Dog Tails 93

Flora & Fauna
How Does Your Garden Grow?. 96
Life With Mushrooms 98
The Bear's Favors and Favorite Meals 99
Animal Instincts 101
Lie Down With the Dogs... 103
Of Fish and Cockroaches 105
Vegetarian Disses and Disguises 107

Moscow & St. Petersburg
Moscow in Sunshine and Tears 110
Dueling Capitals 111

Life & Death
How Do We Feel, Doctor?. 116
Still Alive, Smoker?. 118
Matters of Life and Death 120

Women & Men
Talking Man-to-Man. 124
The Language of Love 126
Fishing for Tenderness 128
Flirting and Courting 129

Figures & Measures
Better Than a Hundred Rubles. 132
The Power of Seven 133
Just a Minute. 135
50 and Counting. 136

Music & Art
Can I Sip on Your Tchaikovsky?..248
Who Shall Judge?...142
Lights, Camera..144
Drag Yourself to This!..146
Painting in Bedroom Tones 147
Stomping on the Throat...149

Food & Drink
When the Foam Goes Down......................................152
To Tula, Samovar Optional 153
A Tale of Three Sandpipers..155
Here's to You and Us..157
Cooling Off the Tubes 159

Etiquette & Deceptions
It's the Little Things That Count 162
A Little Filler, You Know, Goes a Long Way.........................163
The Enobling Deception 165
Promises, Promises 166
All Play and No Work..168
The Discreet Charm of Avos 169
He Who Laughs Last..171

Linguistics & Ephemera
Fishing With Dried Pasta 174
Getting the Endings Right 175
An Introduction to Russian Acronyms 177
A Small Crowd of Oxymorons.....................................179
Virtual Russian 180
Repeat and Ye Shall Learn 182

Study Guide 185

Word & Phrase Index 236

Subject Index 250

Dedication

To my mother, for instilling in me a talent for languages.
To my wife, for putting up with that talent.

– Mikhail Ivanov

Preface

This book's title may give the wrong impression.

The Russian you can learn from this book is not about survival in the sense of getting by. It is about surviving in the sense of successfully blending in: achieving a superior level of cultural awareness and distinction with your Russian. A run of the mill Russian text might teach you how to ask, "Which way to the bathroom?" The culturally-savvy *Survival Russian* in this book teaches you instead euphemisms like, **куда́ царь пешко́м ходи́л** (where the tsar went on foot – page 84) and **места́ не столь отдалённые** (not so distant places – page 47).

Survival Russian would not have been born or have matured into one of the favorite columns in our magazine, **Russian Life**, were it not for Mikhail Ivanov. It is a column he was born (and educated) to write, so attuned is he to Russian and American (and French) linguistic and cultural differences.

Thanks to Mikhail, *Survival Russian* is about much more than language. Even a casual reading of these columns shows that they present a culturo-linguistic history of Russia in transformation, from 1995 to 2007. Through the essays in this book, you can follow the linguistic adventures of reformers and communists, feel once again the uncertainty of the 1996 elections, and relive the tumultuous era of Boris Yeltsin. To help readers understand context, we note the author and original publication date at the end of each column.

In all, this volume compiles 12 years of *Survival Russian* columns. Of the 95 columns published here, 81 were written by Mikhail Ivanov between 1995 and the end of 2006. Eleven were written by Lina Rozovskaya, and one each were contributed by guest columnists Alex Lane, Naum Sindalovsky and Lynn Visson. Cartoonists for the column over the years (reprinted here) have included: Vladimir Mochalov, Valery Mokhov, Victor Bogorad and Alex Barrett.

While the columns are essentially reproduced here as they were printed in **Russian Life**, in some instances this book's looser limitations on space have allowed us to include bits of columns that had to be cut from the magazine. Most significantly, presentation in book format allows us to make this collection more useful to students and teachers. To that end, we have included a Subject Index, a Word and Phrase Index and a chapter-by-chapter Study Guide. This latter is designed so that the student can write definitions in the right column, then quiz himself or herself by covering up the left or right columns.

Наслаждайтесь!

Paul E. Richardson
Publisher

Compliments

Insults

"You Look Like a Cucumber" and Other Compliments

Differences in national etiquette can prove a virtual minefield. What's accepted in the U.S. can be impolite in Russia. To give a very simple example: Russians don't usually find it polite to ask over the phone: "Who's calling please?" ("**Кто его / её спрáшивает?**") This question is considered indiscreet. Don't ask why – just mark it up to cultural differences.

Similarly, it is considered rude in the U.S. to ask someone how much they make, but in Russia most people (with the exception of the *nouveaux riches* and the mafia) would be happy to tell you their salary. There are a number of ways to ask this question. So, be prepared to hear "**Скóлько ты получáешь?**" or "**Скóлько ты зарабáтываешь?**" every now and then. A true Russian would phrase it as follows: "**Скóлько у тебя выхóдит в мéсяц?**" Or, even more to the point, "**Скóлько у тебя выхóдит в мéсяц 'чи́стыми'?**" (literally: "How much clean money do you bring home?"). The opposite of net salary is "dirty money": "**Скóлько у тебя выхóдит 'гря́зными'?**" (i.e. not taking account of deductions).

Russians working in the private sector are gradually getting used to keeping their salaries secret. In face-to-face conversation you may come across the humorous subterfuge "**Это не телефóнный разговóр**" (it's not something we should talk about over the phone). Take note of it and use it in difficult situations.

Speaking of politesse, paying compliments to Russians, particularly men, is an art in itself. The best way for one middle-aged man to praise another of would be to say, "**Я бы с ним в развéдку пошёл**" ("I'd go with him on a reconnaissance mission"). This is the top compliment amongst Russian men, dating back to World War II. People would trust each other like brothers once they had been together on a reconnaissance mission. Younger generations like this expression too.

Another compliment goes: "**Ты сегóдня вы́глядишь как огурéц (огýрчик)**" ("You look like a cucumber today"). This might sound strange to an American, but the implication is that you look fresh, not green, waxen, or crunchy.

"**Ты настоя́щий мужи́к**" ("You're a real *muzhik*," i.e. regular guy) stresses a man's macho side. As does "**Ты настоя́щий пáрень**" ("You're a real guy"). Also use "**Стари́к, ты сегóдня в удáре**" ("Hey old buddy, you're in great shape today") or "**Ты сегóдня превзошёл самогó себя́**" ("You've surpassed yourself today").

The younger generation of Russians, especially the *nouveaux-riches*, like to be complimented on their expensive purchases. Do not ignore your Russian friend's new tie from Pierre Cardin or Yves Saint-Laurent. Say: "**кла́ссный га́лстук**" or "**кла́ссный пиджа́к**" ("classy tie, classy jacket"). You do not need much linguistic variety with New Russians – you can get away with just the adjective **кла́ссный**.

Compliments for Russian women are easier. First and foremost, remember that just like elsewhere, Russian women do not like to be asked about their age and welcome remarks like "I would not have guessed so many years." (**Я бы Вам сто́лько не дал**). If you do dare ask a woman about her age, the likely answer would be "**А ско́лько бы Вы мне да́ли?**" ("How many years would you give me?").

And yet in some exceptional cases it's good to mention a woman's age. For instance, if you're invited to a birthday party and the host is a woman who just turned 45, toast her and say "**В со́рок пять ба́ба я́годка опя́ть**" ("A woman at 45 is a berry again"). According to Russian beliefs, 45 is a renaissance age for women.

"**Ты сего́дня вы́глядишь на 100 рубле́й**" ("You look like 100 rubles today") was something people used to say amongst friends back in Soviet times, when 100 rubles was a fortune. It can still be used, even though a R100 note is now no more than a souvenir. Today, "you look like R100,000" would be more logical if it did not sound so awkward. So, try something less inflationary, like "**Ты сего́дня вы́глядишь на 'пять с плю́сом'**" ("You look like a 'five plus' today" – the highest mark in the Russian educational system).

A still better option is to say something classical, like: "**Ты сего́дня вы́глядишь бесподо́бно / блестя́ще / восхити́тельно / сногсшиба́тельно**" ("Nobody compares to you, you look radiant, you look terrific, you knock me out").

You can also be almost certain to please a Russian woman if you tell her you think she's lost weight. "**Мне ка́жется, ты похуде́ла.**" It's especially pertinent now that most spouses of New Russians undergo weight loss programs, gorging themselves on kilos of Herbalife.

Accordingly, if you see that a Russian woman has put on weight, keep your observations to yourself. If you really want to spoil your relationship, take note of the Russian for "you put on weight": **ты попра́вилась**.

Women's clothes are another potential object of flattery. The conventional phrase would be "**Это пла́тье тебе́ о́чень идёт**" ("This dress becomes you"). But more typically Russian is "**Это пла́тье на тебе́ сиди́т, как влито́е**" – the equivalent of the English "it fits you like a glove."

Finally, even if you forget all these phrases, just say something positive and your compliment will hit the target. As the Russian saying goes, **До́брое сло́во и ко́шке прия́тно** (Even a cat likes a good word).

Mikhail Ivanov (November 1995)

What's in a Name?

Astrologists claim that first names can have an impact on people's destinies: a Victor will always be victorious, a Yevgeny noble, etc. Hardcore Marxists preaching the priority of the material over the spiritual might disagree, but sometimes common sense is a factor too.

After all, the most ardent of these materialists baptized their children with names like Vladlen, Ninel or Marlen. Now in their late seventies, the persons carrying these names probably regret their parents' hasty decisions. Why? Because they are no longer "on the side of history," so to speak. Vladlen, which at first simply sounds corny, is actually an acronym for Vladimir Lenin. The girl's name Ninel, as you can probably guess, is just 'Lenin' spelled backwards, and Marlen? Marx and Lenin, of course.

So, using more traditional first names may seem much safer. But is it really? The Russian language, as the writer Ivan Turgenev rightly pointed out, is so "great and mighty," that it can turn the most innocuous linguistic term upside down and make a mockery of it.

For example, if you hear someone say about a girl: "she's just some Masha" [the diminutive for Maria] (**она какая-то Маша**), it means she has simple, provincial looks or manners (or both). There is a more positive idiom for Masha too – when someone admires something or someone (usually a girl) with envy because it/he/she cannot be acquired or conquered, he may say: "**хороша Маша – да не наша**," ("Masha's good but she's not ours").

Another meaningful first name is Vasya (the diminutive of Vassily). "Oh, you Vasya!" a Russian might say about a hapless buffoon or simpleton. Fedya (from Fyodor) has similar connotations, and yet a common schoolboy **дразнилка** (tease) is: **Федя-Бредя съел медведя** (Fedya-Bredya ate a bear). Someone with Vasya-style proletarian looks and manners could also be called a **Паша с Уралмаша** – Pasha from Uralmash (a huge machine factory in the Urals).

Ваня and **Ванёк** (diminutives of Ivan) have similar meanings. For instance, someone who does not know his past or shows no interest in the history of his country or family is called **Иван, не помнящий родства** (Ivan Who Doesn't Remember His Roots).

If you know someone's telling you lies or talking sheer bull, you may invoke another name by saying "**Мели Емеля – твоя неделя**" ("Go on with your idle talk!" – Yemelya is a diminutive of Yemelyan).

There is at least one other idiom using a Russian first name – Kuzma – which became world-famous. Nikita Khrushchev promised the world on many occasions to show the USSR's enemies **Кузькину мать** ("Kuzka's mother" – Kuzka is a diminutive of Kuzma). **Показать Кузькину мать** means "to give someone a hard time."

Which brings to mind first names that can be hidden in verbs. For Kuzma is the root of the verb **подкузьмить** – to do something nasty to someone. The first name **Егор**, meanwhile, is part of the verb **объегорить** – to cheat or make a fool of someone.

These two verbs brought infamy to another communist leader, Boris Yeltsin's sworn enemy, the hardliner Yegor Ligachyov. Democrats supporting Yeltsin's liberal reforms used to carry banners saying things like **Нас не объегоришь и нас не подкузьмишь** (You won't fool us or best us), referring to Ligachyov's first name and patronymic – **Егор Кузьмич**.

Kuzmich would very much have liked to send Boris **куда Макар телят не гонял** – where Makar didn't send his calves (i.e. a long way away). In general, beware of Makars – in Russian, this first name is associated with poor luck, hence the proverb, **На бедного Макара все шишки валятся** (A person on whose head every imaginable misfortune rains).

In the end, Mikhail Gorbachev managed to **объего́рить** Ligachyov, and finally fired him. What Ligachyov and other ousted hardliners still say about their nemesis can be summed up in another name-derived saying, **Федо́т – да не тот** ("Fedot, but not the one I want" – i.e. not quite the person we wanted). Gorbachev might reply, "**по Се́ньке и ша́пка**" ("Everyone gets exactly what he deserves" – Senka is a diminutive of Semyon).

The evasive style Gorbachev adopted in press-conferences and interviews suggests another idiom with two more first names – **Фома́** and **Ерёма**. Journalists might say about Gorby – "**Ему́ про Фому́, а он – про Ерёму**" ("We ask him about one thing and he talks about something completely different.").

Speaking of Mikhails – at first sight this name looks unassailable. But don't be too sure. Russian kids tease Mikhails, saying "**Михаи́л коро́в дои́л**" ("Mikhail milked cows"). In Gorbachev's case this tease was quite suitable – he was once responsible for agriculture in the Politburo. Another expression, "**Ми́шка-Ми́шка, где твоя́ улы́бка?**" ("Mishka, Mishka, where's your smile?" – taken from a 1950s film soundtrack) became appropriate last year, when Gorby got less than 1% in Russia's 1996 Presidential elections.

That's about it for first name idioms. By the way, there are also some great teases with Volodya (the diminutive of Vladimir) and Anton which, unfortunately, we can't share with you here. They're not quite printable, but they're certainly fun and the rhyme's perfect. If you're dying to know more, just ask a Russian friend!

Mikhail Ivanov (Jan. 1997)

Russian You'd Rather Not Hear

There are many phrases in Russian that you'd rather not hear, particularly while doing business in Russia.

Begin with **разбо́рка**. This new, and very popular slang word literally means "a settling of accounts," and is derived from the verb **разбира́ться**.

The noun phrase derived from the newly active **престу́пный мир** (criminal world). If a resident of this world wants to threaten a competitor, he calls the **братва́** (literally, the brethren, but in fact a gang) to organize a **разбо́рка**.

The word also has seeped over into the political and business worlds.

Even Evgeny Kiselyov, anchor of the popular political TV news show *Itogi* uses the word now and again while talking about arguments in parliament or differences between political factions, e.g. "**разбо́рки** broke out at a meeting of the Russian Security Council when President Yeltsin reprimanded Defense Minister Grachev for poor command of Russian troops in Chechnya."

As if this were not enough, the book that topped the Russian hardcover bestseller list on March 1 was a novel titled *Razborka*.

Russian intellectuals cringe when they hear such un-schooled language in everyday speech. But you may well win some points with business acquaintances by casually tossing this word into discussions.

A second, less colloquial, but no less common phrase is, **в при́нципе, да**. It means, quite literally, "quite possibly, maybe." Try to obtain a definite "yes" or "no." **В при́нципе** has (in principle) become a tool for linguistic evasiveness.

Speaking of evasiveness, be sure to memorize the Russian equivalent for "let's do lunch": **созво́нимся** (literally: "Let's call each other"). This means, in fact: "You may call me if you want, but I won't bother calling you." If someone says, in parting, "**Я Вам сам позвоню́**" or "**Перезвоню́**," the message is clear: consider our business relationship ended.

Such verbal parrying is best described by another popular expression (which you could, in fact, use to accuse someone of evasiveness): **ве́шать лапшу́ на у́ши** (literally: to hang noodles on someone's ears). If someone hangs noodles from your ears, they are just pretending to be serious and are using lies or falsehoods to avoid you.

Not quite in the noodle-hanging class, but nonetheless diversionary, is the widespread use of the adverb **норма́льно**. A stock answer among acquaintances for the ubiquitous "**Как дела́?**," this word can mean anything from "not bad" to "OK" to "not so good." So, when a business partner or employee says things are going **норма́льно**, you might well want to probe a bit deeper.

If you can deal with these and other verbal deflections, your Russian partner may well describe you as savvy: "**Его го́лыми рука́ми не возмёшь**" ("This one cannot be taken barehanded"). Which sure beats going around with noodles on your ears or ending up in a **разбо́рка** with your partner.

Mikhail Ivanov (April 1995)

Insults That Taste Russian

With so many borrowings entering the language of those who once called themselves *russichi*, it is getting harder and harder to tell what is a true Russian word, if there even is such a thing. To paraphrase the famous saying: scratch a Russian word and you will find a Turkish, Tartar or a Greek root. Well, except perhaps for authentically Slavic words like Yarilo (the Sun God in pagan Rus).

But let's forget about etymology – an all-too-serious science for this space. Instead, we will simply consider some descriptive words which sound and look authentically Russian, and which are fun to say and use (if not always a good choice among "educated folk").

Start with **хмырь**, which forced its way into the language from criminal argot. How do we translate this? Forget the dictionary. As one of my teachers used to say, "true translation begins where the dictionary ends." A **хмырь** is an obnoxious, arrogant and unrefined person whose very appearance makes you cringe. A sleezeball with a slovenly gait who makes passes at your daughter would be a **хмырь**. An arrogant, ill-shaven tourist, smelling of booze and trying to jump the queue at Sheremetyevo customs? Definitely a **хмырь**.

Another pejorative of this ilk is **прохиндей**, best defined as "a sly dog." The film *Прохиндиада*, is the story of such a **прохиндей** – a Soviet-style fixer with contacts in both high and low places, someone who could open any door. A **прохиндей** could thus be seen as an entrepreneurial **хмырь**. An unscrupulous, obnoxious salesperson could well fit this image, but then in today's Russia, those characteristics are less pejorative than they used to be.

Here's another: **разгильдяй**. This is someone who may be nice, but who has a low sense of discipline, commitment and no goals in life. It is someone you cannot trust with anything serious.

Халдей is another tasty Russian word. Formerly a synonym for "lackey" (in pre-revolutionary Russia), in post-revolutionary Russia it is applied almost exclusively to waiters or barmen. It is almost an onomatopoeia that conveys all of the distaste that Russians harbor for waiters. If you are having lunch with a New Russian – a real **хмырь** – and want to watch his jaw drop, say: "Let's call the **халдей**!"

To similarly mesmerize a Russian professor with a colloquialism is considerably more difficult, but still possible. It's a matter of timing. For instance, if you meet a stereotypical absent-minded professor who is surrounded by piles of dusty books and has trouble focusing, take a deep breath and say: "**У Вас тут такáя катавáсия!**" Instead of taking offense, the prof will tip his battered hat to you. **Катавáсия**, as it turns out, has a Greek root (*katabasis*

– a canticle sung by two choirs) and means – in a figurative sense, mess, muddle, disorder, piles of problems and troubles.

To the new Russian with whom you supped, such a professor is a **грамотей** – a good-for-nothing scholar or scribe. Meanwhile, to the professor, the New Russian *parvenu* is a **невежда** (ignoramus), who sees little use in knowledge for its own sake.

You can hardly be accused of sinking to either of these extremes if you take the trouble to add these **словечки** (little words) to your linguistic **кондуит**, so that you might at some point **козырнуть этими словами** (use these words as a trump card).

Now a **грамотей** might tell you that **кондуит** (from the French *conduite* – conduct, behavior) is hardly a tasty "Russian" word. Plus, it means at best a "conduct sheet," not a "notebook for new vocabulary." But, well, in modern Russian life, **кондуит** is used to mean a thick diary or a heavy notebook where one can store names, data, planned meetings and other information. So there really is no problem storing tasty new Russian words there. All the more so that you can later pronounce them with gusto – **со смаком** that is…

Mikhail Ivanov (September 2005)

Open Sesame, Russian-style

Some phrases in Russian seem at first sight to be normal, harmless everyday expressions. Put in context, though, they prove to be magic words – the equivalent of Ali Baba in the fairytale about the 40 thieves saying "Open Sesame" at the entrance to the cave full of treasures.

Here is a good case in point. At a recent interview with a Russian candidate applying for a position at a Western company, the employer wanted to find out about the candidate's current salary. Not an easy question to ask – at least by Western standards. So what does the Russian manager of the company do? He asks: "**Если не секрет, сколько Вы получаете?**" ("If it's not a secret, how much do you make?"). "If it's not a secret" is a good, disarming linguistic subterfuge, and in this case it worked. The sum in question was revealed. The formula is friendly, almost confidential, and invites the interviewee to be sincere – as if the interviewer were to say: "How could there possibly be any secrets between you and me?!"

Another puzzle. How can you ask someone for a favor and make the plea sound so irresistible that it cannot be refused? There are two options. Instead of a simple: **пожалуйста** (please) try this for a change: "**Не в службу, а в дружбу**" ("For friendship, not as part of your job"). Who would refuse to do a favor for the sake of friendship? "**Не в службу, а в дружбу, принесите нам кофейку**" ("For friendship, not as part of your job, bring us some coffee"), a boss asks his secretary. This formula, combined with a broad smile and a friendly hand on the shoulder, has melted many a hard heart.

A synonymous expression is "**Не сочтите за труд**" ("Don't think of it as a chore"). "**Не сочтите за труд, закройте дверь, а то здесь сквозняк**" ("Would you be so kind as to close the door; there's a draft in here"). It's not a big deal to close a door and nobody would really regard it as labor.

What does a Russian do when he is dying to give his opinion or advice on a subject he has nothing to do with? He starts his monologue with "**Конечно, это не моё дело…**" ("Of course, it's none of my business, but..."). And then he says whatever comes into his head, without really bothering about the other person's reaction. At least this formula helps to sweeten the pill.

What do Russians do when they are not sure of a piece of news but still want to spread it around? If someone questions the truth of it they just say: "**За что купи́л – за то и прода́л**" ("I sold it for the same price I bought it for"), which means "I'm just telling it the way I heard it."

The next "Open Sesame" dates back to Soviet times but is still pertinent today. How can someone jump a long line? Their best bet is to say: "**Я с ребёнком**" ("I have a child"), and then preferably display the child in question as proof. This usually works, but may draw the ire of a queuing *babushka*, who might tell you she has a grandson, but that's no reason for her to jump in. **Я с ребёнком** has evolved into an odd set phrase meaning simply "Let me pass." Some jokers use it when shoving their way onto an overcrowded bus.

One set of magic words, also hung over from the Soviet era, has a very definite purpose – to pave the way for offering a bribe. One example results from that classic situation on the road in Russia – you've been pulled over by the ubiquitous GAI (traffic police) for some obscure offense on the road. A brisk "**Мо́жет *так* договори́мся?**" ("Could we settle this between the two of us?") should obviate the need for a trip to the station.

Yet another magic formula is being used extensively in today's "transition to the market economy." No one in Russia can avoid dealing with plumbers, given the terrible state of most plumbing here. Whenever one comes to stop a leak which flooded a neighbor below, he'll likely start in with complaints about a shortage of spare parts, or by telling you he's not supposed to do this or that kind of work. To keep things brief, just tell him "**Я Вас отблагодарю́**" ("You'll be rewarded"), a euphemism for "I'll tip you." Whenever a little tribute is involved, remember this key phrase – you will make yourself clear. But don't forget to "reward" him or your neighbors can expect more deluges.

There is an alternative to the "rewarding" phrase: "**За мной не заржаве́ет**" means something like "I won't make you wait until my gratitude gets rusty," or "I owe you one and will reciprocate soon." This is not quite as universal as "You'll be rewarded," but is quite okay for dealing with plumbers and other proletarian professionals – after all, these guys know all about rust..."

Mikhail Ivanov (September 1995)

Fathers & Sons

No Longer a Comrade, Not Yet a Mister

Хоть горшко́м назови́, то́лько в пе́чку не ставь.
Call me a hot pot if you want, just don't put me in the oven.
Russian proverb

If someone tells you that Russians are no good at paying compliments to the fairer sex, don't take their word for it. Have you never heard a Moskvich call a 50-60-year-old shop assistant **де́вушка** (*devushka* – young lady)? Few shop assistants find this flattering, though, and you might even hear one snap back, "**Я тебе́ в ма́тери гожу́сь!**" ("I'm old enough to be your mother!"), or "**То́же мне де́вушку нашёл?**" ("I don't see any girls here!"). But what's a poor *muzhik* to do? He might call her **же́нщина** (woman), but this isn't very flattering, either. People just don't know what to call each other any more in the new Russia.

The Revolution of 1917 set itself the task of sweeping away old bourgeois forms of address. The resulting vacuum was plugged on every occasion with **това́рищ** (comrade). As a matter of fact, very few people know that in the 1920's and 1930's, there was even a special noun for the female comrade (**това́рка**). The name was so awkward that it didn't last long.

VLADIMIR MOCHALOV

An exception to the **това́рищ** rule was made for those under investigation or in prison. These souls lost the privilege of being called **това́рищ** and were relegated to **граждани́н** or **гражда́нка** (citizen). In Soviet detective movies, militia officers would make a point of harassing suspects with expressions like "**Тамбо́вский волк тебе́ това́рищ**" ("Your comrade is a wolf from Tambov") or "**Кому́ 'това́рищ,' а тебе́ 'граждани́н'**" ("Some people are 'comrades' but you're just a 'citizen'").

Граждани́н is mostly used today in official situations. The word has an urgency about it, as if a cool reminder of some higher authority. Ticket inspectors on buses like to say "**Граждани́н, Ваш биле́т!**" ("Your ticket, citizen!"). Or a *babushka* demanding a seat in the metro might say "**Граждани́н, подви́ньтесь!**" ("Citizen, make some room for me!").

The problem today is that since the latest Russian Revolution, labels like "comrade" and "citizen" no longer seem appropriate, and no consensus has emerged over what should replace them.

Long gone are the pleasant **суда́рыня** or **ба́рышня** (madam) from czarist times, which were applied to commoners as well as nobles. Russian men have hardly been any luckier: gone, too, are the courtly male identifiers **любе́знейший** (most courteous), **суда́рь** (sir), or the beautiful **ми́лостивый госуда́рь** (merciful monarch). Instead, nowadays you can still be in your early fifties and be called **молодо́й челове́к** (young man), or occasionally the more direct **мужчи́на** (man).

Some of the 20-something kiosk-Rockefellers have invented their own classifications, but these are hardly suitable for normal conversation. How can a gentleman call his *devushka* a **клю́шка** (hockey stick), a **моча́лка** (loofah) or **марты́шка** (monkey)? The same goes for men, with **чувáк** (no translation), **мэн** (man), or **братвá** (brethren). Along more traditional lines, there has been a slow revival among all strata of the population of the old words **мужи́к** and **бáба**, which, depending on their use, can be endearing or insulting.

The post-Soviet generation hasn't done much to remedy the situation, either. In business conversations, in official letters, on TV, and in parliamentary debates, **товáрищ** has simply become **господи́н** (mister). For example, ultra-nationalist Duma deputy Vladimir Zhirinovsky would be addressed as "mister," even though, by civilized peoples' standards, he behaves like a "comrade" or even a "citizen."

The most commonly used *tovarishch* replacements seem to be **господи́н** (mister) and **госпожá** (madam), reserved in Soviet times for foreigners from capitalist countries. But no matter how hard ex-Soviet *nomenklatura* and fledgling *bourgeoisie* try to use these once-forgotten terms, old habits die hard.

Even old museum guides resort to the trusty "comrade" in a pinch: "**Дáмы и господá, мину́точку внимáния!**" ("Ladies and gentlemen, may I have your attention for a minute!") But the group keeps on chattering. "**Грáждане, поти́ше пожáлуйста!**" ("Citizens, quiet please!") No effect. Finally, in exasperation the guide sighs "**Я не могу́ рабóтать в такóй обстанóвке, товáрищи!**" ("I just can't work in these conditions, comrades!") Finally, she has made herself clear. The visitors come to order and the tour resumes.

Mikhail Ivanov (August 1995)

You Say You Want a Revolution?

"It is either the revolution – which the Russians have managed to avoid so far, and which can be worse than reforms – or the lack of such."
Russian First Vice-premier Anatoly Chubais

Only a lazy man hasn't blamed the Bolsheviks for what they did to Russia, its economy, its culture, its people, and last but not least, its language.

Clumsy Bolshevik idioms still resonate: **револю́ция** (revolution), **октября́та** (Children of October), **ле́нинец** (Leninist), **меньшеви́к** (Menshevik), **завóд Крáсный Пролетáрий** (Red Proletarian factory), **кулаки́** (*kulaks*), **раскулáчивание** (dekulakization), **совéты** (councils), **колхóзы** (*kolkhozes*), etc. *ad nauseum*.

But little do most students (or teachers) of Russian know about the ways Soviet-style slang is still used in Russia today, by almost all strata of the population. Most usually it is applied in a humorous context. For this is how the pathetic revolutionary idioms sound like today.

If you are saddened by something meaningless, those older and "lucky" enough to have lived under socialism may reassure you with this version of "don't worry, be happy": **Это всё ерундá / фигня́ по сравнéнию с мировóй револю́цией** (this is nothing compared to world revolution).

Speaking of revolution, you might find a humorous context to employ a common rephrasing of the revolutionary song, *The International*. The original goes like this: **Мы стáрый мир разру́шим до основáнья, а затéм...** (We'll tear down the old world and then ...)

In the new interpretation, it is rewritten as: **Мы ста́рый мир разру́шим до основа́нья, а заче́м...** (We'll tear down the old world, but why?) Why indeed?

One idol that has been torn down in the post-Soviet world is the positive connotation of the adjective "proletarian." It is now clearly a pejorative. Thus, if someone criticizes something for no apparent reason or uses physical force immoderately, it is common to comment that this person acted "with all proletarian hatred" – **со всей пролета́рской не́навистью**. This can also be said of clumsy, forceful mistakes that may not be malicious, i.e. a strong kick in a soccer match going way high of the goal.

Recently, a revolutionary catch-phrase – one of the "good old idioms" – was resurrected in a *Nezavisimaya Gazeta* front page commentary forecasting the eventual dismissal of the influential Kremlin politician, Anatoly Chubais. **Револю́ция пожира́ет свои́х дете́й** (The revolution is devouring its own children), the headline read.

Yet New Times have also introduced their own neologisms which sound suspiciously like those of bygone days. Thus, the "red" (pro-Communist) press called privatization (**приватиза́ция**) **чубайсиза́ция страны́** (chubaisization of the country), after the father of privatization. Similarly, Chubais' followers/adepts are pejoratively called **чубайся́та** (hearkening back to the word "**октября́та**", a combination of the words **октя́брь** and **ребя́та**, meaning the Octobrists). Better yet, some call privatization "**прихватиза́ция**" (from the word **прихвати́ть** – to grab), perhaps best translated as "grabization," which of course hints (not so subtly) at the less than legal way Russian entrepreneurs were and still are grabbing state assets for peanuts.

We owe to the political star of *perestroika*, former St. Petersburg Mayor Anatoly Sobchak (who, according to the press, was allegedly engaged in corruption) another great turn of phrase: **Собча́чье се́рдце** (the heart of Sobchak). This is how quick-witted left oppositionists, "with all proletarian hatred," condemned some of Sobchak's schemes. The allusion, of course, is to the title of Bulgakov's famous novel **Соба́чье Се́рдце** (*The Heart of a Dog*), where, in a masterful allegory, a professor transplants parts of a criminal into a dog, and gets a despicable proletarian. [This phrase now has an additional, quite poignant allusion, as Sobchak died an early death after heart trouble.]

Russian democrats, for their part, excoriate their adversaries with the widespread idioms **краснокори́чневые** (red-browns) and **коммуня́ки** (little communists), which, while accurate, are far from as witty as the remarks of the old communist guard.

This is not to say the rulers of the New Russia are only capable of lackluster phrases. Suffice it to mention Prime Minister Viktor Chernomyrdin's historical phrase, "**Хоте́ли как лу́чше, а получи́лось как всегда́**" ("We meant it to be the best ever, but it turned out the usual way"). This contemporary idiom is being quoted and paraphrased throughout the media since the prime minister voiced it two years ago, and no other politician/art figure/writer has so far come close to this linguistic *tour de force*.

Another more recent pearl is **семибанки́рщина** (copied from a period in Russian history called *semiboyarshchina*). Such is the epithet given by Russian observers to the period of Russia in late 1990s – characterized by the creation of an oligarchy, where power and finances are controlled by seven major banks.

Unfortunately, the new political language has also been impregnated with argot from the milieu of mafia and bandits. Thus, back when President Boris Yeltsin's bodyguard, Alexander Korzhakov held sway in the Kremlin, the press used such phrases as **его́ заказа́ли** (he was contracted), derived from the notion of someone being the object of a contract killing. And the recently dismissed chairman of the National Sports Fund, Boris Fyodorov, was said to be "put on a meter" (**поста́вить на счётчик**). This is a loan-sharking term which means that, from now on, the debtor will daily pay the compounded interest on his debt.

The newest slang relating to New Russians is the odd term, **новари́щи**, invented by acrimonious French hotel managers in the Cote d'Azur. By combining the words *nouveaux-riches* and *tovarishchi* (comrades) they gave a very apropos assessment of the *novarishchi's* "distinguished taste and fine manners."

So, as you can see, not only the October Revolution but also the new era of wild capitalism *a la Russe* has had a negative impact on the "great and mighty" Russian language. But, of course, "this is nothing as compared" to what might have been the impact of an eventual world revolution.

Mikhail Ivanov (November 1997)

From *Devushka* to *Babushka*, Non-Stop

A major challenge that students of Russian (and even native Russians) face daily is how to address a stranger (**незнако́мый челове́к**). As politically incorrect as it may seem, humans have a habit of distinguishing strangers first by their sex. And, right away, problems start to arise.

When addressing a strange woman you can call her **да́ма** (lady or madam), which is courteous, but a bit overdone, and, of course, sounds very awkward when applied to anyone under 50. It is best applied to a **соли́дная** (respectable) woman sporting a fur-coat (**шу́ба**) and diamonds (**брилли́анты**). In fact, sometimes it can sound pretty sarcastic, as in "**Да́ма, вы мне все но́ги оттопта́ли**" ("Madam, you have been stepping all over my feet"), addressed to the elephantine woman carrying a dozen plastic bags and muscling against you for space in a crowded metro car.

You may very rarely hear outdated pre-Revolutionary forms of address like **ба́рышня** (young lady), usually used by older men when speaking to young women, or **суда́рыня** (madam). The latter might make the woman addressed feel like she is an entertainer at a *kitschy* Russian restaurant, decked out like a live *matryoshka* in traditional Russian costume. But you may hear this form of address in less likely places as well. I once quit a very good

yoga (**йо́га**) school after the first class because the guru addressed the women in the class as **суда́рыни**. He said something like "**Суда́рыни, бо́льше растяни́те подмы́шечные впа́дины!**" ("Madams, stretch out your axillas further!"). Somehow, this linguistic disconnect totally killed my desire to do yoga under his guidance.

A dictionary will tell you that "sir" and "madam" are, respectively, **господи́н** and **госпожа́**. But the Soviet era slogan, **У нас госпо́д нет!** (We have no sirs/masters!), has tainted these words, and you will only find them used in business correspondence or discussions, usually when foreigners are involved. Otherwise, these forms of address are quite awkward. You would not hear a Moscow policeman, for instance, say "**Госпожа́, сержа́нт Смирно́в. Разреши́те Ва́ши докуме́нты.**" ("Madam, I am Sergeant Smirnov. May I please see your documents?")

Thus, since all the words mentioned above will do you little or no good, the most universal form of address in today's Russia is **де́вушка**, which means "young girl," but is used to refer to women of all ages. Many Russians, trying to get the attention of, say, a middle-aged saleswoman (**продавщи́ца**), will use the term **де́вушка**. Which means Russian women turn from a *devushka* straight into a *babushka* (**ба́бушка**), deprived of any chance to enjoy the mature years of womanhood.

There is, in fact, little alternative to *devushka* – if we do not count the rigid and impersonal **же́нщина** (woman). The latter is often heard in the street or on public transport, as in "**Же́нщина, вы кошелёк урони́ли**" ("Woman, you dropped your purse") or "**Же́нщина, вы выхо́дите на сле́дующей?**" ("Woman, are you getting off at the next stop?"). While in Russian such usage is a bit less harsh than in English (where "woman" sounds like it needs to be proceeded with a "hey"), it is still best avoided.

A similar problem arises when addressing a strange man. The twin-brother of *devushka* is **молодо́й челове́к** (young man). In the absence of other options, Russians use **молодо́й челове́к** to address "young" men aged from three to 63. And then they switch to **де́душка**, which is the male counterpart of the internationally known *babushka*. Men apparently age quickly here as well...

In polite company, women are addressed as **да́мы**, as in **Да́мы и господа́**! (Ladies and gentlemen!). References to women "as a class" range from the sublime **прекра́сный пол** (the fair sex) to the colloquial and quite coarse **ба́бы**. While this word sounds a bit like the English word "babe," it was originally used to refer to lower class women, e.g. peasants. Yet in contemporary Russian it has become a pejorative for "women" in general. It is actually used in such sexist expressions as **не ба́бье э́то де́ло** (this is not a woman's job) and **ба́бские разгово́ры** (women-talk).

A group of women, discussing someone's private life, can say, for instance: **он нашёл себе́ но́вую ба́бу** (he found himself a new plaything). Someone who has new "arm candy" every month can be called a **бабник**. By the way, the (non-derogatory) Russian word for "Indian summer" is **бабье ле́то** (*babas'* summer). Oh, and if a man is called a **ба́ба**, it means he is considered a sissy.

On the other end of the scale from the *baba*-man is the **мужи́к** (*muzhik*), which connotes manliness and toughness. A man who possesses all the typical male qualities can be praised with: **Он настоя́щий мужи́к** (He is a Real Man). Feminists (**феминистки**) – this word, by the way, still carries negative connotations in Russia, especially when used by a Real Man – will be repulsed to learn that, in some traditional Russian families, to pass for an authentic *muzhik*, one must know the crafts of a **водопрово́дчик** (plumber) and **пло́тник** (carpenter), while the dishes (**посу́да**) and the cleaning (**убо́рка**) are left to the **хозя́йка** (lady of the house). The Real Man's salary (**зарпла́та**) must always exceed that of his wife, who often chooses the humble role of housewife (**домохозя́йка**), if the family can afford that. However, sexist traditions are giving way, and the number of business-women (**би́знес-ву́ман**) is steadily rising.

Due to the difficulties in addressing men and women in Russian, one might simply want to give up and stick to the neutral and impersonal **прости́те** or **извини́те** (excuse me) to get someone's attention. Like "**Прости́те, вы не подска́жете, кото́рый час?**" ("Excuse me, could you tell me, what time it is?"). This is safe, polite and, of course, 100% P.C.

Lina Rozovskaya (May 2004)

The *Babushka* Factor

Understanding the *babushka* factor is key to grasping many things Russian. Often one of the first Russian words foreigners know, they pronounce **Ба́бушка**! with gusto. Which is easy, since it is so simple, compact and colorful. But little do they know that this word is steeped with cultural connotations.

The *babushka* is omnipresent in Russian folklore, culture and even economics. In the mid-1990s, analysts often talked of "the *babushka* segment" of the economy – the lines of *babushka*-pensioners selling "impulse-buy" items near metro stations. This "segment" once accounted for 40% of total Russian retail tobacco sales.

Pushkin's *babushka*, Maria Alexeyevna, unwittingly participated in the creation of many literary masterpieces, through her retelling of fairy tales to her soon-to-be famous grandson. Mikhail Lermontov's *babushka*, Elizaveta Arsenieva, was also instrumental in the brilliant yet short-lived military and poetic career of her beloved Misha.

Ба́бушка has many tender, diminutive suffixes – e.g. **бабу́ля** – yet they are not always used tenderly. "**Самому́ не хвата́ет, бабу́ля!**" ("I don't have enough (money) myself"), a New Russian was overheard replying to a begging **бабушка** outside a McDonald's. And the hero of the film, *The Meeting Place Cannot Be Changed*, Vladimir Sharapov, mimicking folksy speaking habits, would say over the phone: "**Ну спаси́бо тебе́, ба́банька!**" ("Thanks a lot, you old woman!")

Perhaps the rudest way to address an elderly woman is to call her **ба́бка** (**ба́бки** in plural, but not to be confused with **ба́бки** or **ба́бульки**, slang words for money). To wit: "**Что ты ворчи́шь, как ста́рая ба́бка?!**" ("Why are you as grumpy as an old woman?") In the same vein, when you feel like "sending somebody to hell," you can send him **к чёртовой бабушке** – "to the devil's grandma." Tennis megastar Marat Safin once lobbed out a rather crude *babushka*-related proverb to deride those who were second-guessing his performance at a Kremlin Cup tournament. To a bewildered crowd of international journalists, he proclaimed: "**Ёсли, ёсли... Ёсли бы бабушка была дедушкой, у бабушки были бы яйца...**" Which can be mildly translated as, "If grandma were a grampa, she would have had all of grampa's parts."

That *babushka* is normally seen as a font of truth has given rise to other, more socially-acceptable idioms, such as **Бабушка надвое сказала** ("it remains to be seen," or literally, "*Babushka* was ambiguous, so we can't take anything for granted"). When someone is really sure of something, it is good to say, "**И к бабке не ходи**" – (literally, "I'm so sure of this, you don't even have to ask grandma.") Synonymously: "**и к гадалке** (fortune-teller) **не ходи**."

What about the humorous and elegant proverb, **Вот тебе, бабушка, и Юрьев день**? Yury's Day was an annual holiday of sorts when unencumbered Russian serfs could leave their landlord without explanation and move to live under another landlord or settle in virgin lands. Ivan the Terrible banned Yury's Day in the late 16th century, tying serfs to the land and taking away one of the few freedoms Russians then enjoyed. Thus was the proverb born. Ever since, it has been used to express a disagreeable surprise resulting from governmental resolutions or decisions.

Finally, when Russians talk about a person who wants to spite someone, albeit to their own detriment, they say, "**назло бабушке отморозить себе уши**" ("to freeze one's ears to spite the *babushka*"). This proverb evokes the classic situation where a *babushka* forces a recalcitrant grandson to put on his hat before going outside in winter... But, once he is out of the house, he takes off the hat to spite his grandma, only to freeze his ears and catch cold. A synonymous expression is "**назло бабушке отрезать себе ухо**" ("to cut off one's ear to spite *babushka*"). Or, as it is said in English, "to cut off one's nose to spite their face."

When the famous impressionist Vincent Van Gogh in 1888 cut off his right ear, he doubtless had nothing against his *babushka*. It is believed he did the deed in an act of self-loathing or disease-ridden rage. (Another theory has it that his right ear was cut off by his friend Paul Gauguin in a drunken brawl.) Be that as it may, Van Gogh's *Self-Portrait with a Bound Up Ear*, where he wears a bandage and a fur *shapka* of sorts, is now worth fabulous **бабульки** – a few million at least. **И к бабке не ходи!**

Mikhail Ivanov (July 2006)

The Flowers of Life on Their Parents' Grave

That the birth rate in Russia is plummeting does not exactly mean Russians don't love kids – they do, it's just that Russia can't afford large families anymore.

Parents here now pay an arm and a leg to support a newborn baby – what with all these Pampers and other Western stuff on offer. To say nothing of supporting and bringing up older kids. For, as the Russians say, "small children, small worries; big children, big worries" (**маленькие детки – маленькие бедки, а вырастут велики – будут большие**). Nevertheless, as Sting sang in a song that went over very well in Russia: "...Russians love their children too." Those parents who have both a daughter and a son are thought to be especially lucky, for they have what old Russians call "golden children" – **золотые дети**.

The father of Soviet literature, Maxim Gorky, had this to say about kids: "Children are the flowers of life" (**Дети – цветы жизни**). Hopeless cynics rephrased the stock phrase to: "Children are the flowers of life on their parent's grave" (**Дети – цветы жизни на могиле родителей**). But then this was probably invented in a moment of despair and most likely refers to the big worries brought on by big children...

These same cynics probably belong to the category of parents who hire babysitters and will not consider making any sacrifices to bring up their children in a healthy, homey atmosphere. About such parents, Russians have a fairly morbid saying: **у семи нянек дитя без глазу** ("seven babysitters can't say why their only baby lost her eye," or, if your prefer a looser translation, "too many cooks spoil the broth"). Neglectful parents never bother finding out why their baby cries. Instead of checking the baby's diapers or stopping for a few minutes to play with the child, they would rather give him something to play with, to distract its attention. For, as Russians say, **чем бы дитя не тешилось, лишь бы не плакало** (anything to keep the baby quiet). And the children of such parents? They will probably bring up their kids in the same fashion. After all, **яблоко от яблочка недалеко падает** (the apple never falls far from the tree).

In the Soviet era, kid-idioms were often used in an adult context. Suffice it to mention Lenin's famous book, **Детская болезнь левизны в коммунизме** (*The Infantile Disease of Leftist Communism*). And there is the cliché Lenin used when he was disagreeing with his opponents, **думать так было бы ребячеством** (to think so would be childish).

Soviet children were steeped in the spirit and language of communist ideology from the earliest days of their childhood. Or, to put it in an old, bookish way, "from their young fingernails" (**с младых ногтей**).

Meanwhile, the senile ideologues at the top were occasionally entering their second childhood (**впада́ли в де́тство** – literally, "fell back into childhood"). So, in a way, the Soviet children were on a par with their educators. But their parents, disillusioned with the political regime, were unmoved by communist educational dogmas. A famous joke of the late 1970s has it that, when communist leader Leonid Brezhnev professed the famous Soviet cliché, "**на́ши де́ти бу́дут жить при коммуни́зме**" ("our children will live under communism"), a parent in the crowd of listeners chuckled: "**Так им и на́до!**" ("They deserve it!")

Luckily, for Brezhnev, by then surrounded by seven babysitters, he would not have gotten the joke even if he had heard it. By that time, he was already falling deep back into his childhood...

Mikhail Ivanov (June 1997)

No Sweat, Dude, Really!

Since this column began in 1995, our country has raised a whole new generation of teenagers. So it is time we brought you up to speed on the younger generation's slang, to give you a linguistic shot in the arm as it were.

Remember **кру́то/круто́й** (cool), which was all the rage in the 1990s? Well, the word still exists, but is just no longer **кру́то**. Teens now say something is **прико́льно** or **понто́во**. The words are untranslatable, of course, so just memorize them.

Meanwhile, savvy teens sprinkle as many utterances as possible with the rather redundant "**на са́мом де́ле**" ("as a matter of fact"). This phenomenon has grown over the last few years and bothers the older generations to no end (ensuring its continuance).

But the most irritating "cool word" is the verb **па́риться**, in the imperative form – **не па́рься**. Its only plus is that it is a perfect translation for the English, "No sweat!" Indeed, our self-assured teens, with their belly rings and low-waisted jeans drooping like slackened sails, don't like to "sweat." Why work hard and reap the fruits of your labor when you can have it all – and now! This idiom is particularly contagious. The other day, I caught myself saying to my wife – instead of the usual "relax" (**рассла́бься**) – "**не па́рься**." This idiom drives me nuts (**бе́сит меня́**).

And there's another thing: **беси́ть** (to drive someone mad, nuts) has become the universal slang verb for expressing one's discontent: **Меня́ бе́сит шко́ла... меня́ бе́сят роди́тели... это меня́ бе́сит...** You hear it everywhere. A normal verb, used to exhaustion, is enough to drive you mad!

Or take the innocuous **конкре́тно** (concrete, specific). No, we are not talking about its use in the normal context – **конкре́тный отве́т, конкре́тная ситуа́ция**. That wouldn't be slang, would it? The usage is more like: "**прие́хали таки́е конкре́тные ребя́та**" ("some pretty strong and scary guys arrived"). Or: "**Он так конкре́тно его поби́л**" ("He beat the hell out of him"). Actually (**на са́мом де́ле**), **конкре́тно** is on its way out. It has ceded its place to **реа́льно, реа́льный** (real) – which can mean "great, big, superb or very bad," depending on the context or intonation of the speaker.

There is also the new ultimate adverb "**не по-де́тски**" (literally, "not in a childish way"). It means "big time," "greatly," or "superbly." For example, recently, in a city van (**маршру́тка**), a military school student called his friend on his cell phone: "Hey, guys, I got leave until tomorrow morning and Sasha's parents are out. Let's get together at his place – **на́до сего́дня оторва́ться не по-де́тски**." ("We have to have a seriously good time.") Note the use of **оторва́ться** (literally, to cut out, to relax, go on a bender, have fun, or better "to let all hell break loose").

Overhearing this conversation, I felt myself smile bitterly. But, apparently, to the student and his mate, it must have looked more like a cringe. They got my meaning and proceeded to stare at me as if I were a fossil – a mammoth covered with moths. Or, to use their language, a complete **лох** (hapless idiot). Or, better still, the ultimate insult: **лох педа́льный**

(pedaling **лох**). The first time I heard **лох педа́льный**, I asked some teens what on Earth it meant. What have pedals got to do with anything?! No one knew the etymology (or, for that matter, what "etymology" meant).

Is it because the **лох** is riding a bicycle? To this conjecture, one 20-something simply laughed in my face. "I don't know why we say it, simply because **нам так по ка́йфу**" ("simply because we enjoy it"). To do something **по ка́йфу** means to enjoy something, to take pleasure in doing something. Okay, this one I got, because the word **кайф** (pleasure, fun) is something we said in my teen years, in the – *gulp* – late 1970s and early 1980s.

"But you should say '**в кайф**,' not '**по ка́йфу**.' The preposition is wrong," my linguist self asserted.

"No, man," responded the fellow, "maybe you **старпе́ры** (old farts) said '**в кайф**,' but now we say '**по ка́йфу**.' Don't try to fix it, it's too late. **Поздня́к мета́ться**."

My feet felt solid ground again – this final expression (**поздня́к мета́ться**) I understood straight off. It's easy enough. **Поздня́к** comes from the adverb **по́здно** (late) and the verb **мета́ться** is a quite normal verb meaning "to rush about."

"**Действи́тельно, бесполезня́к**," (it is useless indeed), I murmured, dredging up a 20-year-old idiom from my student years. And it turned the tide. The youth praised my linguistic turn.

"How do you say it again? **Бесполезня́к? Прико́льно, чува́к**" ("cool one, dude"). I'll try to remember it."

That "**чува́к**" was music to my ears. An idiom older than even I, it is experiencing a comeback in modern slang, giving hope to those who still feel 20-something inside.

I walked away feeling completely rejuvenated.

Mikhail Ivanov (November 2005)

Out
&
About

Why Going Dutch is not Russian

Once upon a time, waiters were kings in this place. Well, sort of. While they once enjoyed one of the highest incomes in the country, deep down restaurant goers hardly gave them the respect due a sovereign. In fact, there was even a standard parental threat – "if you don't apply yourself at school, you'll become a janitor or waiter."

In short, the profession of waiter in the USSR used to be despised and frowned upon. Waiters – even more than other representatives of the Soviet service sector – were notorious for their **хáмство** (boorishness). Plus, not only did they not smile back at you, they could easily cheat the client by fixing the tab (**обсчитáть**), watering down his cognac (**разбáвить водóй**) or underweighing (**недовéшивать**), thus saving a hundred-odd grams on each portion of veal, sturgeon or whatever, while replenishing their supposedly meager stocks of food at home.

Veteran travelers to Soviet Russia will also remember the ill-fated **швейцáр** (door man) who would let you negotiate the infamous **нет мест** (sorry, we're full) signs for a few rubles.

For Homo Sovieticus, known for his high endurance, the **нет мест** obstacle was no more daunting than any other obstacle put before him by the inefficient system. You overcame it simply by buttering up the staff. Anyone with a friend among the **официáнты** (waiters) had a key which could open many doors – particularly if you knew all the waiters by their first names.

Anyone who didn't hold that key had to accept a famous maxim, interpreted the Soviet way: **клиéнт всегдá непрáв** (the customer is always wrong). While the **пронЫра/прохиндéй** (fixer) usually knew all waiters by their first names, the average, battered Soviet customer without **связи** (connections) – who went to restaurants at best twice a year – didn't even know how to address waiters.

Back in tsarist times it was so easy. A waiter working in a **трактúр** (a kind of Russian pub serving food) was officially called **половóй** (literally, floor man). Yet clients addressed him simply as **человéк** (man). In translation, a dialogue between customers and waiters in a Russian **трактúр** might sound something like a conversation in a Brooklyn bar –"Two more beers, man!" "Make it fast, man!" "Keep the change, man!"

After October 1917, *traktirs* slowly disappeared, as did good and affable waiters. Nobody calls them **человéк** anymore.

In Stalin's time, waiters' behavior was more or less acceptable – unfriendly service could be easily interpreted as sabotage. So for a while waiters were just called **официáнты**.

But in the 1970s and '80s, during the Stagnation Period, the now infamous boorishness of the Soviet waiter appeared. Clients had no recourse against shoddy service but for the virtually ignored **жа́лобная кни́га** (book of complaints), where one could write comments about bad service without having any major effect on it.

In that period, calling a waiter "waiter" earned you no points (this is equally true today). So customers racked their brains to find a good euphemism for the despicable **официа́нт**. Some would implore the prideful waiter with **маэ́стро** (maestro) or **брато́к** (little brother). However, the most frequent formulae were the anonymous and beseeching, "**Мо́жно Вас на мину́точку?**" ("Can I speak to you for a second?") and "**Бу́дьте добры́**"("Would you be so kind?")

In today's consumer society, though, some Russian waiters have actually take to *smiling* at customers. They bring you the menu (**меню́**), give you clean napkins (**салфе́тки**) and even let you take your time in making your choice. When you're ready, they typically ask you politely, "**Вы уже́ вы́брали?**" ("Have you chosen already?"). Some even adopt good old phrases from Chekhovian times, like, "**Чего́ жела́ете?**" ("What would you like?") or "**Жела́ете что́-нибудь на десе́рт?**" ("Care for a dessert?").

Then they patiently note down your order, which will normally include **заку́ски** (starters), **пе́рвое** (soups), **второ́е** (hot meals), and **десе́рт** (dessert). What is more, many now speak English, so you may not need to learn the words for various dishes. Still, your waiter will certainly be charmed if you drop a few, key Russian phrases. For example, if you want to order the same meal as your host say, "**мне то же са́мое**" ("The same for me") or something like, "**А Вы что рекоменду́ете?**" ("What would you recommend?") Or, "**Я полага́юсь на Ваш вкус**"("I'll rely on your taste").

The waiter may respond to your inquiry by offering you their favorite special dish (**фи́рменное блю́до**) and **что́-нибудь из напи́тков** (something to drink). When your meal is served, it is customary for the waiter to wish you **прия́тного аппети́та** (have a nice meal). Once in a while they might ask to change your ash tray (**поменя́ть пе́пельницу**) and as soon as you're finished they may ask: "**Я могу́ э́то убра́ть/ унести́?**" ("Can I take this away?").

When the solemn moment of payment comes, take note of the formula: "**Счёт, пожа́луйста/посчита́йте нам пожа́луйста**" ("Can I have the bill, please?").

And how do you finesse the everpresent social challenge of deciding who picks up the tab? Well, usually when a Russian asks you "**В како́й рестора́н пойдём?**" ("Which restaurant are we going to?") or says "**Я приглаша́ю Вас в рестора́н**" ("I'm inviting you"), it's on him or her. Likewise, when you hear your Russian friends say, "**Я плачу́**" ("I am buying") or "**Я угоща́ю**" (I'm treating you) "**Я сего́дня гуля́ю**" ("I'm letting my hair down today"), don't even offer to go Dutch. While you are at it, don't look for an equivalent to "going Dutch" in Russian. In theory you can say "**ка́ждый пла́тит за себя́**" ("everyone pays for himself") but in practice nobody either says or does this.

If you invite a Russian out to dinner – especially a lady – you're buying. If you don't, your Russian friend may complain the next day to his/her friends that "**он меня не по́нял**" ("he didn't get me"). Your man the waiter may make the same remark if you don't leave a tip (**чаевы́е**). By the way, don't take the word **чаевы́е** (tea money) literally – like the guy from the Russian joke who gave his waiter two pieces of sugar instead of money. By Russian standards, if the service was good, your tip has to be worth more than a cup of tea.

Mikhail Ivanov (June 1996)

Ending Telephone Hangups

It is impossible to spend time in Russia without picking up the phone. And for the visitor using Russian phones, there are two potential sources of frustration: the system itself and Russian phone culture. Unfortunately, we can't do much about the infrastructure of the phone system, some of which dates back to before the revolution (!), but we can offer some help on the cultural side.

Russian phone culture, like anything in today's Russia, is in a state of transition – and yet, the remarkable linguistic hiccup from the past "telephone law" – **телефо́нное пра́во** still holds true. This phrase dates to the Soviet era of management when a simple phone call from a properly placed *apparatchik* was enough to, say, stop a criminal investigation, secure a lucrative job for a Politburo son in the Foreign Ministry, or obtain the best seats in the Bolshoi.

Many innovations in the phone lexicon have been introduced with the dissemination of modern means of communications among "New Russians" (**Но́вые Ру́сские**) who moved from using the once-fashionable pager (**пе́йджер**) to state-of-the art cellular and mobile phones **со́товые / моби́льные телефо́ны**. The proper usage, by the way, for contacting someone by pager is: "to drop a message on one's pager" – **сбрось / скинь мне на пе́йджер**. Interestingly, since the pager is usually worn on the waist, inventive Russians have come up with a humorous replacement for "low blow," now literally a blow below the pager (**уда́р ни́же пе́йджера**). Compare with **уда́р ни́же по́яса**. There is also a current famous joke about the son of a new Russian using his mobile phone as a spade in a sandbox. "What are you doing?" his sandbox buddy says. "You'll break the phone." "Big deal," he replies. "Daddy will buy me another one." "Yeah, but it will take him at least couple of days to buy and register it. In the meantime, you will have to resort to using a pager, like an idiot."

Back to some more practical tips. Before you make any attempt to converse **по телефо́ну** in Russia, there are a few things you should know. Despite a general improvement in phone etiquette, you will still often encounter, in business or other non-personal conversations, a very abrupt and to-the-point manner that you may construe as rude. And you may get hung up on if your Russian is halting. As well, Russians still don't fully trust the phone lines to be secure (witness the culturally-embedded phrase, **э́то не телефо́нный разгово́р**). Many still prefer to handle important (and sometimes not-so-important) issues face to face. This said, pick up the phone and start dialing...

There are a number of ways to ask for your intended recipient. In Russian, a phrase such as, "Can I please speak with Ivan Ivanov?" can be spoken in several variants:

Formal: "**Попроси́те, пожа́луйста / Позови́те Ива́на Ивано́ва.**"

Less formal: "**Бу́дьте добры́, Ива́на Ивано́ва.**"

Informal, though still polite: "**Здра́вствуйте, мо́жно Ива́на Ивано́ва?**" A blunt **мо́жно** without **здра́вствуйте** is commonly heard but is impolite.

In business, the phrase should be split into two sentences: "**Ива́н Ивано́в на ме́сте?** If you get a "**Да,**" then follow with: **Переда́йте ему́, пожа́луйста, тру́бку.**" ("Would you please pass the receiver to him?") This phrase is used even if you know the business has a modern phone system and there will be no *trubka*-passing.

Visitors often err in using the Russian literal equivalent for "Mr. Smith, please." "**Пожа́луйста, господи́на Сми́та.**" Do this if for some reason you wish to underline your status as a foreigner.

When answering the phone, you can use the international "**Алло́**" or the typical and impersonal: "**Вас слу́шают**," literally: "you are being listened to" (still a possibility in this part of the world).

An old-fashioned receptionist working at Aeroflot's **спра́вочная** (information service) or at the railway station might simply blurt: "**Говори́те!**" ("Talk!")

"**Говори́те!**" in a well-cultivated voice is intended to discourage the caller from further inquiries.

If you ask to speak to a particular person and that person is the one who answered the phone, this person may reply: "**Он / она́ / я у телефо́на.**"

There are many ways to be put on hold in Russian: "**Подожди́те, пожа́луйста**" ("Please wait"), "**Одну́ мину́ту**" ("Just a minute") and "**Одну́ секу́нду**" ("Just a second").

Russians are also fond of diminutives and might add the suffix "**чк**," as in "**Одну́ мину́точку.**"

Note however that, to the Russian ear, these forms can sound a bit "sweet" coming from a man.

There is no direct equivalent for the English "to leave a message" or "to take a message." The closest version is **оста́вить запи́ску** (leave a note).

If you want a message to be relayed, you can say, "**Переда́йте пожа́луйста, что...**" This implies that the information will be transmitted in written form. As you will likely find, however, such **запи́ски** are rare.

For "He is on another line, would you like to hold?" or "Can I take a message?" Russians would usually say, "**Он говори́т по друго́му телефо́ну. Вы подождёте или позвони́те попо́зже?**"

The English, "Can I take a message?" is usually given as "**Что ему́ переда́ть?**" ("What shall I relay to him?")

"He will call you back" is "**Он Вам перезвони́т.**" But don't count on this unless you owe someone a lot of money. Not returning calls is an important feature of Russian phone culture, and in fact, the parting words "**Созвони́мся!**" ("Let's be in touch by phone!") is kind of like "Let's do lunch!" in English. The speaker usually has the exact opposite intention.

The Russian language does have an exact equivalent for "Who's calling, please?" It is "**Кто его́ спра́шивает?**" But this phrase can imply that the called party is screening incoming calls. In this instance, if your call is not welcome, you will likely hear "**Его нет**" ("He's out," which could be either true or false). The worst permutation of this has become a set phrase: "He is out and nobody knows when he'll be in." ("**Его нет и неизве́стно, когда́ он бу́дет**.") This is not unlike the Russian joke about a little boy saying over the phone: "Daddy says he is out."

Now the easy part. You may be surprised when, at just the point in your conversation when you are preparing to say "good-bye", the other person simply hangs up. Russian phone etiquette is not big on the sign off, and when business is concluded, Russians will often hang up the phone without formality. Don't take it personally. However, it is also quite common to conclude with "**до свида́ния**" ("goodbye," literally, "until next time"), or between friends, "**пока́**" (more like "bye-bye").

Mikhail Ivanov (October 1998)

Of Tickets, Hares and Dozing Fathers

За двумя́ за́йцами пого́нишься, ни одного́ не пойма́ешь.
If you run after two hares you will catch neither.
Russian proverb

When Moscow hosted the 1980 Olympic Games, a trip on the city transportation network was simple for foreign tourists: there were no crowds (all non-Muscovites had to leave the city), and the names of metro stations were even announced in English at each stop. Granted, Russia's invasion of Afghanistan (and the resultant boycott by Western nations) put a damper on visitor turnout, but those who made the trip must still remember how comforting it was to hear the words "Next stop: Polyezhayevskaya" in a familiar tongue.

The Olympics are history. So are those temporary linguistic concessions. As a visitor, you're on your own on Russian public transport, so a user-friendly transport vocabulary will come in handy. Of course, you can always use your hands – or better still your elbows – to communicate. But you will have a much smoother ride with a few choice expressions at your disposal – useful to counter that over-aggressive *babushka* stabbing you in the ribs with her umbrella.

It may be that you are not responding to her "**да́йте пройти́**" ("let me pass") or "**уступи́те ме́сто**" ("give up your seat"). If she is pushing too hard, however, you can always respond with "**не толка́йтесь**" or "**не пиха́йтесь**" ("stop shoving").

If a *babushka* does make it clear that she wants your seat, you'd better give it up, or you may wind up in an altercation with indignant fellow passengers. The Russian film comedy *Mission Ы and Other Adventures of Shurik* affords a classic parody of metro seating protocol: "**Молодо́й челове́к, как Вам не сты́дно, уступи́те ме́сто же́нщине – она́ гото́вится стать ма́терью**," says a *babushka* pointing toward a pregnant woman. ("Young man, shame on you, give up your seat to the lady. She's soon to be a mother").

"**А я гото́влюсь стать отцо́м.**" ("Yeah, well, I'm going to be a father soon."), the 40-something thug snaps back before falling back to sleep in his seat.

Of course, if you want to enjoy the show, you have to purchase your ticket. When you're buying a metro token (**жето́н**), a simple **пожа́луйста** (please), plus the number of tokens you want will be enough to make you understood.

Above-ground transport is a little more complicated. Ticket booklets used for trolleys, trams, and buses are called an **абоне́нтная кни́жечка**. If on a crowded bus someone taps you on the shoulder and passes you some money, it's not because they think you look needy. He/she wants you to pass it on to the driver, who also acts as ticket seller. The key phrase here is, "**Переда́йте, пожа́луйста, на кни́жечку**" ("Pass it on please, it's for tickets"). If you forget to buy your ticket, the driver might remind you by announcing, "**Своевре́менно и пра́вильно опла́чивайте прое́зд**" ("Buy your tickets correctly and in good time").

Someone traveling without a ticket is called a **безбиле́тник** (ticketless person) by transport officials, and a **за́яц** (hare) by everyone else. The origin of this colloquial term is shrouded in mystery, but it probably refers to the nervous demeanor of those who **е́здят за́йцем** (ride like hares), ready to flee the undercover **контролёр** (controller) at any moment, lest they be forced to pay the **штраф** (fine).

The Russian for "tickets, please" is **предъяви́те Ваш биле́т**. If you don't have one, and aren't ready to cough up a fine on the spot, the controller may say "**Пройдёмте в мили́цию**." ("Let's go to the police station"). He means it, and you'll have to get off with him at the next stop.

Getting off of a metro, trolley, bus, or tram car can sometimes be trickier than getting on. If your way is blocked by a dozen women with heavy bags, you should ask them: "**Вы выхо́дите / схо́дите на сле́дующей?**" ("Are you getting off at the next stop?").

If your obstructers are getting off, you can go with the flow. If not, and the bus is crowded, you should suggest switching places: "**Дава́йте с Ва́ми поменя́емся**" and start moving toward the exit. The more polite ones will offer to let you through with the words "**Я Вас вы́пущу**" ("I'll let you out.")

Here are some other situational phrases to remember:

If you see an empty train approaching the platform and nobody gets on, you are likely to hear: "**На по́езд поса́дки нет**." ("This train is not taking passengers"). On the other hand, if your train stops and everybody suddenly clears out, the conductor may be announcing: "**По́езд да́льше не идёт, про́сьба освободи́ть ваго́ны**." ("This train goes no further, please exit the cars.") In this case you will have to get off and wait for the next train.

Recently, metro passengers have been hearing a new announcement as their train pulls into each station: **"Уважа́емые пассажи́ры, не забыва́йте свой ве́щи."** ("Respected passengers, don't forget your belongings.") This started soon after the war in Chechnya began.

If you do happen to forget something and want to get it back, you should contact the **"Бюро́ нахо́док"** (literally: Office of Found Items). But in today's less disciplined environment, "finders keepers" (**кто́-то теря́ет, кто́-то нахо́дит**) is more the rule. So keep a close eye on your valuables, and Russian public transport will be an adventure, not a disaster.

Mikhail Ivanov (March 1996)

Update: Needless to say, the Moscow metro no longer uses **жето́ны** and you don't buy an **абоне́нтная кни́жечка** to ride buses. Things are in the process of modernization (with magnetic code swipe cards, etc.), yet these linguistic relics are still inbued with enough meaning that they bear learning and understanding.

Beware the Teapots and Snowdrops

Driving in Russia is, by all accounts, a nerve-racking experience. So basic road vocabulary is this column's theme – because rare are those who have been able to avoid communicating with the notoriously corrupt Russian road police (**ГАИ: Госуда́рственная автоинспе́кция**) or with fellow drivers. Of course "fellow" is probably too nice a word, since every second "fellow" will attempt to **подре́зать** (cut you off), thus creating what they call in GAI parlance an **авари́йная ситуа́ция** (accident-prone situation).

Indeed, courteous behavior is hard to come by on Russian roads strewn with **я́мы** (potholes). Novices are advised to stick a picture of a teapot (**ча́йник**) in the back window of their car, as a warning for other drivers. But also note that **ча́йник** is slang for a "poor driver." Women, whether they put up a sign or not, should be ready to hear more than their fair share of criticisms, since men do most of the driving here. A common sexist proverb is: **же́нщина за рулём – что фаши́ст на та́нке** (a woman at the wheel is like a fascist driving a tank).

Another category of drivers commonly derided by other drivers are the **подсне́жники** ("snowdrops" – a spring flower). These are **автолюби́тели** ("car lovers," or amateurs, as opposed to professional drivers) who prefer to store their cars in a garage during the winter, only venturing out on the roads again in spring – showing up like snowdrops.

Snowdrops are actually famous for keeping their car in good order and usually have no problem passing the **техосмо́тр** (technical inspection) at GAI, which is supposed to identify – and thus eliminate – any technical deficiencies of a car. But, of course, the **техосмо́тр** is just a ruse to generate bribes. A recent nationwide campaign, the **заме́на води́тельских прав** (exchange of driving licenses, not to be confused with the old exchange of party cards campaign which Soviet era leaders used to root out potential opposition) introduced a new unified license which looks like a credit card. This of course was another source of bribe revenue. For any drivers who did not meet the January 1, 2000, deadline for exchange of documents surely had to line GAI pockets.

If you **нарушили правила дорожного движения** (violated traffic rules) and a GAI officer catches you red-handed, you will pay. Certain violations they will not let slide, such as **превышение скорости** (speeding), **проезд на красный сигнал светофора** (running a red light), **вождение в нетрезвом состоянии** (driving "under the influence"). This latter violation is the bread and butter of your typical Russian **гаишник**. Late at night and holidays are ideal times for the **гаишник** to catch drunk drivers and feather his nest, so to speak. DUI in Russia can cost you between $100 and $200 cash, unless you want to face the official punishment, which normally involves confiscation of one's driver's license for a year (**лишение водительских прав сроком на год**) and a requirement to retake a driving exam with GAI (**повторный экзамен в ГАИ**).

So, after a night with the Green Dragon, catch a **тачка** (literally, "wheelbarrow") or **мотор** (engine) – the two slang words for "car." In this instance, it is helpful to know how to talk to **частники** (gypsy drivers), who like to **бомбить** (to make money on the side and/or by deceit) or to taxi drivers (**таксисты**). To win their favors, local passengers usually address them as "boss" (**шеф**) or "commander" (**командир**), while, in common usage, drivers call one another **водила** (derived from **водитель**, driver).

The first question your **частник** will ask is short and simple: "**Сколько?**" ("How much?") Be ready to toss out offers the Russian way: **десятку / десяточку** (a ten), **двадцатку / двадцаточку** (a twenty), **тридцатник** (a thirty), **полтинник** (a fifty), **стольник** (a hundred). Just using the simple cardinal numbers you learned in school will help mark you as a foreigner, or worse, a novice, and you can count on paying more.

If you are stopped by a GAI officer, you will be asked to show your **водительские права** or, more formally, **водительское удостоверение**. This usually means the **инспектор ГАИ** intends to withdraw your license and issue a fine (**штраф**). Fines can be paid either on the spot or via Sberbank (in which case the driver gives proof of bank transfer payment to the GAI division in their residential district to reclaim their **права**). The alternative, of course, is if the **гаишник** gives you a sly look and asks, "**Квитанция нужна?**" ("Do you need a receipt?") which means he is ready to **договориться** (settle) – take a bribe that is. You can be proactive and say, "**Мне не нужна квитанция!**" ("I don't need a receipt").

Not surprisingly, GAI officers are the butt of numerous jokes. The shortest is about a GAI inspector who introduces himself to drivers as "**Инспе́ктор Си́доров, тро́е дете́й!**" ("Inspector Sidorov, three children!").

In another joke, GAI Lieutenant Petrov asks his superior for a raise, since he has just married and needs to buy a new apartment. The superior picks up the phone and barks out: "Sergeant! Lieutenant Petrov is coming to see you. Please give him a new road sign."

The infamy of the GAI has in fact reached such pandemic proportions that the organization recently resorted to a name change, from **ГАИ** to the clumsy **ГИБДД** (**Госуда́рственная Инспе́кция по Безопа́сности Доро́жного Движе́ния** – Main Inspectorate for Road Safety, to emphasize their public safety role). But battered Russian drivers were quick to decifer the acronym as "**Гони́ инспе́ктору ба́бки и дви́гай да́льше!**" ("Give the inspector some dough and drive on!"). Folk wisdom, indeed, knows no bounds. For now this is surely the "safest" way to travel Russian roads.

Mikhail Ivanov (March 2000)

To Queue or Not to Queue

The image of an **о́чередь** (queue), winding around a street corner and stretching beyond the horizon may well be imprinted on the collective unconscious (**коллекти́вное бессозна́тельное**) of Russians, even those lucky enough to have been born in the abundant mid-90s.

Queuing (**стоя́ть в о́череди** – to stand in a queue, often shortened to simply **стоя́ть** – stand) for food and other essential items was a routine pastime of every Soviet citizen, with the exception of the **сли́вки** (cream) of the party elite. One often stood in queues for toilet paper – strictly four rolls for every pair of hands (**четы́ре руло́на в одни́ ру́ки**), for bananas, vegetable oil, for tights, for imported boots (even if only size 40 was left – **оста́лся то́лько сороково́й разме́р**)... in short, for just about any consumer good in short supply (**дефици́т**).

This is why a resourceful *homo sovieticus* (**сове́тский челове́к**) always carried in his case or her handbag an **аво́ська** – a string-bag that could be rolled up into a very small space, but which was always at the ready, "just in case" its owner came across a queue.

The first step would be to secure a place in the queue (**встать в о́чередь**). Only then would the new arrival ask, "**За чем стои́м?**" ("What are we queuing for?") or "**Что даю́т?**" ("What are they giving out?").

Today, the horrors of communal queuing are long gone, yet one can still spend plenty of time standing in line. In the last year, I can recall queuing for several things for over an hour: for plane tickets (**за биле́тами на самолёт**), to get into a photo exhibition (**на вы́ставку**), to get a visa at the Italian embassy (**в италья́нское посо́льство за ви́зой**), and with my dog at the vet (**на приём к ветерина́ру**).

Russian queuing has its own etiquette. Before taking a place in a queue, try asking, "**Кто после́дний?**" ("Who's last in line?"). Then you can occupy your place and patiently stand or sit. Alternatively, you could try to dodge the queue by what is called **заня́ть о́чередь** – securing your place by declaring to the person in front of you, "**Я за ва́ми**" ("I am behind you") and abandoning the queue for the time you estimate it would take you to reach its head. Before leaving, be sure to warn the people in front of you and behind: "**Я отойду́ на мину́тку**" ("I am leaving for just a moment"), to make sure they know you will be coming back. Then, theoretically, you could leave the standing to others and retire to a nearby café.

If you want to secure a place in a virtual queue, such as a waiting list for a plane ticket, you can ask the responsible person, "**Поста́вьте меня́ на лист ожида́ния.**" ("Put me on the waiting list.")

In a situation similar to queuing, if you find yourself in a stuffed metro car and want to make sure you can get out at the next stop, you may want to ask the people between you and the door, "**Вы выхо́дите на сле́дующей?**" ("Are you getting off at the next stop?"). It's kind of a polite advance notice that you will soon be shouldering your way by them.

Life is short and, if you have the guts, you can try to get what you want **без о́череди** (jumping the line). But if you try this, be bold and confident and quite prepared to hear something rude and humiliating, such as "**Вас здесь не стоя́ло.**" ("You weren't standing here.") This phrase, because of its awkward grammatical structure, is a rather rude way to evict someone from a queue. The phrase dates at least to the Stalin era, since Anna Akhmatova reportedly used it mockingly to say that a person had not stood in lines outside prisons with parcels for loved ones.

It will be a while before the word **о́чередь** ceases to have negative connotations for Russians. As the dog Sharik, newly transformed into comrade Sharikov in Mikhail Bulgakov's *Heart of a Dog* liked to shout, "**В о́чередь, су́кины де́ти, в о́чередь!**" ("Get in line, you S.O.B.s, get in line!")

Lina Rozovskaya (September 2004)

Euphemisms
&
Expletives

Show Your Colors

Ка́ждый охо́тник жела́ет знать, где сиди́т фаза́н.
Every hunter wants to know where the pheasant sits.

This seemingly stupid phrase is actually a trick to help you learn Russian colors. Each initial letter corresponds to the colors of the rainbow **кра́сный, ора́нжевый, жёлтый, зелёный, голубо́й, си́ний, фиоле́товый**. Russian schoolchildren are taught it in natural science or physics and it's so catchy that once you've learned it you are bound to remember these Russian colors' names.

No, this isn't a lesson in elementary physics. But colors are essential in linguistics too: they help you make your language more sophisticated, or just more colorful.

The first thing every foreign student in Russian should know is the role of red. Anyone who's been to Red Square will remember that **кра́сный** in old Russian means "beautiful" – like **кра́сная де́вица** (pretty girl).

Centuries later, red became the symbol of revolution – associated with the color of the blood shed by its heroes. Therefore everything beautiful or glorious became red, hence the Red Army, Red October Chocolate Factory, etc.

Over the years, the word **кра́сный** lost its old meaning. As for the new meaning, Russians came to realize there's nothing beautiful or glorious about bloodshed – even in the name of revolution.

Today even New Russians have stopped wearing tasteless red jackets and opted for more discreet colors. Maybe they're getting more stylish, maybe Yeltsin's [1996] victory over Zyuganov played its role, or maybe somebody told them about the famous folk saying, **дура́к лю́бит кра́сное** (fools love red).

Whatever the explanation, in post-communist Russia, red is associated with danger. You go red from anger or shame (**покрасне́ть от зло́сти / стыда́**). Your eyes go red from crying (or drinking). If you get cold water from the red tap in a hotel in a remote Russian town, don't blame cultural differences. Red means hot in Russia, too – so either the hot water was cut off or the plumbers' eyes were red and he confused the colors.

Not all colors are as popular. It's hard to find anything with orange in it, only the lyrics of a mid-1960s song which goes: **ора́нжевые ма́мы ора́нжевые пе́сни ора́нжево пою́т** (orange mothers sing orange songs in an orange way). This anthem to color-blindness sounds a little bizarre today, but for people living in the Khrushchev thaw, it was refreshing to sing something light and easy instead of proletarian hits about the red cavalry.

Yellow (**жёлтый**) is used more extensively, but usually has pejorative connotations. One example is **желторо́тик** (yellow-mouth), meaning someone inexperienced and cowardly.

Зелёный is worth remembering if only because of the almighty dollar, in Russian **зелёные** (greenbacks), and here they give the green light too (**даю́т зелёный свет**).

Like in the U.S., **голубо́й** (blue) isn't just a color of the rainbow. Don't try to use it with its American meaning (sadness) here, however, because it most often means someone with homosexual tendencies. Other meanings include **голуба́я мечта́** (a blue dream), i.e. the dream of your life. Ostap Bender, meanwhile, hero of the comic novel *The Twelve Chairs*, dreamed of someone bringing him a million rubles on a small plate with a blue border (**на блю́дечке с голубо́й каёмочкой**). Like many quotes from the novel, this became proverbial, meaning wanting to have one's cake and eat it too.

Синий (dark blue) is associated with cold. You can say your nose is blue from cold (**синий от холода**). If you shave closely, a Russian will say you're shaven blue: **до синевы выбрит**. Hence the joke: What's the difference between a White officer and a Soviet officer? The former was always a bit drunk and shaven blue (**слегка пьян, до синевы выбрит**) while the latter was a bit shaven and drunk blue (**до синевы пьян, слегка выбрит**).

Speaking of White officers, **белый** (white) has plenty of other meanings. Geographers will remind you of "white spots" on the map (**белые пятна на карте**), i.e. undiscovered regions. Russian history still has far too many white (unknown) pages (**белые страницы**). Someone who wants to start from scratch can say he's starting from white (**начать набело**). Fear is also associated with white: like Americans, Russians go white with fear (**побелеть от страха**).

Russians consider white a color which stands out. If you wore jeans to a cocktail party, a Russian would say you looked like a white crow (**выглядеть, как белая ворона**), i.e. you stuck out like a sore thumb.

Серый (grey) is, of course, the color of mediocrity, referring to dull and illiterate people. Yet Russians call influential politicians who keep a low-profile **серые кардиналы** (grey cardinals), the best known being Brezhnev's ideology chief Mikhail Suslov.

Like in English, **чёрный** (black) is reserved for the macabre, like black days in history (**чёрные дни в истории**) or black humor (**чёрный юмор**).

Russians might also feel **чёрная зависть** (black envy). Yet, some English phrases have a slightly different equivalent – a black sheep in the family is not the **чёрная** but the **паршивая** (lousy) **овца в стаде** (in the herd).

To end on a brighter note, remember the meaning of the word **розовый** (pink). Looking pink means looking healthy and rejuvenated. As Russians tend to look at things with Dostoyevskian pessimism, they might say that someone who seems too jovial sees everything in pink (**всё видит в розовом свете**) or looks at the world through rose-colored glasses (**смотрит на мир сквозь розовые очки**). Little wonder that you will see few Russians smiling on the street. Which is one reason why smiling Americans look like white crows in a Russian crowd.

Mikhail Ivanov (September 1996)

Of Despicable Metal and Easy Behavior

The guardian of order should not be putting it behind the collar, hanging out with women of easy behavior or wantonly tossing about despicable metal. This is particularly true when the best part of humanity is in the situation. At best, this is incompatible activity; at worst, it may draw the attention of sharks of the plume.

Sounds like a conundrum, doesn't it? Welcome to the jungle of Russian euphemisms. Bearing in mind their importance in everyday language, demonstrating a knowledge euphemisms them can be considered a linguistic *tour de force*.

Despicable metal (**презре́нный мета́лл**) is a nice, subtle paraphrase for money (the Russian equivalent of "the root of all evil"). Although, come to think of it, you could have a hard time finding a Russian who despises it, so perhaps "cherished metal" or "beloved metal" would be more appropriate.

A breadwinner (**корми́лец**) should not put behind the collar (**закла́дывать за воротни́к** – drink) unless he wants his family to be short of this metal. On the contrary, he should take good care of his other half (**втора́я полови́на** – spouse) especially if she is in the situation (**в положе́нии** – pregnant) rather than пуска́ться во все тя́жкие (go on a bender) or meet with "representatives of the oldest profession" (**представи́тельницы древне́йшей профе́ссии**). Another Russian euphemism for this profession, less familiar to English speakers, is **же́нщины лёгкого поведе́ния** (women of easy behavior).

The Cold War years were, of course, a golden age of euphemisms. These women of easy behavior were often planted in Moscow hotel rooms on direct orders from **ры́цари плаща́ и кинжа́ла** (cloak-and-dagger knights), a euphemism for the secret service and also reminiscent of an expression in English.

When sent abroad on missions, "knights" collected information on their own. If they got over-enthusiastic and got themselves exposed, local **стра́жи поря́дка** ("guardians of order" – i.e. officers of the law) might issue a special statement for the "sharks of the plume" (**аку́лы пера́** – journalists) pointing out that the knights' "activities were incompatible with their official status" (**их де́ятельность несовмести́ма с их официа́льным ста́тусом** – a lengthy euphemism for spying).

This type of incompatible activity reached its peak in the early 1980s, when Leonid Brezhnev "ordered us to live a long time" (**приказа́л до́лго жить** – a euphemism for dying) and **отошёл в лу́чший мир** (passed on to a better world).

His successor, Yuri Andropov (who issued the same "order" soon after Brezhnev), headed the KGB for many years – coordinating both cloak and dagger knights and guardians of order. Then, in his brief period as General Secretary, Andropov cracked down on corruption in the Interior Ministry and its boss Shchelokov, who happened to be Brezhnev's brother-in-law. Shchelokov was notorious for being "unclean-handed" (**нечист на руку** – corrupt) so he ultimately decided to "settle accounts with life" (**свести счёты с жизнью** – commit suicide) instead of being sent to "very remote places" (**места весьма отдалённые** – prison.) Incidentally, don't confuse this phrase with "not such remote places" (**места не столь отдалённые** – the bathroom).

In the meantime, Brezhnev's son-in-law, Yuri Churbanov (who by pure coincidence made a vertiginous carrier in the same ministry), also attracted the attention of the guardians of order. He was not only unclean-handed but also hung out with women of easy behavior, invoking the ire of his better half, Galina Brezhneva (who, incidentally, was famous for putting it behind her collar).

When he found out, Churbanov ended up in a very remote place after the guardians of order got onto him (his guardian angel, Brezhnev, having passed from the scene too long hence). Churbanov's marriage of convenience with Galina was not exceptional – back then it was common practice for the Russian "stronger sex" (**сильный пол** – men) to look for their other half among daughters of the high-ranking Soviet *nomenklatura*.

Nowadays in Russia, roles have changed somewhat. It is not uncommon for the **лучшая половина человечества** ("the best part of humanity," i.e. the fairer sex) to marry the "strong of this world" (**сильные мира сего** – people with power or money or both: politicians, bank presidents, managing directors, etc.) who work stressful 16-hour days. Even though these people don't usually excel at "fulfilling their conjugal duties" (**исполнять свои супружеские обязанности**), at least they can provide their better halves with plenty of despicable metal before ordering them to live long.

Of course, it could be argued that in Russia some of the strong of this world may be unclean-handed, but the local fairer sex doesn't seem particularly worried about that. Unlike so many of their compatriots, the Russian strong of this world at least don't tend to put it behind the collar beyond reasonable limits. After all, this type of activity could be considered incompatible with their status.

Mikhail Ivanov (October 1996)

Swearing, by Japanese God!

The Sun of Russian poetry, Alexander Pushkin, a notorious rake, loved to indulge in linguistic hooliganism. (By the way, the word "Pushkin" is now the latest slang among Russian youth for "cool" – e.g. when someone asks "How was the movie? (or jeans or coat)" the reply is "Oh Pushkin!" instead of "Oh, cool!") In his lesser-known verses, diaries and private correspondences, the great Russian poet didn't mince words, often employing a vivid arsenal of Russian *mat* (curse words).

In modern reprints of his works, his countrymen find many omissions or elipses replacing unprintable vocabulary. But then he was Pushkin! (And his verses were "Pushkin" too.) So he could afford linguistically what we, simple mortals, simply cannot.

But we can't just deprive ourselves of swearing, can we? For it is arguably one of the best ways of letting off steam. And, for those who want to express themselves colorfully, but shun outright obscenity, there are some now traditional *mat*-surrogates. One of the most popular is the infamous **блин** (literally "pancake"), which every Russian teenager uses extensively. For all our love for pancake eating, when someone yells "**Блин!**" all of sudden, he is not voicing an uncontrollable craving for this crisp, porous and fluffy-battered stuff. In fact, **блин** is a standard euphemism for what "a known Russia basher" (as Western journalist Jean McKenzie once introduced herself) called this "naughty word" that means "whore" (also beginning with a "bl") and is used "where English speakers normally utter their own favorite four-letter expletive."

In a hilarious contemporaneous development, Russian linguiphiles, led by stand-up comedian Yelena Stepanenko, have taken to calling Bill Clinton "Blin Clinton" or "Klin Blinton" (ironically, "klin" translates as "wedge" or "gore" – the verb, not the vice-president).

A longer synonym for **блин**, the phrase "**Болят мои раны**" (literally "my wounds hurt") is based on the same similarity in pronunciation. It also starts with a "**Б**," so everyone gets the hint, but it is "formally" decent and the cursor's face is saved.

The second most popular curse is when Russians profane another's mother. It starts with a "yo" sound, so inventive Russians have crafted a "civilized" subterfuge which unfortunately is not favorable to citizens of the Country of the Rising Sun: **Японский Бог** (Japanese God!). A less frequent synomym of the Japanese God is the Japanese cop! (**Японский городовой**!). The explanation for both is pretty simple – in pronunciation they start with a "yo," just like the infamous idiom. Alternatively, one could say "**Ё моё!**" (literally "my 'yo'") which is tolerated in informal oral speech.

Russian inventiveness in euphemisms knows no boundaries. If a Muscovite sees a lady of ill-repute walking along Tverskaya street, he might say "God forgive"(**Прости Господи!**), but he may or may not be offering up a prayer. For, it is simply a euphemism for the word prostitute (**проститутка**), which sounds similar. No, there is no etymological connection, just a polite name for Moscow's "moths" (**ночные бабочки**).

Actually, call them what you will – it won't have any impact on the number of Moscow's *godforgives*. Their position is very strong. Likely because, as in any big city, they are in cahoots with the **русский городовой**. Or perhaps because demand for local "**прости Господи**" is steady and increasing. In fact, a recent Potemkin village-like raid on the Moscow's *godforgives* by then Interior Ministry Kulikov cleaned up the city for a couple of hours. But the next day, **японский городовой!**, things were back to "normal." All Kulikov could say was that "his wounds hurt."

As we attempt to be a respectable magazine on Russian culture, we definitely can't elaborate on this list, which, of course, is far from complete. But if you know at least these few key euphemisms, your chances to pass for a local – or at least to score some linguistic points with locals – are much higher. But then, don't abuse the privilege, Japanese God forbid! For instance, parents daring to claim their place in the ranks of the Russian *intelligentsia* give their kids a hard time for using this ubiquitous "pancake" word – including yours truly. It may seem a linguistic hypocrisy, since quite a few such *intelligents* often spruce up their speech with *mat*. But then, that's the way we are. You never know with these Russians, **блин!**

Mikhail Ivanov (June 1996)

Invoking Heaven and Hell

Не упоминай имя Господа своего всуе.
Don't speak the Lord's name in vain.

If there is one commandment that Russians ignore the most, this is definitely it. One can hear **слава Богу** (Thank God) in Russia almost as often as "please" or "thank you."

Over the course of 74 years, atheist Bolshevism failed miserably at driving religious idiom from the Russian language. Phrases invoking the Almighty proved so deep-rooted that even Party leaders peppered their oral and written speech with them. Lenin himself was known to take the Lord's name in vain while driving home a point in one of his fervent diatribes against the enemies of world socialism, perhaps in deference to his famous maxim that "anything which serves the communist cause is moral."

Such references are clearly in vogue among today's politicians, including such luminaries as Mikhail Gorbachev, Boris Yeltsin, and current Communist leader Gennady Zyuganov, who may become Russia's next President in a few months, **не дай Бог** (God forbid).

If Zyuganov does win the election, as many experts predict, Russians will either exclaim "**Боже мой!**" ("Oh my God!"), or "**Слава Богу!**" ("Glory to God!"), depending on their political leanings.

Another popular religious phrase is **ради Бога** (for God's sake). "**Ради Бога, перестань называть меня 'малыш'!**" ("For God's sake, stop calling me 'little one!'") says the heroine to her lover in the popular Russian soap opera *Winter Cherry*.

The seemingly synonymous **ради Христа** or **Христа ради** (for Christ's sake) has a different connotation. In old Russia, it was a set-phrase used by beggars. Less charitable members of the public would often reply "**Бог подаст**" ("God will provide"). Which may make it a phrase to use on today's street gypsies.

But, take note. This phrase has been adapted to modern circumstances. For example, your business partner might inform you that he won't do something **Христа ради**, meaning you should have put it in writing, because this is going to cost you extra.

Indeed, the appeal to higher authority is a favorite tactic of Russians in the financial arena. For example, in the vegetable market you will often hear a *babushka* uttering an incredulous **свят-свят** at the price of tomatoes. Literally it means "sacred-sacred," and is used by Orthodox believers and older Russians, accompanied by a sign of the cross, when they find themselves at a disadvantage, like shopping for vegetables in the winter time.

If this *babushka* should decide to take a hard negotiating position with the tomato vendor, she might retort with "**Креста́ на тебе́ нет!**"("shame on you," or, literally, "you don't have a cross on you"). This is an emphatic phrase that could come in handy. For example, if your taxi driver wants $10 for a five-minute ride, it might be helpful to shame him by telling him that he doesn't have a cross on him.

In fact, religious vocabulary is so rich that there is a phrase to suit almost any situation. If you think that someone is telling you lies, or you disagree with them about something, you can say: **Госпо́дь с тобо́й,** a holy Russian equivalent for the English, "Oh, come on!"

However effective the vocabulary of heaven may be, though, sometimes an appeal to the Darker Side is in order. This is where the vocabulary of hell comes in.

For example, a Russian who slips on a watermelon peel might exclaim "**Чёрт побери́**" ("Damn!" literally, "The devil take you!"). This is what happened to Semyon Semyonich, the hero of the classic Russian movie, *Diamond Arm*. His inadvertent pronouncement of this phrase, which happens to be some diamond smugglers' password, starts him on the adventure of a lifetime. If, while in Russia, you need to invent a password for any reason, **ра́ди Бо́га**, don't use the phrase – **чёрт побери́**. It is about as rare a password as "How's it going?" would be in English.

Now and then, something a bit stronger is called for, like when you're eating in a Soviet-style restaurant, and you suspect that the waiter has padded your bill (which, **сла́ва Бо́гу**, happens less and less often). In this case, you might try on him, "**Это чёрт зна́ет что!**" ("The devil knows what this is!"). If he doesn't get the hint, it's time to **посла́ть его́ к чёртовой ма́тери / ба́бушке** (send him to the devil's mother/grandmother). Or, if you want to be a little softer, tell him he'll get a balding devil instead of money: "**Чёрта лы́сого ты полу́чишь вме́сто де́нег.**"

Not all "devilish" words in Russian have negative meanings, however. When a man's friends say his new girlfriend is **чертовски хороша́**, there is no reason for him to take offense. It was meant as a compliment. They are saying that she is "devilishly beautiful."

Similarly, if, **не дай Бог**, you try to drink a Russian under the table and succeed, then the next day he may call you a **чертя́ка** (little devil) with heartfelt admiration.

Finally, when you read those apocalyptic scenarios in the press about Russia being doomed to bear its cross (**нести́ свой крест**) until the End Times, try to keep an open mind. As the Russians say: "**Не так стра́шен чёрт, как его́ малю́ют**" ("The devil is not as terrible as he is painted").

Mikhail Ivanov (April 1996)

Walking A Verst in Russia's Lapti

Down through the centuries, Russian reformers have repeatedly said they do not want their country to remain a **лапотная Россия** – Russia of the *laptis*, referring to **лапти**, the traditional footwear made from birch bark. Despite the somewhat romantic refrains of our folk song: "**Лапти, да лапти, да лапти мои!**" ("Oh you, my *laptis-laptis!*"), this and other connotations of **лапти** are often negative, in this case implying backwardness.

The word **лапоть** (singular for **лапти**) also figures in the idiom "**Не лаптем щи хлебаем.**" The literal meaning is "we don't eat our soup with *lapti*," but the real meaning is that "we are not as simple and primitive as you may think; we *do* know how to use a spoon." A similar usage appeared in the famous film, *Moscow Doesn't Believe in Tears*. The heroine is visiting a Soviet TV studio and hears two singers offering up a 1950s-era *chastushka* (humorous, four line rhyme):

Пусть нас "лапотной Россией" называет Вашингтон
Мы недавно запустили лапоть в сорок тысяч тонн
Let Washington call us "Russia of the laptis"
We recently launched a 40-thousand-ton lapti

The 40-thousand-ton reference was to Sputnik.

In the even more famous Russian film, *Gentlemen of Fortune*, when the thieves are driving around Moscow, searching fruitlessly for an address, one of the passengers blames the taxi driver for not being able to find his way in the capital, and says, "**Карту купи, лапоть!**" ("Buy yourself a map, you *lapot!*")

If the outer bark of the birch tree has one meaning, you can be sure the inner bark – **лыко** (bast) – has another, albeit similar meaning. **Лыко** is associated with something primitive or elementary. For example, one of my schoolteachers used to remind us that she took very seriously the writing of her recommendation for our academic files – the **характеристика**. "Please, don't shy from social work," she would say, "You are in your final class and your **характеристика** will have **каждое лыко в строку**." In other words, everything you do or don't do will be reflected there. Likewise, when you say about someone, "**Он не лыком шит**" (literally, "He is not sewn with bast"), it means "He is no idiot." Consequently, when someone drinks himself into oblivion, a folksy way to describe his condition is to say "**Он лыка не вяжет**" (he is so bombed, "He cannot weave bast").

A few words should also be said about the all-important Russian **сапоги́** (boots). These footwear, though not as ancient as *lapti*, also occupy a special place of honor in the Russian lexicon.

For decades, a fine pair of boots has been a sign of prestige and wealth. In Soviet times, women would line up for hours to buy a pair of foreign-made, leather **сапоги́**. So, in the mid-1990s, a TV spot for the infamous MMM pyramid scheme showed the company's happy spokesman, Lenya Golubkov, leaving MMM offices with cash dividends and voicing the now cliché phrase, "**Куплю́ жене́ сапоги́!**" ("Now I am going to buy some boots for my wife!")

When you want to say that two people are very much alike (usually in a bad way), you can say, "**Два сапога́ – па́ра**" ("Two boots make a pair"). And when someone who is good at doing or making something does not take advantage of his own product, you can call him a **Сапо́жник без сапо́г** (a barefoot shoemaker).

Just as in English, you kick someone out of something by "giving them the boot" – **пнуть сапого́м**. Thus, in a song sung by Alexander Malinin (lyrics by Yevgeny Yevtushenko), the author warns against two awful fates:

**Дай Бог, что́бы твоя́ страна́ тебя́ не пну́ла сапожи́щем,
Дай Бог, что́бы твоя́ жена́ тебя́ люби́ла да́же ни́щим!**
*God forbid your country gives you the boot,
And may your wife love you even if you are a beggar!*

Before sending this column to print, I decided to try the latter line out on my wife (a fan of Malinin), to make sure it resonated well (and to make sure I was still in good standing). She reassured me she will love me even if I went bust, adding with a laugh, "Though, I hope it won't happen." After which, I said to myself, "No, dear, you are definitely not sewn with **лы́ко**!"

Or maybe I should have paraphrased Lenya Golubkov and replied to her reassurance with, "Come on, honey, let's go buy you some new boots!"

Mikhail Ivanov (February 2005)

Russlish & Beyond

A Few "False Friends"

Сло́во – не воробе́й, вы́летит – не пойма́ешь.
A word is not a nightingale, once it's out you can't catch it.
Russian proverb

Anyone who has tried to learn a difficult language like Russian understands the relief in finding words that sound just like their native equivalent. When you hear such international words as "metro" or 'taxi' enough times, you can even start to feel that elusive mastery quickening within you.

Unfortunately, time shows this list of "free words" to be a lot shorter than it first seems. What's more, some of these "familiar" words can easily be misused, causing embarrassment. In the theory of translation, such snares are called "false friends of the translator."

As any Russian teacher will tell you, this is a very topical issue. Speaking of which, how would you say in Russian: "It's a topical issue"? The best way is to say **Э́то актуа́льный вопро́с. Актуа́льный** means topical, newsy or urgent, and not "actually," the Russian equivalent of which is **факти́чески** (factually) or **на са́мом де́ле** (in actual fact).

If someone tells you that your tie doesn't look **соли́дно**, they"re not referring to its composition. What your Russian critic means is that your tie isn't presentable. The English "solid" has little in common with the Russian **соли́дный**. The appropriate equivalents would be **про́чный** (strong) or **твёрдый** (hard).

Speaking of ties, if you're shopping in Russia for a "real silk" one, don't look for the easiest Russian equivalent, **реа́льный шёлк**. It should translate as 100 percent (**стопроце́нтный**) **шёлк** or **натура́льный** (natural silk). Unfortunately, the chances of finding such a tie in Moscow at an affordable price are just not **реа́льно** ("realistic" not "real" – another false friend).

If someone does insult your tie, you might reciprocate and tell him that he is not quite **интеллиге́нтный**. This is not to say that this person is not "intelligent." **Интеллиге́нтный** in Russian means decent, discreet, learned and well-mannered. This type of person would be expected to keep negative opinions to himself.

In a related vein, don't try to interrogate someone who is full of **интеллиге́нтность** (the noun for **интеллиге́нтный**) for classified (**секре́тный**) information. This person's discretion is of a different character.

If you want to use a less class-oriented word than **интеллиге́нтный**, try **корре́ктный**. Any athlete, whatever their level of play, will be expected to fit this description. Swearing at the crowd, fouling opponents, or throwing equipment is likely to invite charges of **некорре́ктное поведе́ние** (incorrect, i.e. unsportsmanlike behavior).

Back in the 1980s, when the arms race was at its peak, you might have heard about U.S. spy satellites monitoring very "accurate" Soviet medium-range SS-20 missiles. Had the Soviet General Secretary's interpreter translated this as **аккура́тные**, he would have upset the strategic parity between NATO and the Warsaw Pact, and perhaps lost his job or worse. "Accurate" is a very false friend of military interpreters. The treacherously similar **аккура́тно** means "exact, punctual, careful and conscientious." So the "high accuracy" of an SS-20 should be conveyed as **высо́кая то́чность**.

This subtle difference in the meanings of the English "accurate" and Russian **аккура́тный** can sometimes bring absurd results. The words **аккура́тная фигу́рка**, trans-

late literally into English as "accurate figure." But this might not be music to the ears of a Russian accountant, for to him/her it means "well-proportioned figure."

Further, if someone were to say in public that his boss' new wife looks much younger than he does, Russians may find his remark not **аккура́тная**, even when true. In this context **аккура́тная** means "careful."

An **интеллиге́нтный** employee, meanwhile, would never make such a remark. Not only because it's not **интеллиге́нтно** or **корре́ктно** (discreet) but because it's not right (**пра́вильно**) or intelligent (**умно́**) either. If such an employee demands a large raise, his boss may reply that he doesn't find this figure "accurate." A career-minded person should know how to talk about his superiors in public. This is still an **актуа́льный вопро́с** in today's Russia.

Mikhail Ivanov (January 1996)

Khalyava: All Play and No Work

When I was a child, I got my fair share of Russian **ска́зки** (fairy tales) at bedtime. While they rarely succeeded in putting me to sleep, they did teach me the Russian philosophy of life... while likely negatively affecting my impressionable personality.

Contrary to Soviet mythology, **ска́зки** taught that the world is a cruel place, where one's morality has no influence upon one's fortune. The **ска́зки** swarmed with young fools (**дураки́**) and lazybones (**лентя́и**) who always got the biggest piece of pie at the end of the story.

Take a **неуда́чник** (a loser, today anglicized simply as **лу́зер**) named **Еме́ля** (Yemelya). The youngest son of the prototypical **стари́к со стару́хой** (an old man and his wife), Yemelya was also the stupidest **дура́к** his village ever knew. All he would do was lie on the **печь** (stove) all day **па́льцем не пошеве́ли́т** (not lifting a finger). Then, one day, his family somehow manages to coax him into going down to the river to get water.

As luck would have it, Yemelya catches a miraculous **щу́ка** (pike) in his bucket. It will grant his every wish. All he has to do is say **по щу́чьему веле́нью, по моему́ хоте́нью** ("by the pike's command, by my desire") and any whim is realized. Yemelya started by having the water-filled buckets walk home on their own and finished his wishing spree by marrying the local tsarevna. Somewhere in the middle of the fairy tale, he made his stove drive him all the way to the tsar's palace. The image of a lazy **лу́зер** lying on a **печь** and getting whatever his heart desires firmly imprinted itself in my mind.

This getting everything for nothing is summarized by one of Russia's most untranslatable words – **халя́ва**. It is a word with such a broad semantic field that a single magazine column cannot hope to accommodate all the shadows of its meaning. **Халя́ва** means a freebie, something someone gets for free or without making much effort – **на халя́ву**, e.g. the way Yemelya got himself a tsarevna for a wife. This is not to say that **халя́ва** only applies to things of great value. After all, as modern Russian wisdom has it, **на халя́ву и у́ксус сла́док** ("Even vinegar is sweet when it is *khalyava*").

Халя́ва also means an easy, low-effort (**халя́вный**) job, something that requires little effort and is compensated well. And it means moonlighting too. A person who is good at getting such jobs and at doing the least work possible is called a **халя́вщик**. This is a person who is good at dumping his workload on others, or eating in restaurants at others' expense – a freeloader. The verb is **халя́вить**.

An easy job or moonlighting can also be referred to as **халту́ра**. The person who works carelessly, a hack or potboiler who works without due diligence, follow through or dotting his i's (the verb being **халту́рить**) is called a **халту́рщик**.

In November, as it turns out, the Russian State Duma indulged the national **халя́ва** habit by passing a bill that considerably extends Russia's most celebrated national holiday. Deputies stretched the official New Year's holiday from January 1 to 5, giving Russians five consecutive days to **пра́здновать**. This is not to imply, of course, that, before the bill came into effect, the Russian workforce was universally to be found in offices at 9 AM sharp on January 2 or the first working day (**рабо́чий день**) after the official New Year's break. It is just that now the New Year's **халя́ва** has been made official.

National traditions must be enshrined in law, after all. Work, as we know, can wait. Or, as the familiar Russian adage has it: **Рабо́та не волк, в лес не убежи́т.** (Work is not a wolf, it won't run off into the woods.)

Lina Rozovskaya (January 2005)

Excuse My Russian

There's nothing like the immersion method if you want to speak Russian like a native. One must choose carefully, however, with whom and where to immerse oneself: dialect and poor grammar abound in every nation. This chapter can't point you to the ideal environment for immersion, but it can help you to recognize the wrong one.

For example, though Former Soviet President Mikhail Gorbachev was immensely popular internationally, he's no role model in the elocution department. It is a little-known fact in the West that, despite his prestigious and much-publicized university education, the Soviet Union's last leader regularly stressed the wrong syllable and abused Russian grammar in public speeches, much to the chagrin of intellectuals.

If Ronald Reagan or George Bush had practiced the immersion method with Gorby, in no time at all they would have been saying **нача́ть**, instead of **нача́ть**, (to begin). Other common examples of incorrect stress include **позво́нит** (he will call) instead of **позвони́т**, **кило́метр** instead of **киломе́тр**, and **кварта́л** in place of **кварта́л** (quarter).

Mikhail Sergeyevich was also keen on using savvy foreign words like **консе́нсус** (consensus) where the simple Russian **согла́сие** (agreement) would do. The trouble was, he sometimes failed to grasp the subtleties of the imports. When the media latched onto and broadcast these gaffs, another ungrammatical phrase would enter into common usage.

One legendary pearl of "Gorbachev savvy" is **сохрани́ть ны́нешний ста́тус-кво** (to retain the current status-quo) – the status-quo is current by definition. There was also **друга́я альтернати́ва** (another alternative) and **потенциа́льные возмо́жности** (potential possibilities). In Russian, such linguistic phenomena are called **ма́сло ма́сляное** (buttered butter).

Be on the lookout as well for when Russians abuse complex comparative forms, like **бо́лее** (more) plus an adjective. They might combine **бо́лее**, not with simple adjectives like **хоро́ший** (good), but with comparative adjectives like **лу́чший** to produce the horrific "more better." In Russian as in English, two comparative forms back to back are redundant.

Improper declension is one more thing to look out for. Don't bother declining the word **пальто́** (coat). If you hear someone say **без пальта́** (without a coat), they're not using "Ivy League" Russian. It should be spoken **без пальто́**. The rule is: words of foreign origin ending with an "o" like **пальто́, кино́** and **метро́** don't decline, though they commonly are.

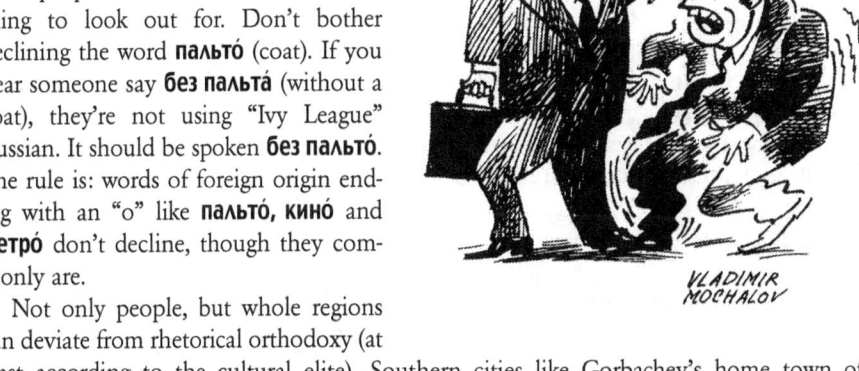

Not only people, but whole regions can deviate from rhetorical orthodoxy (at least according to the cultural elite). Southern cities like Gorbachev's home town of Stavropol are rich in such departures. For example, in the third person, the verb **класть** (to put) declines as **кладёт** (singular) and **кладут** (plural). A Stavropol native might say **ло́жит**

(singular) or **лóжут** (plural), derived from the non-existent infinitive of the verb, **ложи́ть**. In the perfective form, the verb **класть** is **положи́ть**, (to place) or **вложи́ть** (to insert).

If you go to the Crimea for an immersion experience, you might end up saying **и́хний / и́хние**, the local version of **их** (the possessive pronoun meaning "their"). **И́хние** is considered to be a **простре́чие** (literally "simple speech"). If you use it, every Russian will understand you, but you may raise high a few eyebrows.

Speaking of high brows, you can always make out a true Russian **интеллиге́нт** (intellectual) by the way he apologizes. You won't hear him/her use the word **извиня́юсь** – introduced into the language by illiterate sailors in 1917 and regularly substituted for the correct form: **извини́те** (excuse me). The difference between the two is subtle but critical. The reflexive form of the verb **извиня́ть** (to excuse) in literal translation means "I excuse myself."

To those with a refined sense of the language, **извиня́юсь** is an absurdity. If somebody apologizes this way after stepping on your foot on a crowded trolleybus, they would technically not be begging your forgiveness, but forgiving themselves for the transgression. Don't hold it against them, their intentions are pure. Some of the commonly used embellishments to this words are even less apologetic: **я о́чень извиня́юсь** (I excuse myself very much) or **я си́льно извиня́юсь** (I excuse myself strongly).

In the end, if you can't remember how to decline the word **пальто́**, at least bring one with you if you come to Russia at this time of year. Your trip will be much "more better" that way.

Mikhail Ivanov (February 1996)

Survival German

It was 60 years ago that the Soviet Union finally halted the German offensive outside Moscow, turning the tide in the war and overturning Hitler's plan for a **блицкри́г** (*Blitzkrieg*). Yet even for Russians of my generation and younger, the war is still in our hearts and minds, largely because of the heavy toll (27 million lives) of victory.

In 1941, when Hitler was implementing his **план Барбаро́сса** (Barbarossa Plan), Moscow was strewn with **противота́нковые ежи́** (anti-tank "hedgehogs") and the situation was more than grave.

From those days one famous phrase–the slogan of the day–is still well known: **"Вели́ка Росси́я, а отступа́ть не́куда – позади́ Москва́!"** ("Russia is huge, but there is nowhere to retreat, for Moscow is behind us.") In the same vein, at that time the whole country sang a song we still all know by heart:

Встава́й, страна́ огро́мная	*Get up, huge country*
Встава́й на сме́ртный бой	*To a deadly battle*
С фаши́стской си́лой тёмною	*With the dark fascist force*
С прокля́тою ордо́й	*With the damned Horde*

Пусть я́рость благоро́дная
Вскипа́ет как волна́
Идёт война́ наро́дная,
Свяще́нная война́!

Let the noble fury
Mount like a wave
A People's War is raging
A Holy War!

    The lyrics of this song should give pause to those who mistranslate **Вели́кая Оте́чественная Война́** ("Great Patriotic War"; there is even a set acronym for it – **ВОВ**) as World War II (which is actually **втора́я мирова́я война́**).

    Luckily, Moscow's defenders repulsed the enemy. But the true turning of the war's tide would not come until Stalingrad in 1943. And victory was still four years off. Plenty of new phrases and idioms would take root in the Russian language during those difficult years.

    While most borrowings from those times were German (e.g., Germans were commonly referred to as **фри́цы** – Fritzes, from the common German name), some English words did break through our linguistic lines, e.g. **лэнд-ли́з** (Lend-Lease). Many Russians survived on **тушёнка** (canned meat) which came to the USSR **по ленд-ли́зу**. Of course, the USSR most wanted the **откры́тие второ́го фро́нта** (opening of a second front), which finally happened with the allied landing at Normandy (**вы́садка сою́зников в Норма́ндии**). But second front or no, the Soviets were determined to take Berlin by storm, to "kill the fascist beast in its den" (**доби́ть фаши́стскую га́дину в её ло́гове**).

    Besides **блицкри́г**, many more German words invaded our language, most simple transliterations, as they needed no translation. From books and movies, every Russian learned "**Шне́ллер!**" (Faster") and "**Хе́нде Хох**" ("Hands up!") – key words for taking German prisoners, as was the expected German supplication of the Soviet soldier: "**Нихт Ши́ссен!**" ("Don't shoot!")

    As a child, I loved war novels and movies, and learned just enough German, as they say, to make me dangerous. In 1995 – the 50th anniversary of our victory over Germany – I was in Frankfurt for that city's annual book fair. Riding home one night by taxi after an evening sampling the city's fine apple wine and **шнапс** (Schnapps), the linguist in me couldn't help asking for translations of what the driver was saying as he explained where we were driving. He kept saying "haupt," as in "hauptbahnhof" ("main," as in "main railway station"). "Oh, yes, yes, I know that word," I shouted, feeling I had made a great discovery, "it's like **гаупт-шту́рмбанфюрер,**" (*Hauptsturmbanführer* – Head Stormtrooper). Needless to say, this "illumination" did not seem as exciting to our driver, who simply shrugged his shoulders as if a chill were traveling down his spine.

    I was smart enough not to continue with the most popular German phrase from my childhood: "Hitler Kaput!" To cheer him up, I was about to cite a more positive German song I knew from films, "Deutsche Soldaten nicht kapituliren" (German soldiers don't capitulate), but I was also advised against this.

    That night we drank with our hosts to freundshaft (but not the more intimate "Russian" toast **на брудерша́фт**) and I assured our German friends that Russia no longer saw Germany as a threat, that we are trying to put the bitter memories of the Third Reich (**Тре́тий Рейх**) behind us (though some German words are still hard to erase from our minds).

    I can only hope that my grandchildren will be lucky enough never to have to learn any language the way our generation learned German.

Mikhail Ivanov (November 2001)

When P.R. Sounds Like Samovar

The Russian language abhors a vacuum and, as with, say, computer parlance, has a tendency to fill new lacunae with foreign words.

There is hardly any area in the Russian linguistic space like PR – public relations. Here, foreign borrowing has been "met with open arms," so to speak. Even die-hard nationalist Duma deputies are joining in the use of alien vocabulary in this sphere. And it should not be surprising. After all, the very notion of PR was non-existent either in Russian political campaigns or in Russian business. Both were, in a manner of speaking, **виртуáльные** (virtual) realities here. Instead of political campaigns preceding elections, in Soviet times we had what they called **всенарóдный прáздник единéния пáртии и нарóда** ("a national holiday of the union between Party and the people"). Hence, no need for PR. Can you imagine, for instance, Josef Stalin openly vying for the post of party leader with Sergei Kirov, printing a PR article in *Pravda* to present an embellished image of himself in the eyes of party delegates? Not. Easier to simply arrange for Kirov to be shot by a maniac in the corridors of Smolny. Why waste time and money on PR?

Of course, Uncle Joe did use his own brand of PR, but it lacked a certain subtlety. Some would even claim (after he was safely beyond the grave), that it rose to the level of cult-building (a.k.a. the infamous **культ лúчности** – personality cult). As to business – there was none (no business, that is). All we had was the **"нарóдное хозя́йство"** (national economy); PR (not to be confused with propaganda) was rare. Sure, a plant or a factory could promote itself as the "victor of socialist competition" (**победи́тель социалисти́ческого соревновáния**) or claim the dubious **знак кáчества** (symbol of quality) on its products, but these titles were attributed (or rather distributed) in ways that had little to do with true business competition.

Not so today. Politicians and businessmen alike are throwing money at PR (**пиáр**) like there is no tomorrow. The late general Alexander Lebed spared no expense to bring French megastar Alain Delon to Russia to voice his support for Lebed's presidential ambitions. And businessmen of all stripes engage in "capitalist competition" – trying to be seen as frequently as possible on the covers of business and political magazines, paying big bucks (**бáксы**) for a **пиáровская статья́** (a "bought and paid for" article). And, if they want to denigrate a competitor, they resort to **чёрный пиáр** ("black PR" – mudslinging stories published for money). White PR (**бéлый пиáр**) also exists, but this is used mostly by well-established Western companies, who invite local journalists to press-conferences (the invitation greased by the promise of a buffet, of course) in order to spread news about, say, the nomination of a new CEO or the launch of a new model of car.

This alien acronym – PR – has been adapted to Russia so well and "decorated" with so many suffixes and prefixes that it can be difficult to recognize the actual English "public relations" behind it. Take the verb **пиа́риться** – meaning "to promote oneself." It sounds like a normal reflexive Russian verb, right? The same is true of the word **пиа́рщик** (PR officer or expert in PR), and the adjective **пиа́ровский**, which sounds more like the name of a famous field marshal with Polish roots. And finally there is the new word **са́мопиар** (self-promotion) which is utterly detached from its English roots and sounds very Russian – almost like **самова́р**.

Amazingly, even well-honed Russian words which once reflected our reality are now "evicted" by imports. Take the "twin" of PR: HR (human resources). Recently, I was interviewing a candidate for an HR post, only to find that this fellow hated being tagged with the familiar Russian/Soviet word **кадрови́к** (literally, "cadre person"). Nor did he like for his division to be called **отде́л ка́дров** (cadre department). This new breed of **эйча́ровцы** do not want to be associated with old **ка́дровые** realities and prefer to call their personnel **людски́е ресу́рсы** (human resources) and label themselves a **специали́ст по эйча́р** or simply **эйча́ровец**.

In fact, there is a **пиа́ровский** element in this. To be associated, even (or especially?) linguistically, with Stalin-era divisions for human resources is bad PR. So, by calling themselves **эйча́ровцы**, the new Russian **кадровики́** are seeking to promote themselves as representatives of a new generation of Russian business. It is a part of what some are calling **импло́ймент бре́ндинг** (employment branding), which is meant to attract the best young employees. And, to paraphrase Stalin's old maxim: "**Людски́е ресу́рсы** (not **ка́дры**) **реша́ют всё**" ("The human resources decide everything").

Mikhail Ivanov (July 2005)

Excuse My English

Not all anglicisms in Russian are "false friends" (see page 54). For instance, when you hear your Russian friend say he's just eaten a **га́мбургер** (hamburger), there's no linguistic trap – he does mean a piece of ground beef with that distinctively dull, rubbery taste. (Inventive Russian journalists and literary critics have recently created a hybrid borrowing – **ло́вбургер**, "love-burger" – blending the notion of hamburger tediousness with cheap, romantic fiction translated from English.)

Indeed, the list of borrowed Russian words you need not suspect of being false friends of interpreters is lengthy: **такси́, метро́, бар, аэропо́рт, ви́део, шо́у**, etc. Take them for granted and thank modern civilization for sparing you the trouble to learn them. Oh, and don't forget to give thanks for the fall of the USSR. With the arrival of a market economy and a new political era, the list of borrowed words has enlarged considerably.

For instance, even communist leader Gennady Zyuganov, in spite of his paranoic hatred for things foreign, talks about Yeltsin's tarnished **и́мидж** and works on improving his own. His colleagues from the former Soviet Communist Party didn't care much about their **и́мидж**, or **рейти́нг** for that matter – they were always "elected." They could never be impeached either, only "removed" by death or some secret **пле́нум**. Today even children know the word **импи́чмент**, borrowed from U.S. democracy and often brandished so threateningly by the communist faction in the Duma against Yeltsin.

The most difficult wave of borrowings from the English has been adopted by Russian students and vendors, and distorted to such an extent that they have become unrecognizable to native English speakers.

If a Russian asked you how many **ба́ксы** you'd paid for your **трузера́** or **шузы́**, you probably wouldn't realize he was asking you how many bucks you'd paid for your trousers or shoes. Because of linguistic adaptation of borrowings to local pronunciation, Russians tend to pronounce the English plural "s" as well as the Russian plural "ы". This is what makes some borrowings an inalienable part of the slang, e.g.: "**Мои́ пэ́рентцы сего́дня домо́й не приду́т – дава́йте устро́им у меня́ сэ́йшн и позовём герло́в.**" ("My parents won't be coming home tonight, so let's have a party [session] at my place and invite some girls over"). This is the kind of language you'd expect from the son of well-known Russian diplomats who spent a long time in the U.S..

One can only guess how many **батлы́** or **бо́тлы** (from the English "bottles") they might **дринкану́ть** (drink) in the absence of the **пэ́рентцы**. And then, if they have too much **виска́рь** (i.e. whiskey), the next day most of them **бу́дут в дау́не** (will be down).

When trendy Russian students flag down a taxi, meanwhile, they won't be offering the driver **пять ты́сяч рубле́й** (five thousand rubles) but rather a **фа́йфушник** or **тен** (from the English "five" or "ten").

The first thing these guys look for when they buy something for themselves is the **ле́йбл** (label). They hope it is real **стейтсо́вый** (from the States) and not sporting a fake Levi's **ле́йбл** stuck on the **джи́нсы** (jeans) by the vendor. In these circles, people are what they wear, so they would laugh at anyone dressed like a **ка́нтри** or **кантру́шник** (i.e. country bumpkin). They really make you **крейзану́ться** (go crazy), because their primitive mentality fits the look on their **фэйс**. All they dream of is to drive their own **мерс** (Mercedes) or **вольву́шник** (Volvo).

The electronic revolution has inevitably brought another wave of anglicisms to the Russian language. Words like **компью́тер**, **при́нтер** and **факс** are obvious, but many are obscured by that old Russian habit of adding suffixes. Hence a Russian computer programmer might spend a day tuning up his **пи́сюк** (PC) and working on a **файле́ц** (file), then go home and relax in front of the **те́лик** (television) or put on a **ви́дик** (video) or **сидю́к** (CD).

OK, now let's say you're in Moscow. After an long day of exercising your best survival Russian skills, you feel like relaxing your tongue a bit and speaking a bit of pure English with a "local" expat.

Dream on. Once you start talking about local realities, you'll be amazed by the inadequacy of English. Apart from such obvious Russianisms as *borshch* and politburo, you'll hear plenty of novelties taken from contemporary Russian life.

An expat veteran would make a point of telling you that he has just remonted his apartment (a verb from the Russian **ремо́нт** – renovation), and how much *valuta* (currency) or *dengi* (rubles) he has spent to make his *kvartira* (apartment) a place he looks forward to coming home to after a long day.

The seasoned traveler would remind you to buy a *proyezdnoy* (monthly pass) for city transport unless you want to pay a *shtraf* (fine). And note: you never cross a street or transfer trains, you always *perekhod*.

If you ask an expat how to get tickets to the Bolshoi he won't say you have two options but rather two *variants* – to buy the tickets from the *kassa* (cashier) or from *spekulyanty* (black market dealers).

For expats in Russia, the usage of such words as these is a way to show off one's immersion in local culture. The result is the continued mingling of our two languages. Thus, whatever debts Russian owes to English for the borrowing of words have been (or are being) generously paid back. And as the Russian saying goes, **Долг платежо́м кра́сен** (The beauty of a debt is in its payment).

Mikhail Ivanov (July 1996)

Linguistic Escapades in Lingua Russe

Time was, speaking French for the Russian elite was considered **комильфо́** (*comme il faut* or proper) whereas speaking Russian was **моветон** (*mauvaix ton*, bad form). The nobles would occasionally utter some Russians words like *muzhik*, and yet this sounded pejorative – e.g dressed – **а ля мужи́к** (*a la muzhik*).

These days, the Russian elite – the political elite at least – have more or less forgotten **комильфо́** language (and manners for that matter). The only French word that likely is widely spoken in the Kremlin is the non-translatable **брют**, as in champagne. But even this Frenchism may soon disappear. President Yeltsin recently promised President Jacques Chirac that Russian wine producers will stop labeling their wares with the French terms **шампа́нское** or **конья́к** (*champagne, cognac*), words the French consider trademarked. Russians will apparently now call their champagne and cognac "sparkling wine" and "brandy" (**шипу́чее вино́** and **бре́нди**, respectively).

As to the once-pejorative *muzhik*, it is now associated in elite circles with machismo. Public opinion here seems to feel that a president messing around with **куртиза́нки** (*courtisanes* – female aides) is a sign of a "real man" (**настоя́щий мужи́к**). There was even widespread public sympathy for Minister of Justice Sergei Kovalyov, who was fired after he was caught on video cavorting with some **коко́тки** (from the French *cocottes*) in a *banya* (an escapade later dubbed "Banyagate"). Some papers and journals publicly acquitted Kovalyov, saying that the politicians' **аму́рные дела́** (affairs of the heart) or **алько́вные**

стра́сти (from the French *alcove*, bedroom) were his private business and that it is wrong to **буди́ровать э́тот вопро́с** (to hype the issue, from the French *bouder*). This is an example of how poor Russian makes it into media parlance. Interestingly, Lenin once criticized this pretentiously incorrect idiom, for initially **буди́ровать** in Russian meant what it means in French – to be capricious, to show one's discontent.

Given centuries of court French in imperial Russia, French borrowings in Russian are innumerable. For instance, **эскапа́ды** (*escapades*) and *carte blanche* (**карт-бла́нш**) are direct borrowings that could be freely used, say, to discuss recent scandals at the Clinton White House.

But not all borrowings are immediately apparent to an English speaker. Thus, sticking with current events, **манки́ровал свои́ми супру́жескими обя́занностями** means to neglect one's conjugal duties (from the French verb *manquer*, to miss). And, interestingly, the familiar **импи́чмент**, a recent Russian borrowing from English, can be traced back to the French *empecher*.

Valery Mokhov

Linguistic borrowings tend to occur when another culture has a particular strength in an area. Thus, the plethora of Frenchisms in Russian in the area of love and wine. Of course, there is also cuisine. Here, borrowings range from the common **меню́** (*menu*) to **бланманже́** (*blanc-manger*), **пюре́** (*puree*) and **руле́т** (*roulette*). And in ballet we have **па-де-де** (*pas de deux*), **фуэте́** (*fouette*), **пуа́нты** (*pointe*) and what not.

Frenchisms have been sprinkled throughout Russian, to the extent that some are almost **клише́** (*cliche*), like the fatalistic declaration of **форсмажо́рные обстоя́тельства** (*force majeure*). In sports there are terms like **пелето́н** (*peloton* – cycling) or **туше́** (*touche* – in wrestling or fencing). Oh, and the *haute couture* is **высо́кая мо́да** or just **от кутю́р**.

But the most subtle (and interesting) borrowings are those where differences of *nuance* have somehow arisen between the borrowed foreign word and the Russian equivalent, or where the fact of a foreign borrowing is somehow disguised. For instance, it is common to use the word **чу́вства** to mean feelings. But don't use the French borrowing **сантиме́нты** to mean sentiments. For the Russian word has more to do with the English word "sentimental" and can often be pejorative, e.g: **Дава́йте без сантиме́нтов** (Let's proceed without emotions). The French *plaisir* (pleasure) has been disguised as **блези́р** and is often used in the phrase **для блези́ру**, meaning "for fun" or doing something for the heck of it. And then there is the very Russian sounding noun **амикошо́нство**. It is actually a compound borrowing from the French words *ami* (friend) and *cochon* (pig). This has become a phrase (meaning excessive unceremoniousness or familiarity) beloved by the Russian *intelligentsia*.

Finally, it is worth mentioning two borrowings with fascinating historical roots. The first, **шерамы́жник**, is derived from the French *cher ami* (dear friend). Linguistic legend has it that the word was concocted by French prisoners of war who were abandoned by Napoleon in Russia after his 1812 debacle. The Frenchmen in question used the word to address Russian peasants and beg for a piece of bread. So now **шерамы́жник** means an obnoxious cadger.

The French feminine for "dear" (*chere*) is also at the root of another idiom, **шёрочка с машёрочкой** (*chere* + *ma chere*). This phrase refers to years during and after the Great Patriotic War, when there were not enough men for dances and woman-to-woman dancing pairs were common at *soirees*.

In the end, unless you are faced with some **форс-мажо́р** situation requiring use of Frenchisms in Russian (e.g. to impress intellectuals), you can regard this vocabulary as optional (or **факультати́вный**, from the French, *facultatif*), an *a la carte* part of your Survival Russian **меню́**, if you will. It certainly will not add any *couleure locale* to your Russian – though **блези́р** and **шерамы́жник** would be exceptions. But, then again, it doesn't hurt to know the basic French borrowings in Russian. For then you have **карт-бла́нш** to use this or that **клише́**, depending on where your **эскапа́ды** take you.

Mikhail Ivanov (March 1998)

War
& Competition

Russia, Widen Your Step!

Any idea why grandfathers serve in the Russian army? No, it's not because of personnel problems. The army may be understaffed, but not to that extent. For now the Defense Ministry can do without pensioners.

In fact, the "grandfathers" serving in the Russian army are only 20 years old: **деды** (grandfathers) is the slang word for soldiers in their second year of service. Hence the ill-famed **дедовщина** (hazing).

The administrative euphemism for the word **дедовщина** is **неуставные отношения** (literally, "non-statutory relationship," from the word **устав**, meaning statute or army code). So if a **дед** is caught red-handed, bullying or beating a **новобранец** (young conscript), this is what he will be accused of. The **дед** could then be indicted by a military court (**военный трибунал**).

The slang word for **новобранец** is **салага** or **салабон**. According to the unwritten law of **дедовщина**, he's supposed to do anything a **дед** asks him to – polish his boots, do his share of the washing up, or give him a lion's share of a food package received from home.

It takes each **салага** a year to get "promoted" to the rank of **черпак** (from the Russian verb **черпать** – to ladle out). A **черпак** enjoys the "privilege" of ladling soup at the canteen for his platoon. According to the unwritten code of hazing, he is supposed to give priority to **дедам** when putting meat in the soup, but is also allowed to spare a few pieces for himself.

When the Defense Minister issues the annual **приказ о демобилизации** (demobilization decree) the **дед** becomes a **дембель** (slang for both demobilization and a demobilized soldier). A **дембель** may stay in the army for a while before he is discharged, but there is nothing a sergeant can do to him. While a **дембель** will almost certainly get away with going **самоволка** (AWOL), a **салага** would surely be put in the "lip" (**губа**), slang for guardhouse, for the same action.

Official military cliches can be fun to learn too. Like anywhere else in the world, servicemen in Russia tend to express themselves the hard way. Troops don't "eat" in the Russian army, they "ingest food" (**принимают пищу**). So, lunch time is known as a "time for food ingestion" (**время приёма пищи**).

One of the staples of the diet "ingested' by Russian soldiers is **шрапнель** (shrapnel), the slang for **перловая каша** (pearl barley gruel), so called because it's invariably poorly-cooked and therefore as hard to digest as pieces of enemy shell. In the Russian army this is a universal form of "ammunition," ingested on its own or, as a special treat, with fish.

Ordinary civilians in plain clothes usually call themselves **народ** or **люди** (people). Once they put on a military uniform, though, they become **личный состав** ("personnel" or, literally, "personal compound/mixture").

When it comes to killing, Russian soldiers start to use words like **живая сила** (life force). In battle, they will be expected to "eliminate the living force of the adversary' – **поражать живую силу противника**, i.e. kill people (**убивать людей**).

Military commands also sound a little unusual and **салаги** can have a hard time learning them. When a drill sergeant wants a marching soldier to turn right, he will say: "**левое плечо вперёд**" (literally, "left shoulder forward"). Of course the average conscript will need some time to work out that this just means "turn right'. (The same goes for **правое плечо вперёд** – turn left).

War & Competition

Whereas in civilian life Russians just say **быстре́е** (faster) – or **поторопи́сь** (hurry up) – in the army they opt for the enigmatic **ши́ре шаг**, meaning literally "widen your step."

Some awkward phrases from military parlance recited by generations of *dembels* have become proverbial: **Вы тро́е – о́ба ко мне́** (Both you three come here); **Копа́ть от забо́ра и до обе́да** (Dig from the fence till lunchtime); or **Не де́лаете у́мное лицо́ – Вы же офице́р** (Stop trying to look smart – you're an officer).

This doesn't mean all army idioms are funny or clumsy. You should already be familiar with the famous compliment "I'd go with him on a reconnaissance mission" (page 10). There are other positive idioms from army folklore, like **поря́док в та́нковых войска́х** ("the tanks are in order" – a military set-phrase meaning everything's fine).

And even the younger generation likes quoting the famous lyrics from an old wartime air force song: **Пе́рвым де́лом – самолёты, ну а де́вушки – пото́м** (Airplanes come first, girls next). Taken out of context, this just means "first things first."

Civilians generally have no qualms about assimilating military slang. Words like **деды́**, **салага́** and **самово́лка** have long been in wide use. Russian proverbs and sayings with military terms enjoy similar popularity. For instance, in Soviet times employees of state enterprises and organizations would say about their jobs: **Солда́т спит, а слу́жба идёт** ("The soldier sleeps, but his army service goes on"– i.e. what's the point of working if you get paid no matter what?).

Now that a more ambitious generation of self-made Russians has emerged, you might expect their favorite military saying to be: **Плох тот солда́т, кото́рый не мечта́ет стать генера́лом** (It's a poor soldier who never dreams of becoming a general). And, if you take a look at the wealth of the new "generals' of Russian business, you have to admit that their tanks sure are in order.

Mikhail Ivanov (May 1996)

War-Torn Language

Given that, in the 20th century alone, some 30 to 50 million Soviets died as a result of war, it should be no surprise that war has made its mark on the Russian language. To summon up Lenin's famous precept from the Civil War (9 million killed): **Учиться военному делу настоящим образом**, we have "learned the art of war the real way," or perhaps "the hard way." And, as the proverb has it, **Война не лечит, а калечит**. (War does not heal, it scars.)

In the Kievan Rus era, Prince Svyatoslav addressed his warriors on the eve of an enemy invasion with the words: "**Да не посрамим земли Русские, но ляжем костьми, мёртвы ибо срама не имам**" ("Let us be worthy of the Russian land, for the fallen ones know no shame"). A slightly modernized version of the latter portion – **мёртвые срама не имут** – has entered modern usage and is commonly seen in press headlines and word plays (e.g., **компьютеры спаму не имут** – "computers know no spam," replacing **срам**, "shame," with spam).

Closer to our era, General Alexander Suvorov, the great war hero, reminded that: **Воюй не числом, а уменьем** ("make war not with numbers, but with your talents"). Russian linguist Vladimir Dal, meanwhile, collected many sayings from the War of 1812, including these two about Napoleon: **Наступил на землю русскую, да оступился** (He stepped on Russian lands, but stumbled), and **Отогрелся в Москве, да замёрз на Березине** (He warmed up in Moscow, but froze on the Berezina). The latter refers both to the occupation and burning of Moscow, and to the French defeat.

The word **война** (war) is present in many idioms and proverbs, some no longer associated directly with war. For example, when someone says, "**Мы ещё повоюем**" (literally, "We are still warring"), it can mean simply, "We are not done yet," with no particularly martial reference. It can be used as a phrase of self-encouragement ("we have not given up") after a long period of recovery or when someone's career or private life is at a low ebb. More pessimistically, when someone (an athlete, in particular) has been struggling with an injury and decides to quit, he could say: "**Всё, отвоевался**" ("That's it, I'm done warring").

The well-known saying, **На войне, как на войне** ("all's fair in war," or "*a la guerre comme a la guerre*") has also made its way well beyond military life. It now merely implies that drastic conditions require drastic measures – no holds barred (**все средства хороши**).

Unlike today, in Soviet times, particularly after the USSR defeated the Nazis in the Great Patriotic War (**Великая Отечественная Война**, not called WWII here when referring to Russia's war with Germany), our **военные** (servicemen) enjoyed undisputed authority and prestige; anything related to them had a positive connotation. To say someone had **военная выправка** (military bearing) meant that their attire and manner was straight, ordered and attractive. If someone delivered a concise oral report or always spoke to the point, he was complimented for speaking **по-вое́нному чётко** (as concisely as a serviceman).

In recent years, however, things military have become less popular. The obviously negative aspects of war are highlighted in the proverb, **Кому́ война́, а кому́ мать родна́** (To some it is war, to others a dear mother). It means that war is atrocious for some, but others benefit from it. The liberal press likes to employ this proverb when criticizing President Putin and Russian generals on the war in Chechnya.

But of course war is atrocious. The bard Bulat Okudzhava expressed this eloquently in many of his works, including *Do svidaniya, malchiki* (*Goodbye Boys*): **Ах война́, что ж ты, по́длая, сде́лала**? (Akh, war, what have you done to us, you villain?) More recently, the Russian rock group Lyube, in their song *Kombat*, echoed Okudzhava's 40-year-old line with, "**Ах война́, война́-война́, дурна́я де́вка – сте́рва она́.**" (Akh, war, war, she is a nasty girl, just scum.) Put more simply, in the way only proverbs can encapsulate things: **Война́ кро́вь лю́бит** (War loves blood).

Russians of all generations – those who fought in wars and those who have not – would certainly subscribe to these sentiments. We have indeed learned from war "the hard way" and deserve several centuries of peace. As another of our "war-torn" sayings has it, **Повоева́ли – и бу́дет** (We are done warring, and ever will be).

Mikhail Ivanov (May 2005)

It's the Participation That Counts!

Naive journalists have been trying for too long to convince us that sports and politics should be separated. But is it realistic to separate sports from politics or from day-to-day life for that matter? Wasn't it Baron Pierre de Coubertin, the founder of the Contemplation Olympic Movement, who said "Oh, sport, you are Peace!"?

No matter how hard countries have tried to separate sports from politics, they have invariably failed. Proof? The same, "**О спорт! Ты мир!**" was beaten to death by Soviet propagandists in the run-up to the 1980 Moscow Olympics. But this didn't stop the USSR's diplomatic opponents from boycotting the event (because of the USSR's military invasion of Afghanistan).

The linguistic dividing line between politics and sports is even more fragile than the diplomatic one. Today we hear how Russian politics is full of "low blows" (**уда́ры ни́же по́яса**) or how Yeltsin won his second presidential seat by points (**по очка́м**), whereas Yuri Luzhkov knocked his opponents out (**нокаути́ровал**) in the recent mayoral elections.

Thus, a serious foray into the sports lexicon is *de rigueur*. Or, to use a common figure skating term, it should be included in the **обяза́тельная програ́мма** (mandatory program), vs. the **произво́льная програ́мма** (free program). Sports terms, particularly from figure skating (**фигу́рное ката́ние**), can also take on humorous connotations, as this Russian joke illustrates: "A husband watching a couple of ice skaters is gawking at the female partner: 'I would love to skate the free program with her,' he says. 'Well,' his wife responds from the bedroom, 'we'll see how you skate the mandatory one.'" (**Посмо́трим, как ты обяза́тельную отката́ешь.**")

Over the years, sports fashions have varied greatly, according to the changing tastes of Russia's rulers. Of late, tennis parlance has been in vogue in the Kremlin: astute local commentators make a point to say how Yeltsin always tries to play his adversaries "on his favorite surface" (**на своём люби́мом покры́тии**), for this is when his opponents "make double faults" or "unforced errors," one after another (**двойны́е оши́бки, невы́нужденные оши́бки**).

Yet, under Brezhnev, ice hockey was top dog. And, despite the plummeting ratings of Russia's national hockey team, hockey idioms remain quite popular. Take for instance the famous old Soviet **Ша́йбу! Ша́йбу!** (literally "Puck! Puck!," the equivalent of "Go, Russia, Go!") This slogan is still echoed in the stands of many stadiums, regardless of the sport. And, when NHL players were playing too rough, the legendary TV sports commentator Nikolai Ozerov coined the idiom, "We don't need that kind of hockey" ("**Тако́й хокке́й нам не ну́жен**"). This idiom now enjoys wider usage, to express a negative opinion about something. Another pearl spawned by Ozerov was: "Without this, hockey would lose about half of its spectacular attractiveness" ("**Без э́того хокке́й потеря́л бы едва́ ли не полови́ну свое́й зре́лищной привлека́тельности**"). What he meant was that it is the faults, unpredictable defeats and other gaffes which make hockey such a passionate game. Heard out of hockey context, this phrase becomes quite funny.

Of course, the sport for all tastes is soccer. Unfortunately, of late the dirty tricks of this sport have taken root in Kremlin politics. Soon after Boris Berezovsky was expelled from the field (**удалён с по́ля**), observers noted it was a not without Chubais' influence. Yet, as a true sportsman, Berezovsky showed solid endurance (**выно́сливость**) and an ability to take a hit (**держа́ть уда́р**), making sure Chubais at least received a "yellow card" (i.e warning) for his now infamous privatization book. This, of course, means that Chubais' next yellow card would automatically ensue in a red one (i.e expulsion – **удале́ние**). So, for now the Berezovsky-Chubais match has ended in a draw (**зако́нчился ничье́й**), and one may need to resort to the "goal average system" to define the winner (**определи́ть победи́теля по систе́ме "гол+пас"**).

In the meantime, Yeltsin forcibly ended Boris Nemtsov's **беспро́игрышную се́рию** (winning streak) by scolding him in public for unpaid pension arrears. If this continues, Yeltsin's former pet Nemtsov may not "pass the qualification tournament" (**пройти́ отбо́рочный турни́р**) for the Presidential race of 2000. And, almost simultaneously, ex-defense minister Pavel Grachev, having sat for so long "on the bench" (**на скаме́йке запасны́х**) for having let too many goals into Russia's net (**пропусти́ть мно́го мяче́й**) in the past, finally landed a cushy job "in the second league" (**во второ́й ли́ге**), when Yeltsin gave him the post of counsellor at the state arms exporter, Rosvooruzheniye.

Sports terms are certainly not limited to the domestic sphere. Soviet-style political observers love to invoke wrestling terms and cite U.S. "arm-twisting policies" (**поли́тика выкру́чивания рук**), and political historians would justly recall how the USSR's allies tried to "play the clock" (**тяну́ть вре́мя**) before opening the Second Front in WWII. What is more, Yeltsin's critics say Russia keeps finding itself "off-sides" (**вне игры́**) in the international arena and that, because of "liberals like Gorbachev" and "turncoats like Yeltsin," Russia lost the Cold War. Yeltsin and his supporters could reply to all this in a humorous vein by recalling the famous Olympic motto: "Winning is not the main thing, participation is" ("**Гла́вное не побе́да – гла́вное уча́стие**").

Let's face it: more and more often Russian politicians are being booed (**освистаны** – literally "whistled at") by the public for poor performance, both when playing **на своём по́ле** (at home) and away (**в гостя́х** or **на чужо́м по́ле**). And the independent press urges all sides to rid Russian politics and everyday life of the mutual **уда́ры ни́же по́яса** and other **гру́бая игра́** (rough games). However, for now, these sports-related phenomena seem to be too deeply-rooted in the life and language of Russia. And, frankly, both foreign and domestic observers would agree that, without these "rule violations" (**нарушéния пра́вил**), Russian life would lose just about half of its spectacular attractiveness.

Mikhail Ivanov (February 1998)

Setting the Bar High

Since Russian sport seems to be witnessing a track and field revival, it is worth looking at this topic from a linguistic angle. The bard Vladimir Vysotsky dedicated several songs to the Queen of Sports (**Короле́ва спо́рта**) as some like to call track and field (including Moscow Mayor Yuri Luzhkov, at Moscow's 2006 World Indoor Championships, where he added the prefix, "Her Majesty").

Begin with a misnomer: **лёгкая атле́тика**. Literally "light athletics" or even "easy athletics," track and field is anything but easy. Just watch long-distance runners cruising at their 10,000 meter pace – roughly equivalent to what we mere mortals call our 60 meter sprint pace – and you see that **лёгкая атле́тика** is in fact very **тяжёлая** (hard). Note: in sports terminology, **тяжёлая атле́тика** is weight-lifting.

In one Vysotsky sports song (OK, dedicated to a speed skater, but applicable to track anyway) the hero admits to overestimating his physical reserves, as a result of which he burned out: "I made my kick in the 10,000 meter race as if it were a 500 meter run – and I flattened out" ("**Я на де́сять тыщ рвану́л, как на пятьсо́т, и спёкся**").

The lesson is clear: in sports (and in life) one should not **сбить дыха́лку** (lose one's breathing rhythm) and you should always conserve energy for the final kick (**фи́нишный рыво́к**).

Not surprisingly, the idiom **фи́нишный рыво́к** appears in countless articles dedicated to presidential races or, better yet, to a presidential marathon (**президе́нтский марафо́н**). Analogies between athletics and politics are as ubiquitous in Russian as they are in English: just like runners, political contenders can **пойма́ть второ́е дыха́ние** (catch their second wind) or may **сойти́ с диста́нции** (withdraw from the race). Some candidates have a **фальста́рт** (false start) and are disqualified. Those who remain in the race are ever watchful for the right moment to **нача́ть спуртова́ть** – to make their move (literally, "to spurt").

Outgoing politicos may "pass the baton" (**передáть эстафéтную пáлочку**) to their successors, who will **принять эстафéту** ("assume the relay," or carry the torch onward).

The idea of the political relay was frequently cited in Soviet political texts, usually praising the connection between generations – thus the idiom **эстафéта поколéний** (generational relay). Open up a *Pravda* archive from the 1930s-1970s and you are sure to eventually read about a veteran, record-setting Stakhanovite miner who is passing the baton on to a young colleague.

Jumping is another area ripe for metaphors. As in the high jump or pole vault, it is common to talk about "raising the bar" (**поднять плáнку**), raising it too high (**задрáть плáнку до заоблáчных высóт** – literally setting it "above the clouds"), or keeping it "just high enough" (**высокó держáть плáнку**).

In jumping, success often boils down to hitting the right (correct) take-off foot – **толчкóвая ногá**. Most jumpers' **толчкóвая** is their left. But, as Vysotsky sang in his **Пéсенка прыгунá в высотý** (*Song of a High Jumper*): "**У когó толчкóвая – лéвая, а у меня толчкóвая – прáвая!**" ("Some people take off with their left foot, but I take off with my right" – i.e. I do things my way). Like no one else, Vysotsky grasped the essence of high jumping and sports:

Разбéг, толчóк... И – стыдно подымáться:	*I run, I jump ... I am ashamed to get up:*
Во ртý опилки, слёзы из-под век,	*I've a mouthful of sawdust, tears in my eyes*
На рубежé проклятом два двенáдцать	*The bar has kept me from beating*
Мне плáнка преградила путь наверх.	*The damned 2.12 meter barrier*
Я признаюсь вам, как на духý:	*I confess to you, as if to my soul:*
Таковá вся спортивная жизнь,	*This is what the sporting life is all about,*
Лишь мгновéние ты наверхý –	*You are at the top for just a moment*
И стремительно пáдаешь вниз.	*And then you come crashing down.*

If there was anyone who set the bar high in life, it was Vladimir Vysotsky. Russia has yet to see a contemporary bard who could **принять эстафéту поколéний** from Vysotsky, who sadly died during... the 1980 Moscow Olympics. Such is the fate of Russians who take paths less traveled. Or who take off from their right foot.

Mikhail Ivanov (May 2006)

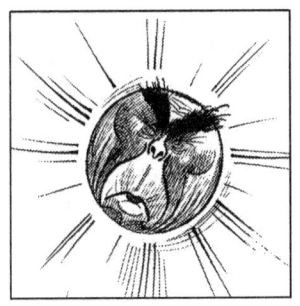

Weather & Seasons

Don't Ask Me for Snow in Winter

То ли до́ждь – то ли снег, то ли бу́дет – то ли нет.
Maybe rain, maybe snow, maybe yes or maybe no.

There's nothing like this good old Russian proverb to characterize this year's winter, as well as Russia's general political and economic situation. For, if you take this idiom in its figurative sense, it means "everything is up in the air, it's hard to tell right now."

This is an apt description for Russia in her current period of transition, when the Communists keep making apocalyptic prophesies, calling for the President's and Prime Minister's resignation every time they attend the Duma. Their political colors don't vary much, so you could label them all with the answer to the wintery riddle: **зимо́й и ле́том одни́м цве́том** – ("What is the same color be it winter or summer?" – if politics is not one of your passions, the usual answer to this riddle is a fir tree).

The "ones who show the same colors in all seasons" have been trying vainly – or better yet, trying **как ры́ба об лёд** (like a fish flopping on the ice) – to improve their flagging political fortunes by taking advantage of Yeltsin's prolonged absence. Now, as the president gets back into his working rhythm, he may well demonstrate another famous winter phrase, invented by the writers Ilf and Petrov: **Лёд тро́нулся, кома́ндовать пара́дом бу́ду я** (The ice is broken, it is I who will lead the parade), while his subordinates, as well as ordinary

Russians, might welcome him back with: **Ско́лько лет, ско́лько зим!** – the Russian wintery equivalent of the English, "Long time no see!"

On the other hand, if you take the "maybe rain, maybe snow" proverb at face value, you could easily apply it to the weather we've been having in Moscow of late.

Last November and December, temperatures hit all-time highs for this time of year. As Alexander Pushkin would have put it, **Зимы́ ждала́, ждала́ приро́да!** (Nature was waiting, waiting for winter.) – but in vain. At press time, there was no snow at all – just some ridiculously light precipitation, which Russians call "white flies" (**бе́лые му́хи**) and can't even be taken as real snow in a country which is traditionally rich in this natural resource.

Therefore, when Russians want to suggest that someone is extremely mean, they say: "**У него́ зимо́й сне́га не вы́просишь**" ("You can't even ask him for snow in winter"). Of course, the saying is very applicable to this winter. Our present snow-free conditions may even make snow a sort of hard currency and send demand for the white flakes skyrocketing.

Perhaps soon, in order to keep their offspring happy, New Russians will be spending Christmas and New Year's in Switzerland, or will buy imported snow for outrageous sums from enterprising northern minorities. Knowing New Russians, who want everything that's expensive or hard to come by, and want it now, the idea may not be so far-fetched. This season, snow-making or snow-selling could become a lucrative business in the European part of Russia. Consequently, the Chukchis [indigenous people native to the Chukotka peninsula and ethnically tied to North American Eskimos] could make a good business selling snow. Why not set up a company called, for example, **Снег Лимитэд** (Snow Limited)? Snow supplies are limited indeed.

In the meantime, Russian children won't be able to play with snowflakes (**играть в снежки**), let alone make snow *babas* (**лепить снежную бабу**) or frolic *en masse* in **сугробы** (snow drifts).

Those who favor this new shortage – climatic this time around – are definitely the municipal services, which have been traditionally plagued by slippery roads and haunted by the severe problems of black ice (**гололёд**) or snowstorms (**метель; снежная буря**). A continuing shortage of adequate snowplows (**снегоуборочная машина**) is usually the talk of the town – and will be again – as winter **вступит в свои права** (comes into its own).

To paraphrase a great winter-related proverb, the city should be preparing its cart in December and its snowplows (sledges) in July (**Готовь сани летом, а телегу – зимой**) so that problems don't come suddenly and unexpectedly – or, better said, **как снег на голову** (like snow on one's head).

With luck, these weather-cliches will stay with you **и в зной, и в стужу** (in heat and in cold), will have a snowball effect (**эффект снежного кома**) on your vocabularly growth, and won't melt like the first snow (**растает как первый снег**).

Mikhail Ivanov (February 1997)

It's Spring, Say "Thank You" to the Party!

Time was, Russians would bless the Communist party for everything they had (or did not have). So, whoever took the floor at the rostrum of a communist meeting (dedicated to the spring field work, to the completion of the Five-Year Plan, what have you) would end his speech with a mandatory "thanks" to the party. This gave birth to the satiric short poem: **Зима прошла, настало лето – спасибо партии за это**, which can be translated as "Summer has come, winter is gone – so we owe the party one."

It might be appropriate at this point to cite the spring-related idiom about "not believing anyone on April 1" (see "He Who Laughs Last," page 171), but that deals more with humor than with seasons. But Russians are not very trusting in March either. At least they don't trust the weather much. March is considered a very treacherous month: the sun does shine, the snow does melt, but it's still usually very cold, hence the folk wisdom, **На дворе марток, надевай трое порток** (It's March outside, so put on three pairs of trousers). This is to protect against the cold icy wind.

Speaking of winds, when someone – usually at the sight of some enemy, nemesis or persecutor – disappears all of sudden, Russians say **"его как ветром сдуло"** ("he was blown

away by the wind" – of course, not to be confused with the lyrics of the Bob Dylan song). If someone is hard to catch or find, a cynical person might advise you to "go and chase the wind in the field" ("**ищи́ ве́тра в по́ле**"). And if a "blowhard" gives you a lengthy, reprimanding lecture, take heart in the Russian saying **соба́ка ла́ет – ве́тер но́сит** (the dog's barking is carried away by the wind).

Needless to say, spring is associated here with love and good moods – or both. Hence the expression "spring mood" (**весе́ннее настрое́ние**). When men fall prey to this mood they start courting the fair sex and are compared to March cats. Someone who behaves **как кот ма́ртовский** is a promiscuous male. Russian macho types like to say about this time of the year **Весна́ пришла́ – ще́пка на ще́пку па́дает** (Spring has come, a sliver falls on a sliver). The creators of the U.S. suspense film *Sliver* (in Russian **Ще́пка**) were inspired by architecture and not this saying, yet it is ironic that the film's mood reflects the meaning of the proverb quite well. (In any event, the Russian language owns the copyright).

Come May and Russian peasants start to predict the fall harvest by the spring weather. If May is cold, they say: "**Май холо́дный – год хлебор́одный**" ("A cold May means a rich harvest").

The great Russian poet Fyodor Tyutchev had a more poetic way of describing this month. Take note of his now proverbial two line poem:

Люблю́ грозу́ в нача́ле ма́я, когда́ весе́нний пе́рвый гром,
Сло́вно резвя́ся и игра́я, грохо́чет в не́бе голубо́м

*I love thunderstorm in early May, when the first spring thunder
is rolling up in the blue sky as it were frisking and playing.*

Back in pagan times, Russians (their ancestors, that is) greatly feared thunder. It was usually associated with something unexpected, usually a disagreeable surprise, hence the saying: **Как гром среди́ я́сного не́ба** (Like thunder amidst the clear sky).

Another thunder-related idiom reflects on stereotypical Russian nonchalance: **Гром не гря́нет – мужи́к не перекре́стится** (A peasant will cross himself only if there is thunder). This is applicable to someone who never meets a deadline and who needs disasters or crises to be motivated.

Who says May, says rain, so Russians love rain-related sayings this time of year as well. Russians don't say "to mushroom" but rather "**расти́, как грибы́ по́сле дождя́**" ("to grow like mushrooms after a rain"). Great lovers of mushroom-picking, Russians know that mushrooms love sun and rain – especially if it's simultaneous – so when you see the sun in the sky but drops of rain fall on your head, it is called "a mushroom rain" – **грибно́й дождь**. To say it's raining cats and dogs – you have a couple of immediate choices: "**льёт,** как из ведра" ("it's pouring as if from a bucket"), or "дождь стеной" ("it's like a wall of rain"). There are plenty of others, but let's make one final comment on "rainy" sayings.

Russia's leaders recently postponed indefinitely the deadline for payment of workers' wage arrears. Such "manana-style" scheduling is brilliantly summed up by the phrase about indefinite time: после дождичка в четверг (after a little bit of rain on Thursday). But in Russia's tough socio-political situation, this answer may not work. For all these workers, miners and teachers have been waiting desperately for their paychecks. Or, as Russians would say, they have be "waiting for an answer like the nightingale waits for the summer" ("Жду ответа, как соловей лета"). And it looks like they won't take the "Thursday rain story" for an answer...

Mikhail Ivanov (May 1997)

The General Zima Factor

As I write these lines, Moscow is being assaulted by a brutal cold spell surrounding the date of Orthodox Epiphany (**Крещение**), a time of traditionally cold weather long known as **Крещенские морозы** (Epiphany frosts). This prompted a local humorist to rephrase Pushkin's famous winter line: **И рады мы проказам матушки зимы** ("We are pleased with Mother Winter's mischief.") by adding a "**ль**" between **рады** and **мы**, changing the meaning to "Are we really pleased...?"

January's freeze would seem to indicate that global warming is far from imminent. Weather forecasters promised that the mercury would dip to -37° Celsius – apparently a low not hit since 1940. At such times, we writers cannot help but consider the role of winter in Russian history and culture.

Winter weather lasts a good six months here – from mid-October through early April. So perhaps it is not surprising that many Russians adore this season, tenderly calling winter (a feminine noun in Russian) **зима-красна** (winter the pretty), or **Зимушка-зима** (little winter).

For the Germans and French, however, winter in Russia probably has fewer positive connotations. They came up with their own militaristic appellation of winter – **генерал Зима** – who, as they claim, "fought" alongside Kutuzov against Napoleon, and beside Zhukov against Hitler. Certainly many give General Winter more than his due in these wars (at the expense of human factors), but it is unquestioned that he had a role in leading many thousands of German and French soldiers to their eternal **зимовье** (winter quarters) on the fields surrounding Moscow in 1941 and 1812.

Truth be told, not all Russians are huge fans of bitter cold. As the saying goes, **русская кость тепло любит** (the Russian bone likes warmth). But, then again, being winter-hardy (**зимостойкий**) is largely a matter of preparation: **лето пролежишь, зимой с сумой побежишь** (if you lay idle in summer, you will go crazy in winter). For what Russian does not know, deep in their warmth-loving bones, the axiomatic proverb, **готовь сани летом, а телегу – зимой** (prepare your sled in summer and your cart in winter)?

Not surprisingly, then, winter is associated with more than simply poetic "sun and frost" – **мороз и солнце**, which make for a marvelous day – "**день чудесный**" (*a la* Pushkin:

"Моро́з и со́лнце, день чуде́сный"). Unlike fall (о́сень), that exuberant season when, as a favorite proverb has it, "even a sparrow can afford some beer" (в о́сень и у воробья́ пи́во), winter is a time of tribulation, of rationing the fruits of summer's labor, that they may last until spring: ле́то припаси́-ка, а зима́ прибери́-ка (winter consumes what summer has stored up).

Thus, the verb перезимова́ть (literally, "to winter over") is not always used in its direct sense. When you hear a Russian say: "Ничего́, ка́к-нибудь перезиму́ем" (literally: "It's all right, we'll live through the winter"), it simply means – "Oh, it's OK, we'll make it through somehow." This "ка́к-нибудь" and "перезиму́ем" are so deeply Russian, they are surely two keys to the much-vaunted mystery of the Russian soul.

Another important idiom based on the verb зимова́ть builds around the phrase, где ра́ки зиму́ют ("where the crayfish spend their winters"). Someone who is clever is someone who knows where to find crayfish in winter – зна́ет, где ра́ки зиму́ют. And, if you want to "show someone a thing or two," you can показа́ть, где ра́ки зиму́ют, e.g.: "Сейча́с я ему́ покажу́, где ра́ки зиму́ют" ("Now, you wait, I'll show him a thing or two.") If you are on the receiving end of difficulties or punishment, you will узна́ть, где ра́ки зиму́ют.

As to the eternal debate between generations of Russians over when зима́ was настоя́щая (real) – now or in the mid-20th century, the lexicographer Vladimir Dal captured all that needed saying back in the 19th century. As a proverb recorded in his dictionary so eloquently puts it: не по образца́м зима́ и ле́то быва́ет, по во́ле бо́жьей (Winter and summer are not made according to patterns, but according to God's will).

Mikhail Ivanov (March 2006)

Power & Glory

Dear Demosthenes

There are plenty of phrases in common usage that Russians associate with Leonid Brezhnev. According to one such formulation, Brezhnev may go down in history as a **мелкий политический деятель эпохи Аллы Пугачёвой** ("a minor politician in the era of Alla Pugachyova" – a top Russian pop star of the 1970s and 80s). Ordinary Russians used to call him either Lyonya (the familiar form of Leonid) or Ilyich (his patronymic, shared with Lenin, hence the humorous slogan of the time **от Ильича до Ильича** (from Ilyich to Ilyich). Official propaganda, meanwhile, called him a **верный ленинец** (a loyal Leninist).

In his later years, Lyonya could hardly put two words together. So, when speaking in public, he simply read a prepared text. This was called **по бумажке** – to do everything from paper. This is why ill-wishers claimed that he started his opening speech at the 1980 Olympics with five exclamations ("O! O! O! O! O!") – he had simply read the Olympic logo.

Though his writing skills were questionable at best, at the end of his career Leonid Ilyich discovered a penchant for literature. So much so that the Union of Soviet Writers awarded him the Lenin Prize for his memoir trilogy *Little Land*, *Renaissance* and *Virgin Lands* – mandatory reading at all high schools. The last of these started with the great platitude **будет хлеб – будет и песня** (if there's bread there'll be songs), still famous because aging Soviet actor and sex symbol Vyacheslav Tikhonov read excerpts from these "masterpieces" on prime time TV.

Vulnerable to flattery and awards, Brezhnev liked getting medals and freely distributed them to his retinue. Since gerontocracy prevailed in the Kremlin back then, the cliché phrase for the occasion was: **За большие заслуги в области науки/культуры/военного строительства ... и в связи с 80-летием** (For great merits in the sphere of science/culture/military construction ... and on the occasion of ...'s 80th birthday). In response, the lucky old fellow would always "thank the beloved Communist Party... and personally Leonid Ilyich Brezhnev for this high appraisal of my modest contribution..." (**"поблагодарить родную Коммунистическую партию и лично Леонида Ильича Брежнева за высокую оценку моего скромного вклада..."**) This famous "...и лично" is still used when Russians congratulate each other. Knowing Brezhnev's weakness for flattery, everybody who spoke with him in public called him "dear Leonid Ilyich (thus prompting the joke about Brezhnev picking up the receiver and saying: "Hello, this is dear Leonid Ilyich" – "**Алло, дорогой Леонид Ильич слушает...**")

When Leonid mumbled from the rostrum, the most innocuous Soviet clichés and set phrases became proverbial colloquialisms because of his endless slips of the tongue. At times it seemed like he had a mouthful of stones – like the ancient Greek Demosthenes who honed his speaking skills thus on the seashore. The only difference was that Brezhnev's diction remained lousy until his death, and Demosthenes became a famous orator.

Ilyich was particularly bad at such combinations of letters as "st" or "str." When, in his final report to the Congress of Communist Parties, Brezhnev came to the chapter, 'Relations with Socialist Countries,' TV viewers became glued to the screen in expectation – just to hear him call these countries "s----y sausages." Not because the idea of socialist internationalism was alien to the "loyal Leninist," but because his slurred pronunciation turned the words **социалисти́ческие стра́ны** into **соси́ски сра́ные**. That was especially funny because the presence (or absence) of cheap sausage in stores is still for many Russians one of the main criteria of well-being.

In point of fact, it was under Brezhnev that the quality of Russian sausage began to deteriorate – well-informed experts at a meat-processing factory claim research students wrote dissertations on "sausage hydrolysis" – a process whereby water was added to the meat to make up for shortages. Which of course made the sausages taste just the way Brezhnev described.

Speaking of well-being and economics – Brezhnev had another memorable phrase: **эконо́мика должна́ быть эконо́мной** (economics should be economical). A word play rather than a meaningful formula, this idiom gave rise to another phrase about Brezhnev's U.S. counterpart, **рейгано́мика должна́ быть рейгано́мной** (reaganomics should be reagonomical).

To euphemize the condemnation of party brethren, Ilyich would usually say the party was giving someone a **принципиа́льную оце́нку** (an assessment on principle). Such an assessment seems to have been made of the USSR's neighboring Afghan regime. When the USSR invaded in December 1979, Lyonya's ideologues invented a brezhnevism still fresh in the memory – "the introduction of a limited contingent of Soviet troops at the request of the Afghan government." That prompted the most daring Soviet historians to say that the Mongol-Tatar yoke was "the introduction of a limited contingent of Mongol-Tatar troops at the request of Russian princes."

But the key word of Brezhnev's time was **хала́тность** (negligence). Sometimes it was called **престу́пная хала́тность** (criminal negligence), which became a legal term.

In this era, only "big" things (those with international exposure) met international standards – e.g. ballet, space technology or construction of hydroelectric power stations. Hence the famous verses of the time:

Зато́ мы де́лаем раке́ты и покоря́ем Енисе́й,
а та́кже в о́бласти бале́та мы впереди́ плане́ты всей"

*But, on the other hand, we build rockets and conquer the Yenisei,
and lead the whole planet in ballet.*

Yet anything catering to simple everyday needs – such as hairdressing or restaurant service – was well behind, earning the tag of **хала́тность**. Even funerals were done sloppily. In fact during Brezhnev's funeral, the gravediggers dropped the coffin as they were lowering it into the ground. As the ceremony was broadcast live, the noise they made had worldwide repercussions. Thus did history "assess on principle" the Brezhnev era...

Mikhail Ivanov (December 1996)

Tsar Struck

Despite 70 years of communism and nearly 10 years of reform, plenty of "tsarist" imprints have survived into the modern Russian lexicon. Regular readers of Survival Russian will recall the beautiful form of address "merciful monarch" – **ми́лостивый госуда́рь**, which was a polite *comme il faut* (proper) formula once used by the educated and noble classes.

It is common for domestic political observers to draw parallels between the present day and the tsarist era, comparing the rule of President Boris Yeltsin during his second term to the reign of a tsar. But then President Yeltsin himself, addressing members of his inner ruling circle, was recently quoted as saying: "Listen to what the tsar says" – **Слу́шай, что тебе́ царь говори́т**. (Incidentally, an off-handed reference to "Tsar Boris" can be a humorous flourish: making reference to Tsar Boris Godunov). And some observers, reflecting on Yeltsin's authoritarian style of dealing with his subordinates, may comment that he is acting in accordance with the tsarist principle, "**хочу́ – ка́зню, хочу́ – ми́лую**" ("I'll execute or pardone you, as I like").

Most luminaries of Russian literature from Pushkin onwards were at odds with the Russian autocracy – likely because they did not want the fate of their literary works to depend on the caprices of the tsar. Yet many rank and file Russians loved their tsars. Some historians would even argue that Russians cannot live without a tsar-like regime. The national anthem used to be titled **Бо́же царя́ храни́**, (*God Save the Tsar*). And the old motto **За царя́, за Ро́дину, за ве́ру**, (For the Tsar, for the Fatherland, for the Faith) still strikes a chord with many Russians. Therefore, the word "tsar" often has a positive connotation. When somebody gives you a gorgeous expensive gift you may say he rewarded you "tsar-style" – **награди́л по-ца́рски**. Moreover, today the word "tsar" is even used for marketing – suffice it to note the names of restaurants like "**Ца́рская охо́та**" or "Tsar's Hunt" (where Yeltsin likes to dine) or dishes like "**олени́на по-ца́рски**" ("venison *a la* tsar"). They would not give a name like that to something inedible, would they?

On the other hand, someone who acts hurriedly, without thinking first, is a person "without a tsar in his head" – **без царя́ в голове́**. And if you really think the task or the work somebody wants you to do is a little beneath you, you can use the good old **не ца́рское э́то де́ло** (this is not a tsar's business) – i.e. it's too small for me to waste my time on it.

But the funniest tsar-related idiom is the euphemism **куда́ царь пешко́м ходи́л** ("I need to go where the tsar went on foot," meaning "I need to go to the washroom." An equivalent English euphemism might be "I've gotta go see a man about a horse"). Even if young Russians may find this expression obsolete, it is pretty-self-explanatory.

Speaking of obsolete, if you want to say "way back when," here is a good one: "in the times of Tsar-Gorokh" (**времена́ царя́-Горо́ха**) – literally the "Pea-Tsar," a popular folklore personage from Russian fairy tales. Another good way of proving your education and deep knowledge of folklore and history is the famous expression **Тяжела́ ты, ша́пка Монома́ха!** (Oh, how heavy your are, the Crown of Tsar's Monomakh!). The hat in question was that of Vladimir Monomakh, of Kiev, ancestor of the Muscovite princes, and it was used down through the ages as an important part of the tsars' coronation rituals. Due to all the jewelry and gold the shapka was decorated with, it was physically quite heavy. But wearing the crown was not just physically heavy; it also constituted a difficult political and moral burden. Today, this particular saying is uttered with a deep sigh, to express the burden's of one's responsibilities (most often in the 1st person). Even so, as far as I can remember, no modern Russian tsar has ever volunteered to ever relinquish the **ша́пка**.

As to the old tsars, luckily for them the **ша́пка** was required attire only on great and solemn occasions. And, needless to say, they didn't wear it when visiting the place where they used to walk to...

Mikhail Ivanov (June 1998)

Pulling the Blanket to One's Side

Russian, like any living language, develops according to its own rules. No matter how high the protectionist barriers put up by linguistic purists around so-called "literary Russian," borrowings from the "less desireable" representatives of Russian society are bound to slip through.

Take the lingo of prisoners. How can one stop Russians from using prison slang when tens of millions of Russians served time under Stalin and when, even now, Russia has the highest per capita prison population in the world? It is no wonder that many idioms that once belonged only in Solovki or Kolyma can now be found in newspaper headlines or heard on the radio.

We hear that our politicians, when forging political alliances or holding negotiations, tend to **тяну́ть на себя́ одея́ло** (pull the blanket to their side), prison argot for trying to secure one-sided benefits or better conditions for oneself. In fact, in the run-up to the 2000 presidential elections, the whole of Russia looked like an immense blanket which each politician was trying to pull to his side.

Nor is it unusual to hear about all sorts of **разбо́рки** in the political arena (**разбо́рки** is slang for "a settling of accounts," which was a term once used only by thick-necked banditos).

By now, most Russians know well how to **бо́тать по фе́ни** (speak thieves' argot). Many idioms born behind bars have become classic, namely thanks to movies inspired by prison topics. Thus, after millions laughed at the 1970s Russian comedy *Gentlemen of Fortune* (**Джентльме́ны уда́чи**), adolescents, let alone adults, began repeating the now famous threats from the film "**Пасть порву́! Морга́лы вы́колю!**" – "I will tear off your mouth and gouge out your blinkers!" (from the verb **морга́ть**, to blink). In another borrowing, one hears Russians call each other **реди́ска** ("radish", a "bad person").

If you really want to make a solemn promise and make it an especially strong one, you can say "**век во́ли не вида́ть!**" ("may I not see freedom again for a whole century"). This

now widely used idiom comes directly from the **зо́на** (prison zone) as Russians call their system of camps and other penitentiary establishments, where they cook their very strong, drug-like tea, **чифи́рь,** and call their uncomfortable collective toilet the **пара́ша**.

In fact, the etymological roots of prison-related colorful idioms no longer seems to bother representatives of the middle- and younger-aged generations. They seem to embrace this heritage of their elders. So you hear them talking about **кати́ть бо́чку** (literally "to roll the barrel," to give somebody a hard time, to be rough with somebody) or **лепи́ть горба́того** (literally "to model a hunchback," to lie).

Thanks to such detective movies as **Ме́сто встре́чи измени́ть нельзя́** (*Don't Change the Meeting Place*), any Russian kid knows at least three synonyms for a police officer: **мент** (cop), **лега́вый** (from **лега́вая соба́ка**, a "hunting dog"), and **му́сор** (literally, "rubbish"). Given the "respect" Russia's law-enforcement bodies have engendered with their lax approach to upholding the law, all three terms are in wide usage.

Во́ры в зако́не ("thieves in law") – the highest rank of thief in the **зо́на** hierarchy – despise not only the "hunting dogs" but also their **стукачи́** ("knockers," i.e informers). When thieves-in-law detect a "knocker" they will **мочи́ть** ("wet," kill) the despicable informer either with a **пу́шка** ("cannon", slang for "gun") or a **перо́** ("feather" slang for "knife"). By the way, the English "wet job" becomes simply **"мо́крое де́ло"** in Russian (from the verb **мочи́ть**, "to wet") and the criminal who commits a murder is a **мокру́шник**. And there is a label for every type of criminal, be they a **дому́шник** ("apartment burglar," from the word **дом**), or a **медвежа́тник** (a "bear's man," someone who specializes in safe cracking). Petty thieves who serve as aides to the big time thieves are called "six" – **шестёрка** – and all they are good for is to **стоя́ть на шу́хере**, to "stand lookout" for cops and other unwanted visitors while a robbery is being commited.

Thieves-in-law certainly have little tolerance for those who spill the beans (**расколо́ться**, literally "to split") during an interrogation. Actually, quite often when the investigator has little evidence he will try to "embroider a case" (**шить де́ло**) on the arrested suspect, meaning to frame them. This prompts the now classic response to false accusations (we Russians have a lot of experience with this): "**обижáешь, начáльник**" ("you're hurtin' me, chief").

This brings to mind a popular joke. It seems there was this nanny in a Soviet kindergarten, watching over kids whose parents were serving time in prison. She spotted a kid who didn't make it to the toilet fast enough: "Ah, Petrov," she said, "I see you peed in your pants again." To which little Petrov replied, "You're hurting me chief! You're stitching a wet job on me."(**Обижáешь, начáльник! Мóкрое дéло шьёшь.**)

If the **мéнты** succeed in "stitching a case" on someone, then the poor guy will have to **срок мотáть** (literally, "wind a term," meaning to serve a term). If, however, a former thief decides to go straight, other thieves will say **он завязáл** (literally "knotted up," quit robbing). This phrase itself has gone "straight" and been assimilated into wider usage. It simply means "to quit."

One who doesn't quit and continues his criminal activities, becomes a repeat offender, a "**рецидивúст**." But this is hardly slang; it is the same as in English. What is a slang word is the **вы́шка** (literally "high tower") that violent recidivists often get. The term derives from the penal code term **вы́сшая мéра наказáния** (supreme measure of punishment), i.e. execution.

Of late, however, Russia has been pressed by the Council of Europe to **завязáть** with **вы́шка**. While some argue leniency lets criminals pull the blanket over to their side, others point out that governments really shouldn't be in the business of carrying out wet jobs.

Mikhail Ivanov (October 1999)

Crisis Russian

It will be some time before historians begin writing the history of Russia's 1998 economic crisis. Responsible academics will wait for the dust to settle (**покá уля́жется пыль**), take a look back and give an appraisal of the tumultous events which led to the "pink" (**рóзовая**) revolution and helped Russia's communists secure their long-awaited political revenge (**взять политúческий ревáнш**).

Linguists, however, needn't wait so long. The essential elements of our Survival Russian linguisitic crisis kit are already clear, even though some might argue over which terms are most important.

For instance, we now know that, in times of crisis, shoppers fall prey to **ажиотáжный спрос** (hyped demand) and panic-buying (**пáника в магазúнах**), desperate to dump their rubles (**сбрóсить рублú**) because hyperinflation (**гиперинфля́ция**) is eating up their ruble savings (**съедáет рублёвые сбережéния**). As a result, the overwhelming majority of Russians find themselves below the poverty line (**за чертóй бéдности**).

What is more, the crisis has only hardened the local wisdom that the most reliable investment is kept under the mattress (**под матрáцем**) or in a stocking (**в чулкé**).

Linguists with a lighter bent will want to file in their kit this telling new folk saying: **Лýчше рубль в рукé, чем два в бáнке** (A ruble in the hand is better than two in a bank).

When the historians do get around to writing their textbooks, they will most likely note that this crisis marked the end of the era of the **младорефóрматоры** ("young reformers" – a poetic name coined by Russian journalists, perhaps alluding to Lenin's derogatory term

младогегельянцы – "young Hegelians") and seriously shook the foundations of Russia's oligarchical capitalism (**олигархи́ческий капитали́зм**).

One can only wonder why Sergei Kiriyenko, the young premier who replaced **тяжелове́с** (heavyweight) Viktor Chernomyrdin, resorted to a government **дефо́лт** (default) on loans. International news agencies quickly spread the terrifying news: "The ruble fell!" ("**Рубль упа́л!**"). Perhaps members of the **аппара́т** found themselves muttering the folk saying: **мо́лодо – зе́лено** (the young are green).

In any event, because of the actions of the young reformers and the Central Bank of Russia, both private bank customers and foreign investors felt fooled. Or, to use a now popular bit of slang, they felt as if they were dumped (**их ки́нули**, from the verb **ки́нуть** – "to

fool, to dump someone"). Of course, it was the government who played the role of **кида́ла** (cheater).

Another popular neologism is the now widespread abuse of the verb **уйти́** to mean "fired." The correct **он ушёл** (he departed) is turned in on itself to create the incorrect **его́ ушли́** (literally "he was departed"). Kiriyenko was "departed" once; his predecesssor/successor Viktor Chernomyrdin enjoyed this privilege twice during the crisis.

Interestingly, the departure of the **младореформа́торы** somehow contradicts the old Russian saying, born in communist times: **молоды́м везде́ у нас доро́га, старика́м везде́ у нас почёт** (We always give way to the young, and respect the aged). Well, partially contradicts it anyway. For, if the young reformers ran into a roadblock, then our aged politicians now enjoy more than simple "respect." Observers correctly note that most of Premier Yevgeny Primakov's team are over 60 – including Primakov himself, as well as new/old Central Bank Chairman Viktor Gerashchenko, who has been dubbed here Hercules (**Гера́кл**), because of his last name and his political weight. Indeed, the new team may mark the comeback of gerontocracy (**геронтокра́тии**) to power in Russia.

In the final analysis, ill-conceived actions causing panic among investors and the public justify the proverb **мо́лодо – зе́лено**. The question is whether our aged politicians with their Soviet pedigrees can bring anything to the table but "good" old recipes, like encouraging domestic producers with a "controlled emission" (**контроли́руемая эми́ссия**).

Unfortunately, the situation in post-crisis Russia is perfectly summed up by another piece of local folk wisdom: **Е́сли бы мо́лодость зна́ла, е́сли бы ста́рость могла́** (If youth but knew, if age but could). The difference being that the aged do not seem to know what to do either.

But, if the "green youth" still has a say in Russia, there is one branch of domestic industry which needs urgent injections of freshly-printed rubles: production of mattresses and stockings. It seems that these consumer goods will enjoy **ажиота́жный спрос** in Mother Russia.

Mikhail Ivanov (January 1999)

Tsar Boris' Firm Handshake

The era of Boris Yeltsin – who ruled Russia through the 1990s – left behind a mixed heritage. Historians will rightfully take their time to issue any final verdicts. Yet, most would agree that one of the indisputable achievements of the "First President of Russia," is a cementing of Russia's newly-won freedom of speech. Taking advantage of this gain, we offer a quick analysis of Boris Nikolayevich's linguistic heritage.

The first "yeltsinism" was just noted. Tsar Boris could not suffer any other title. "Former president" or "Ex-president" was not for him. So the Kremlin PR machine came up with a title that will serve Boris for life: "**пе́рвый президе́нт Росси́и.**"

The earliest stages of Yeltsin's presidential career were especially rich in memorable idioms. One of the first was Yegor Ligachyov's, "**Бори́с, ты не прав!**" ("Boris, you are wrong!") The phrase actually predates Yeltsin's tenure as president, to when Boris Nikolayevich was the maverick communist leader of Moscow. But with Yeltsin's ascension to the Kremlin, it became frequent fodder for headlines and political jokes.

Having won the Russian presidency, Boris Nikolaevich awarded us with more "yeltsinisms". Thus, his promise that, if prices rise, "**я ля́гу на ре́льсы**" ("I will lay on the rails"). Prices did go up and Boris did not lie down, so the phrase became our equivalent of Georges H.W. Bush's famous "Read my lips, no new taxes."

Economic difficulties, the first war in Chechnya and personal health problems led to Yeltsin's decline in popularity. The First President's handsome spokesman, Sergei Yastrzhembsky, became quite adept at deflecting difficult questions about the aging Yeltsin's long absences from the public eye. Kremlinologists had to read between the lines. If Yastrzhembsky said: "**Президе́нт рабо́тает с докуме́нтами**" ("The president is working with documents"), journalists would usually conclude that Boris Nikolayevich could barely stand up. To parry such cynicism, Yastrzhembsky invented still another famous cliché: **у президе́нта кре́пкое рукопожа́тие** (the president has a firm handshake). This was read as "the president is still alive."

Later, despite the very precarious state of his health (particularly his heart problems), Yeltsin ran for reelection in 1996, even dancing on stage with pop singers. That campaign

gave birth to two famous slogans: **Голосу́й, а то проигра́ешь** (Vote, or you will lose.) and the ironic **Голосу́й се́рдцем!** (Vote with your heart). Yeltsin got reelected, his heart barely withstanding the battle. Soon, the Kremlin spokesman had to learn a medical term which became known to millions: **аортокорона́рное шунти́рование** (heart bypass operation).

After his recovery from the quintuple bypass operation, Yeltsin was a different man. His mood changed like the winds blowing over the green roof of the Kremlin palace. "Working with documents" no longer satisfied him and the last months of his presidency were a succession of cabinet and premier reshufflings, which the president dubbed with the chess term **рокиро́вочка** (little castling). On the foreign front, Yeltsin was fond of **встре́ча без га́лстуков** ("meetings without ties," or informal meetings). But, on the domestic front, Tsar Boris was losing control over the country. The power in the Kremlin was usurped by the **семья́** (The Family) conferring a mafia-esque notion to this previously innocuous Russian word. It was the **семья́** which was believed to be behind the **банди́тский капитали́зм** (criminal capitalism), or thieving of state assets.

There was another phrase Boris Nikolayevich uttered which would not have had special linguistic distinction were it not coming from the mouth of a Russian ruler. He said to his fellow Russians: "**Прости́те меня́**" ("Pardon me"). Tsar Boris actually used the phrase in a very public way at least twice. The first time was in August 1991, during the funerals for three young Russians who died during the abortive putsch. The second time was on the last day of 1999, when bidding farewell to his compatriots. This yeltsinism may well remain the most valuable pearl in his linguistic legacy.

Yeltsin's **прее́мник**, (heir apparent) Vladimir Putin, has so far had little time to distinguish himself linguistically. During the transitionary period he focused instead on other fronts, i.e. Chechnya. So it is to this battle that we owe the first "putinism." A law student by education, Putin speaks good, sophisticated Russian. But he does like to color his speech with popular colloquial phrases, like the infamous "**в сорти́ре террори́стов замо́чим**" ("we'll wet [kill] the terrorists even in a water closet"). Some "refined" intellectuals were shocked at this thieves' jargon coming from the mouth of our country's leader. But the average Russian, tired of suffering from **беспреде́л** (slang for "chaos") wrought by bandits of all stripes, obviously enjoyed Putin's linguistic nonchalance.

For, unlike so many of Russia's law faculty graduates, Putin not only knows how to speak, but also how to get business done. This prompts me to quote that other Vladimir, a law graduate to whom Putin's native city owed its former name, Leningrad. That famous leninism has it: **"Интеллиге́нция – г**, а на́до де́ло де́лать"** ("The intelligentsia is just sh**. You have to take care of business"). Let's hope, however, that Russia's new president, the so-called "enlightened Chekist" (**просвещённый чеки́ст**), will do business differently from his infamous namesake.

In any case, in terms of energy levels, Putin is head and shoulders above the **пе́рвый президе́нт Росси́и**. His **рукопожа́тие** is firm, and, unlike the "**дед**" ("grandpa," as they called Yeltsin in the latter days of his Kremlin tenure) Putin can work with more than just documents.

Mikhail Ivanov (May 2000)

Lost in Translation

I recently spotted a curious book in a Moscow bookstore. The softcover yellow volume promised 97 sayings by the Russian president in just 200 pages, covering everything from **олига́рхи** (oligarchs) to **Всевы́шний** (God Almighty), from **манья́ки и шпио́ны** (maniacs and spies) to **пья́ницы и матерши́нники** (drunkards and *matershinniks* [those, who overuse Russian *mat* – extremely rude language]), from **до́йная коро́ва** (milkcow) to **карма́ны Гуси́нского** (Gusinsky's pockets). Intrigued, I put out 78 rubles for **Пу́тинки. Кра́ткий сбо́рник изрече́ний президе́нта (Пе́рвый срок)** – *Putinki. A Concise Collection of the President's Aphorisms (First Term)*.

President Putin's dictums, just as those of President Bush, have entered everyday speech. Linguists and speech writers argue that most Russians like the way their president speaks and do not mind his occasional use of slang or even inappropriate language.

The president first revealed his taste for a strong word (**кре́пкое сло́во**), when, at the beginning of his career as state leader, he promised to "wet" terrorists in the "outhouse" (**мочи́ть в сорти́ре**), or when he suggested to a critical French journalist that he come to Moscow to get circumcised (**сде́лать обреза́ние**).

Unfortunately, politicians' aphorisms are often lost in translation. However, while to an English-speaking Russian Bushisms (**бушиз́мы**) present mainly a grammatical challenge, **пу́тинки** offer a different kind of challenge to outsiders. Highly metaphoric and allusive, they often defy translation as a **непереводи́мая игра́ слов** (untranslateable wordplay).

Last fall, at a press conference in Yalta, after Russia's signing of the Agreement of Common Economic Space with Belarus, Kazakhstan and Ukraine, Putin was asked if this agreement meant a return to the USSR. His reply was: **"Э́то по́лная чушь, несура́зица, сапоги́ всмя́тку."** ("This is total nonsense, absurdity, soft-boiled boots.") The word **всмя́тку** is usually applied to eggs – **яйцо́ всмя́тку** is a soft-boiled egg. By applying it to boots, Putin gave a colorful, if difficult to translate, image of complete idiocy.

Some of the dictums quoted in *Putinki* stand a good chance of becoming proverbial. For instance, commenting on Russians' eagerness to find scapegoats (**найти́ козла́ отпуще́ния**) Putin waxed thus: "**У нас есть стари́нная ру́сская заба́ва – по́иск вино́вных.**" ("We have an ancient Russian pastime – searching for people to blame.") Or there was this: "**Если мозги́ утека́ют, зна́чит они́ есть**" ("If there is a brain-drain, that means they are there [in the first place]").

One basis for this book is that the president's political philosophy could be said to reside in his aphorisms: "**Лю́ди простя́т все, кро́ме вранья́**" ("The people will forgive everything but lies"); "**Проси́ бо́льше, даду́т, ско́лько ну́жно.**" ("Ask for more, they will give you what you need."); "**Вертика́ль не абсолю́т**" ("The vertical [of power] is not an absolute.") If that is the case, then these quotes at least show a distinctly pragmatic politician.

While all quotes in the book are meticulously dated and attributed to a printed source, they are, of course, presented out of context and could be said to be taking a point too far. As the president, who once called himself a **раскру́ченный бренд** (a well-advertised brand), once said about a biography of him, "**Я вообще́ не зна́ю, что там мо́жно написа́ть. Я бы ли́чно про себя́ сто́лько не смог написа́ть**" ("I do not know what could be written there. I personally could not write so much about myself").

But, as long as there is a president and the semblance of a free press, there will be books about him. And, back in 2001, Putin was quoted as saying "**Перефрази́руя Ма́рка Тве́на, могу́ сказа́ть: информа́ция о кончи́не свобо́дной пре́ссы в на́шей стране́ си́льно преувели́чена.**" ("Paraphrasing Mark Twain, I can say: 'reports about the death of the free press in our country have been greatly exaggerated.'")

Only time will tell whether that statement will hold true four years from now, when (and if) **Пу́тинки** (**Второ́й срок**) – *Putinki (Second Term)* is published.

Lina Rozovskaya (July 2004)

Dog Tails

Russian President Vladimir Putin is a well-known dog lover. It is not uncommon to see an official photo of him in his Kremlin office, meeting with some high official, and there, in the foreground, a black Labrador retriever – Connie – reclines on the floor.

In 2004, the children's book *Connie's Stories* was published. But it was not a salacious, ground's eye view of Kremlin life. In fact, the word "Putin" does not appear in the book; usually the dog Connie refers simply to his **хозяин** (master).

In Russia, long before Putin came to power, dogs roamed the halls of power and the alleyways of slums. But everywhere they were considered loyal friends. In the movie *Diamond Arm*, when the boorish Upravdom [head of the house committee] blames a dog owner for letting his pet "do his thing" on the courtyard grass, the hapless Semyon Semyonovich Gorbunkov recalls his experience in London, where dogs are allowed everywhere – because, he insists, **"собака друг человека"** ("dog is friend to man"). To which the lady retorts, **"Не знаю, как там в Лондоне, не была. Может, там собака друг человека. А у нас – управдом друг человека."** ("I don't know how things are in London – never been there. Maybe there, the dog is friend to man. But here it is the Upravdom who is friend to man.") That famous exchange from this 1970s movie suggested what a hard life – **собачья жизнь** – Soviets had, if their best friend really were the Upravdom. (Yet, if you have walked through enough Russian courtyards, you may well agree that Gorbunkov's Upravdom had a point about dogs leaving their mark.)

The classic Russian dog story, however (which has an even more obnoxious Upravdom, named Shvonder), is Mikhail Bulgakov's novel, *Heart of the Dog*. In that story, a Professor Preobrazhensky turns the **бродячая собака** (stray dog) **Шарик** (Sharik) into a man named Sharikov. Alas, the transformation is a bust. The professor made dog into man by transplanting into him the pituitary and testes of a drunken worker, so Sharikov turns into a boorish Bolshevik, forcing Preobrazhensky to eventually turn Sharikov back into Sharik. To this day, a rude primitive with base proletarian instincts is called **Шариков**. The phenomenon is known as **шариковщина**. Unfortunately, this species is not yet extinct here – you can still meet many on the metro. They are the ones who elbow you like an NHL defender.

Not surprisingly, dog proverbs and sayings abound in local culture and folklore. When a wound heals quickly, you can say – **"заживает как на собаке"** ("it heals like on a dog"). If someone is holding onto something (or someone) he doesn't need – he is behaving like "a dog in the manger" – **"как собака на сене."** If a person is short and has a childlike appearance, even in his forties, you can say **"маленькая собачка – до старости щенок"** ("a small dog is a puppy even into his old age"). In a situation that results from poor management without advanced planning, when you are doing everything at the very last moment and putting out fires, you can highlight the absurdity of the situation by saying, **"на охоту ехать – собак кормить"** ("it's time to go hunting, feed the dogs" – which no smart hunter would do). Of something superfluous or redundant, you can suggest that you need it "**как собáке пя́тая ногá**" ("like a dog needs a fifth leg"). And when, after thinking long and hard, or, after a lengthy discussion, you finally get the hidden meaning of something, you can utter, "**Ах, вот где собáка зары́та**" ("Ah, this is where the dog is buried.")

It would be impossible to list all dog-related idioms in one short column. So better to finish things up with a joke. It is also an appropriate commentary on safety of the mail in Russia...

A wife tells her husband:

– **У нас такóй у́мный пёсик! Кáждое у́тро бежи́т к почтóвому я́щику и забирáет в дом газéты**. ("We have such a smart doggy. Every morning he runs to the mailbox and picks up the newspapers and brings them home.")

– **Ну и что, мнóгие собáки так умéют...** ("Well, many dogs do that.")

– **Но мы ни на какúе газéты не подпúсывались!** ("Yes, but we don't subscribe to any newspapers!")

Certainly, Putin's Connie does not have to resort to such tricks. But Connie does complain that her **хозя́ин** reads the papers too much: "He reads a lot of papers every day. Is it important? Is reading papers more important than a walk? It cannot be more important than romping, can it?"

Clearly, Connie needs newspapers just like a **пя́тая ногá**... After all, she can get all the information she needs straight from the source.

One can't help wondering what kind of stories Connie could tell if a modern-day Preobrazhensky were to turn her into a human being. It would make any publisher a millionaire. But surely Connie would not be better off.

Mikhail Ivanov (September 2006)

Flora & Fauna

How Does Your Garden Grow?

As we like to say here: **Каждому овощу – свой срок** (For everything there is a season, or literally, "Every vegetable ripens at its own speed"). Given that this is harvest time, it seemed appropriate to consider how vegetables and fruit appear in our language.

Of course, the first vegetable among equals is our "second bread" (**второй хлеб**), the potato. Yet, as readers of *Russian Life* will know, the potato was not welcomed when Peter I brought it to Russia from Europe. The peasants' infamous potato riots (**картофельные бунты**) were one of the earliest protests against reform from the top in Russia.

Luckily, those times are gone. The potato is now a beloved part of the Russian diet and local folklore. All children know the song "**Антошка-Антошка – пойдём копать картошку**" ("Little Anton, come on let's go dig up potatoes"). And most adults recall Vysotsky's song urging Russian workers and students not to dodge the famous "potato missions," when hundreds of thousands of students and workers were sent to collective farms in the fall to help lazy Soviet farmers dig potatoes: **Небось картошку все мы уважаем, если намять её с сольцой?** (We all like potatoes don't we? Especially if you mash them, and eat them with a little salt.)

There are also some negative associations with the potato, however. For instance, Tsar Paul I was said to have a potato nose (**нос картошкой**). More recently, Russian tennis star Yevgeny Kafelnikov, after tanking two Davis Cup singles matches in 1999, compared the Australian tennis courts to a **картофельное поле** (a potato field), meaning the grass court was too uneven. Finally, in thieves' parlance a hand grenade is called a **картошка**.

The carrot is nowhere near as popular as the potato here, and thus its linguistic references are fewer. Aside from the appellation given to hack poetry – **кровь-морковь** – only one cultural reference comes to mind, and it is, well, unprintable. In fact, when I was first taught this risqué **кровь-морковь** rhyme, I **покраснел, как помидор** (turned as red as a tomato), which one can do either from shame or anger.

Needless to say, risqué was not the norm in the Soviet era. In fact, many children were taught the now-famous idiomatic phrase: **детей находят в капусте** (children are found in cabbage). The cabbage connection follows them into toddlerhood. When Russian children are wrapped up in thick clothing, they are said to be **укутан как капуста** (bundled-up like a cabbage). Of course, these days, **капуста** (slang for "money") has become all-important to all but those still wrapped in it.

Other vegetables make cameo appearances in our idioms and slang: **редиска** (radish) is thieves' slang for a bad person; you can pay someone a compliment if you say they look like a little cucumber (**как огурчик**); if somebody behaves like a buffoon, he may be called a **шут гороховый** (Buffoon of Peas); when a parent or teacher realizes their words fall on deaf ears, they may say in irritation "**как об стенку горох**" ("like peas bouncing off the wall").

Fruits don't grow as well in Russia as vegetables, so fruity idioms are often associated with something alien, exotic or even hostile. If someone sees something unexpected or unusual, they might say "**Какой фрукт выискался.**" ("Look at this [strange] fruit we've found!"). When a child has inherited a (usually negative) trait from their parent, we say "**Яблоко от яблони недалеко падает**" ("The apple does not fall far from the tree").

But not all fruit phrases have negative connotations. A well-proportioned woman may be called **спелый персик** (a ripe peach). And when a woman has reached her "ideal" mar-

rying (or dating) age, men might say between themselves that "she is like a ripe pear, ready to fall from the tree" (**"Её мо́жно трясти́, как гру́шу"**).

In reference to film erotica, a steamy love scene is called a **клубни́чка** (strawberry). Meanwhile a sappy romantic scene or film (e.g *Notting Hill* or *Pretty Woman*) is called a **клю́ква** (cranberry).

Another berry, the raspberry – **мали́на** – is a rich source of expressions, all reflecting the high regard the fruit enjoys here. First of all, **мали́на** is crook's argot for "a place to rendezvous" (most often an apartment). Second, when someone spoils a party or a pleasure, you can say they **"всю мали́ну испо́ртил"** ("spoiled the whole raspberry"). Finally, if a man finds himself surrounded by women, someone might jokingly say **"Како́й мали́нник"** or **"В како́й мали́нник ты попа́л!"** ("What a raspberry patch you have fallen into!")

The garden – **огоро́д** – where all these fruits and vegetables grow, is itself a source of linguistic creativity. For example, when someone makes critical comments that allude to someone else (e.g. "Some people are so stubborn!"), the person who is the object of the reproach, if they "get it," might say **"Э́то ка́мень в мой огоро́д?"** ("Is this a stone cast into my garden?") Only rarely would this phrase be used to refer to positive comments thought to be about oneself.

Finally, when someone makes an argument with irrelevant or illogical facts, you can point out the flawed thinking with the Russian proverb: **В огоро́де бузина́ – а в Ки́еве дя́дька** (There is the *buzina** in the garden and an uncle in Kiev).

Needless to say, it might not be wise to use this proverb with a Russian-speaking Ukrainian. There's no telling what kinds of "stones" he might throw into your garden...

Mikhail Ivanov (September 2000)

---

*a wild berry that should not be eaten.

Life With Mushrooms

It ought to be a folk saying: "He who picks mushrooms as a child is addicted for life." My addiction to **грибы** began at the age of four. Ever since, these "meat of the forest" have been a beloved part of my life.

This addiction is hard to explain to the uninitiated. What's so attractive about combing through the moss under pine trees in search of the most precious and noble of all mushrooms – the **бе́лый гриб** (white mushroom, a.k.a. **борови́к**)? Or why should one endure countless mosquito bites just to spot the brown cap of a **подберёзовик** (literally, "the one under the birch tree")? But do it once – uncover these mushrooms on your own and then sup on soup made from them an hour later – and you'll hardly notice the scratches on your face from tree branches or how soaked your feet are from tromping through a swamp in search of a cool, red-haired **подоси́новик** (literally "the one under the aspen tree," this mushroom, in fact, often prefers to nest under ferns near former swamps.

If the early bird gets the worm, he also gets the best mushrooms. A dedicated mushroom hunter sets out no later than 5 AM, better yet 3 or 4 o'clock. That way, he has the forest all to himself – before less avid **грибники́** go on the prowl. Of course, it's tough to get up so early, but then, as the proverb has it, **назва́лся гру́здем – полеза́й в ку́зов** (literally, "if you want to call yourself a big white mushroom, you have to get into the basket").

Regardless of the time of day, the best time for mushroom "shopping" in the forest is shortly after a **грибно́й дождь** (a mushroom rain), a very special, light rain that falls when the sun is shining and stimulates the growth of the tender **грибни́ца** – the mushroom root.

By the way, here is a linguistic secret: The regular way to say "picking mushrooms" is **ходи́ть за гриба́ми**. But when your *dacha* neighbor sees you in rubber boots, carrying a woven basket and asks, "**Куда́?**" ("Where are you off to?"), it is much more stylish (and worthy of a true **грибни́к**) to respond "**По грибы́!**" (rather than "**за гриба́ми!**")

Of course, the truly competitive **грибни́к** may try to put his neighbor off the scent by saying he is going berry picking. Every **грибни́к** has his own special **грибны́е места́** (mushroom-rich places), and the best way to keep those places secret is (aside from getting up very early) to never let anyone know when you are going to visit them.

When something is taking off in Russia, just as in English, it can be said that this thing (say, the number of restaurants) is mushrooming, but we say it more literally, that they "are growing like mushrooms after rain" – "**расту́т, как грибы́ по́сле дождя́.**"

But mushrooms do not always have positive connotations. A grumpy old person can be called a **старый гриб** (old mushroom), and if someone has a wrinkled, weatherbeaten face, we say he is "like a wrinkled mushroom" ("**как сморщенный гриб**").

The poisonous toadstool called the **поганка** is known to all Russian mushroomers, especially its most lethal variety, the **бледная поганка** (pale toadstool). Such notoriety was bound to work its way into slang, and parents in the 1930s-1940s, when angry with their progeny, might say: "**Ах ты, поганка!**" ("Oh, you toadstool!") A popular TV cartoon in the 1970s featured a **водяной** (a sort of water demon) who sang:

Я водяной – я водяной
Никто не водится со мной
Эх, жизнь моя жестянка – ну её в болото
Живу я, как поганка – а мне летать охота!

I am the water demon, I am
Nobody wants to deal with me
My life is like a tin can, it belongs in a swamp
I live like a toadstool, yet I dream of flying!

There is also the popular folk saying, **Если бы да кабы, да во рту росли грибы (то был бы не рот, а целый огород)**. Literally, it means "If it weren't for this and that, mushrooms would be growing in one's mouth (but then it wouldn't be a mouth, but a whole garden)." It means stop indulging in wishful thinking, stop fantasizing.

Finally, there is the proverb popular during the Stalin era: **Ешь пирог с грибами, а язык держи за зубами** (Eat your pie with mushrooms, but keep your tongue behind your teeth.) In other words, "Hear much, speak little." This was quite useful wisdom then, when the price of a wrong word could be imprisonment or worse. But it has relevance for an avid **грибник** – for he who wants to eat mushroom pie had better keep quiet about his **грибные места**!

Mikhail Ivanov (September 2002)

The Bear's Favors and Favorite Meals

Come summer, Russians rush to the *dacha*, where they work like crazy in their individual garden plots (**участки**). Actually, it is more appropriate to say "they work like bees" (**трудятся как пчёлки**), for the bee never sits idle during its short (30-40 days), but bright life.

Perhaps it is little wonder that Russians, often stereotyped as a country of "bears," use their language to pay tribute to the bear's favorite meal, honey. Okay, so Russians don't call their loved ones "honey" (a simple **дорогая** – "dear" – will do), but honey-related idioms are deep-rooted.

Regular readers of this column will recall how to say "honeymoon" – **медовый месяц** (see page 127), supposedly the happiest period in one's conjugal life. Of course, this is not always the case, for, as Russians say: **сколько мёд ни говори – во рту слаще не станет** (no matter how often you say the word honey, it doesn't taste any sweeter in your mouth).

As to bears, they have clawed their way into Russian idioms as well. Suffice it to mention the famous "bear's favor." This originates in a fable by Ivan Krylov, whose hero, a bear, rushed to do a favor for his master. The overzealous bear, anxious to kill a fly sitting on his master's face, killed the master along with the fly. So, to do a bear's favor (**оказа́ть медве́жью услу́гу**) for someone means to render someone a service with opposite, and negative results.

Other ursine idioms are no more flattering to bears. Someone who is lazy is compared to a bear in his den – **как медве́дь в берло́ге**. And, for some unknown reason, when someone has the jitters, even to the point of having neurotic diarrhea, it is called a bear's disease – **медве́жья боле́знь**. Finally, when someone tries to play, sing or whistle something by ear and misses the tune, Russians may say, "the bear has stomped on his ear" – **медве́дь на́ ухо наступи́л**.

So, if you are looking for idioms with positive connotations, stay away from bears; stick to their favorite meal...

For instance, when you see a busy office, full of intense staff, you can say that it **гуди́т как у́лей** (buzzes like a beehive). When a press-conference is announced or a newsmaker enters the room, journalists will rush forward **как пчёлы на мёд** (like bees on honey). When someone is proud of his company's success, he might say **есть и моя́ до́ля в бо́чке мёда** (there is my little drop in the common honey pot). It follows, then, that less zealous employees can spoil general, positive results with one negative deed. Or, as Russians would say, their "contribution" is like **ло́жка дёгтя в бо́чке мёда** (a spoonful of tar in a barrel of honey). And, when sergeants in the Russian army give their soldiers a hard time (always unjustifiably), they tell the soldiers they are doing it **что́бы жизнь мёдом не каза́лась** (so that life doesn't taste like honey).

The positive pull of honey is not lost on free marketeers. Uzbek melon sellers at Moscow farmers' markets can often be heard touting that their sweet melons are "half-sugar-half honey" (**полови́на саха́р – полови́на мёд**). If the customer wants to question the quality of the melon, he can say: "**Твои́ми уста́ми да мёд пить**" ("I wish I were drinking honey with your mouth").

Speaking of sugar, it can't hurt to pick up a few sugar-related idioms. To begin with, Russians, following the advice of doctors, have baptized sugar **бе́лая смерть** (white death), due to its potentially hazardous health impact. On the other hand, while the standard of living of Russian pensioners and war veterans plummets, you may hear them say **жизнь – не са́хар** (life is not sugar). True, the government is trying to **подсласти́ть пилю́лю** (sweeten the pill) by throwing in some one-shot payments or benefits, but that doesn't make their life taste like honey. Pensioners can, however, console themselves with the thought that **на халя́ву – и у́ксус сла́док** (even vinegar tastes good if it's free).

But take note: never tell a Russian war veteran that you pity him or something of this nature. They are poor, but their pride runs deep. In fact, when some of them hear the word **жа́лко** (pity), they may reply with a funny – if somewhat rude – bee-related wordplay (**жа́лко** is also the diminutive of **жа́ло** – the bee's stinger): "**Жа́лко у пчёлки зна́ешь где?**" ("You know where you'll find 'pity' on a bee?") For a less Aesopian version of this idiom, you will have to read the short stories of Vasily Shukshin.

Mikhail Ivanov (July 1997)

Animal Instincts

Even professional interpreters know very few translations for onomatopeias. They may tell you that a rooster goes **ку-ка-ре-ку́** (cock-a-doodle-doo) and that the respective verb is **кукаре́кать** (to crow). And the better ones may know that, in some cases of bird-related content, they would not translate **Пе́тя** as "Little Peter," but as "rooster." Our inventive language has turned **пету́х** into **Пе́тя** (or even the more tender **Пе́тя-петушо́к**), since the noun and first name are so similar.

Perhaps some interpreters know that meowing in Russian is **мя́укать**, so the sound reads as **мя́у-мя́у**. But that will be probably all that most would be able to come up with off the top of their heads. OK, maybe some other verbs like **мыча́ть** (to moo: **му-у-у**) or **ка́ркать** (to caw) are also known, but not the actual exact sound produced by the crow – as adopted in literature/fiction books. For when you read **кар-кар** (caw, caw) in a Russian book, is it a sound made by a **воро́на** (crow), and not a dog or cat?

So, why not learn some other basic animal sounds? What does a horse do, eh? The verb designating the sound a Russian horse makes is **ржать** (to neigh) and the sound is **и-го-го́**. The horse's hooves **цо́кают** (infinitive is **цо́кать** – clatter) and the sound is **цок-цок**.

What does a dog do to discourage someone from entering a house? Right: he **ла́ет** (barks). But the "literary" sound for "woof-woof" is **гав-гав**.

Hens, as we know, cackle (**куда́хтать**): **куда́х-тах-тах**. Remember that phrase from the famous fairy tale about how a hen laid a golden egg? **Дед пла́чет, ба́бка пла́чет – а ку́рочка куда́хчет: "Не плачь дед, не плачь ба́бка, я снесу́ Вам друго́е яи́чко – не просто́е, а золото́е.**" ("The grandfather cries, the grandmother cries, but the hen cackles: 'Don't

cry grandfather and grandmother, I will lay you another egg, not a ordinary egg, but a golden one.'")

Other examples (verbs followed by actual sounds made) from the animal kingdom are:

Duck	у́тка	кря́кать (quack)	кря-кря
Chicken	цыплёнок	куда́хтать (cluck, cackle)	цып-цып-цып
Goat	коза́	бле́ять (bleat)	м-е-е
Pig	свинья́	хрю́кать (grunt)	хрю-хрю
Snake	змея́	шипе́ть (hiss)	ш-ш-ш
Sparrow	воробе́й	чири́кать (chirp)	чик-чири́к, чик-чири́к

With time, some of these animal verbs and sounds have acquired additional, indirect meanings. For example, when someone tells you: "**Не ка́ркай**" ("Don't caw"), it means "Don't jinx it." When a husband says to his wife, "**Раскуда́хталась!**" ("There you go cackling again!"), it means he thinks the wife is panicking without reason.

When someone wants to shut someone up rather abruptly and rudely, he can say: "**Сиди́ – не кукаре́кай!**" ("Just sit and don't cock-a-doodle-do!").

And, as we know (see Mikhail Butov's fiction in *Russian Life*, Jan/Feb 2002), the verb **ла́ять**, if used in the reflexive form, can be colloquial for quarelling. Note the difference: to literally bark at someone is "**ла́ять на кого́-то**," whereas **ла́яться с ке́м-то** means "quarrelling."

Nor should we forget about another bird, the **куку́шка** (cuckoo), which goes **ку-ку**. In Russian folklore, the cuckoo has a special meaning. According to legend, one can stop in a forest when hearing the sound of a cuckoo and ask the bird: "Cuckoo, how much longer will I live?" ("**Куку́шка-куку́шка, ско́лько мне жить?**") The number of "cuckoos" that follow will be the answer.

In a related joke, a Russian guy asks a cuckoo:
"**Куку́шка-куку́шка, ско́лько мне жить?**"
"**Ку–**" (says the cuckoo)
"**А почему́ так ма́–?**" (answers the guy, his **ма́ло** –"little"– cut off by his death).

The lesson is clearly not to tempt fate by asking stupid questions of a cuckoo. Who knows – maybe the cuckoo will **нака́ркать** something way too short? Personally, I would prefer to gauge my life expectancy by the song of the trusty sparrow, which goes **чик-чири́к** non-stop, thus instilling more **уве́ренность в за́втрашнем дне** (confidence in tomorrow), to use a tried and true Soviet cliché.

Mikhail Ivanov (March 2002)

Lie Down With the Dogs...

If, by some bizarre miracle, George Orwell's anti-Stalinist novel, *Animal Farm*, had been published in Soviet Russia, it would have struck a popular chord – if only because animals were important elements in Russian idioms and proverbs long before Stalin's time (remember the famous, "work is not a wolf...?"). Actually, the phrase, "your comrade is a wolf from Tambov..." (see page 20) was born under Stalin and his sycophants, like the venomous State Prosecutor Andrei Vyshinsky, who loved to call the people's enemies "cunning foxes" and "chain dogs."

Well, enough about Stalin. There are plenty of animal expressions without bringing him into things. In fact, today there is hardly an animal which is not part of a set phrase in Russian. Even the exotic koala bear is not exempt, thanks to a poem by Yevgeny Yevtushenko, where he stigmatizes the negative traits in the Russian character – such as laxism, passiveness and nonchalance ("**О, наши русские коалы!**").

But let's start with some animals better suited to Russia's climate. How about the wolf, the bear and the dog?

The wolf is an omnipresent hero of Russian fairy tales, fables and idioms. And who better to illustrate the survivalist principles of the thorny forest that is today's Russian economy: **с волками жить – по-волчьи выть** (living with wolves makes one howl like a wolf). But I personally prefer this one: **Волка ноги кормят** (the legs feed the wolf), a perfect motto for local salesmen.

If you are hungry, you can confess to a wolf's appetite, **волчий аппетит**. This idiom, based on the normal perception of the wolf's role in nature, is understandable without much explanation. Other wolf-related idioms are unique to one language – e.g the English "cry wolf" in Russian becomes a simple "**Прости, дяденька**" ("Forgive me, uncle!"). And the French "speak of the wolf and you will see his tail" ("speak of the devil") also has no direct equivalent in Russian.

Speaking of the French: their invasion and debacle in Russia in 1812 inspired Ivan Krylov to write the fable *A Wolf at a Kennel*. In it, he uses the image of the wolf as the incarnation of an evil enemy (Napoleon and his army). In the end, Krylov sums up his experience in dealing with wolves: "**А потому обычай мой: с волками иначе не делать мировой, как снявши шкуру с них долой**" ("My principle is: never make peace with wolves unless you have already skinned them"). Whoever has dealt with the wolves of this world will confirm that Krylov's popular expression makes perfect sense.

A different Krylov fable evokes yet another popular hero of Russian sayings – the bear. In this fable, the bear slaps his master on the face to kill a fly sitting there, and ends up killing his master in this "rescue operation" – hence the idiom **медвежья услуга** (a bear's favor – see page 100).

We also say of someone who has no ear for music, "a bear stomped on his ear" ("**ему́ медве́дь на́ ухо наступи́л**"). And a stay-at-home kind of person is often compared to a bear in his den (**как медве́дь в берло́ге**). The same applies to someone who hides in some remote corner, waiting to see the outcome of something before acting.

The dog? "**Соба́ка – друг челове́ка!**" ("The dog is man's friend!"). We owe this platitude at least in part to Semyon Semyonovich, the immortal hero of the comedy film, *Diamond Arm*. Semyon touts the phrase to defend the hapless owner of a dog who is being scolded by a pushy lady, a local housing boss, because the dog soiled the grass in the courtyard (see page 93 for the full quote).

Dogs are known for recovering quickly from their wounds. Hence the phrase : "**На нём, как на соба́ке, всё зажива́ет**" ("he heals as quickly as a dog"), meaning it heals really fast.

A less humane idiom: **Соба́ке – соба́чья смерть** (a dog dies like a dog), applies to those who deserved their atrocious death – like bandits, serial killers etc. This is what a sheriff might say to a really nasty criminal after gunning him down in the final scene of a Western.

If someone offers you something futile or completely useless, you can say: "I need this like a dog needs a fifth leg" (**как соба́ке пя́тая нога́**). It is not, of course, a very polite phrase, but your message will surely come across.

You need not go very far to find a Russian reality to which you can apply all these animal-related pictures – just consider the political situation in Russia in the last quarter of 1998. The communists, each an archetypical **волк в ове́чьей шку́ре** (wolf in sheep's clothing), look on President Yeltsin in his presidential seat as a dog in the manger (**как соба́ка на се́не**). Meaning, that the incapacitated Yeltsin is barring others from access to something which he himself can't fully enjoy – the presidency. The manger in this case is his presidential seat and the dog is Yeltsin himself. An old and sick one at that. And, unfortunately, of late the president's wounds have not been healing at dog's speed.

But whatever they all say, Yeltsin and his retinue seem to take the position whereby **соба́ка ла́ет – ве́тер но́сит** ("the dog barks and the wind carries it off," meaning the complaints of the "lesser folk" don't reach the pinnacles of power). Which would be really wise, if only Russians were not so tired of their **соба́чья жизнь** (dog's life). Many have pinned their hopes on Premier Yevgeny Primakov, whose compromise figure fits well with yet another animal-related saying: **и о́вцы це́лы – и во́лки сы́ты** (the wolves are fed and the sheeps are safe).

Everyone knows (**ка́ждая соба́ка зна́ет**) that papering over problems is not wise, but it is surely better than a comeback for communism! Thanks, but no thanks. Been there, done that. Or, as Russians say, **зна́ем, проходи́ли!**.

We need a second dose of communism like a dog needs a fifth leg.

Mikhail Ivanov (February 1999)

Of Fish and Cockroaches

If you have trouble telling the difference between a **форе́ль** and an **осетри́на**, or between **селёдка** and **сёмга**, the following may help.

In Lewis Carroll's *Alice in Wonderland*, there is a chapter titled "Lobster Quadrille." In it, The Mock Turtle and the Gryphon tell Alice that a whiting is called a whiting because it "does the boots and shoes." Alice finds out that, under the sea, shoes are done with "whiting" instead of "blacking" and made of "soles and eels," and that "no wise fish would go anywhere without a porpoise."

In Nina Demurova's able "transculturation" of Carroll's book, the whiting became **треска́** (cod), about which it is said: **Ры́ба она́ так себе́, то́лку от неё ма́ло, а тре́ску мно́го. Как начнёт треща́ть – хоть вон беги́.** The wordplay is on the verb **треща́ть**, which means to crackle, but it also means to jabber. So a translation might be: "As a fish, she is not much, you get very little from her, but she jabbers a lot. And as soon as the jabbering starts, you want to run away." Notably, you can also use **треща́ть**, to describe a headache: **"У меня́ голова́ трещи́т."**

Треска́ is visited by **Старичо́к Судачо́к** (diminutive from **суда́к** – pike perch), called a **суда́к** for his constant gossiping – **с утра́ до но́чи суда́чит** (**суда́чить**: to tittle-tattle). The two chatterboxes are sometimes joined by a **щу́ка** (pike) – **она́ всех щу́чит** – she is always scolding everyone (**щу́чить**: to scold). In this noisy bedlam, the poor **белу́га** (sturgeon) can only **"реве́ть белу́гой"** (cry hysterically).

The word "fish" (**ры́ба**) itself offers quite a pronunciation challenge to those not accustomed to rolling their Рs and squeezing out ыs. In a popular Russian film, *По семе́йным обстоя́тельствам* (*Due to Family Circumstances*), a little girl's speech therapist says to her, **"Фе́фочка, скажи́: ыы́ба."** Since he cannot roll his Рs, "fish" comes out something like "iish". The clever girl, not wanting to repeat the therapist's mistake, replies: **"Селёдка"** ("Herring").

It is actually funny how fishy idioms travel from one language to another. Some translate well: **Лови́ть ры́бу в му́тной воде́** (to fish in troubled waters); **ни ры́ба, не мя́со** (neither fish nor fowl); **как се́льди в бо́чке** (packed like sardines); **как ры́ба в воде́** (like a fish to water); and **би́ться, как ры́ба об лёд** (thrash about like fish on the ice).

But don't jump to the conclusion that any ichthyological idiom will work in both languages. For example, Russians don't drink like fish, but like shoemakers (**пить как сапо́жник**). And **на безры́бье и рак ры́ба** (when there are no fish, even a crawfish is a fish) does not translate directly ("Something is better than nothing" would be a good translation). And, feminists take note, "like a fish needs a bicycle" should translate as **как ры́бке зо́нтик** (umbrella).

One of my favorite fish idioms is **Ма́ленькая ры́бка лу́чше большо́го тарака́на** (A small fish is better than a large cockroach). This hardly needs explanation, and it provides an excellent segue to the poems of Nikolai Oleynikov, a 1920s avant-garde poet who paid homage to both of these most persecuted animals. First, Oleynikov sympathizes with the **тарака́н**, trapped in a glass and chewing on his leg while waiting to be dissected:

Тарака́н сиди́т в стака́не,	*The cockroach sits in the glass,*
Но́жку ры́жую сосёт.	*Gnawing on his rust-colored leg.*
Он попа́лся. Он в капка́не.	*He's done for. Doomed.*
И тепе́рь он ка́зни ждёт.	*And awaits his execution.*

Then there is Oleynikov's requiem for a **кара́сь** (carp) who is frying in a pan:

Жа́реная ры́бка,	*Frying fish,*
Ма́ленький кара́сь,	*Little carp,*
Где ж твоя́ улы́бка,	*Where is your smile,*
Что была́ вчера́сь?	*The one you had yesterday?*

It turns out the carp committed suicide – swimming into a net – after his love was rejected by a cruel coquette:

И реши́л несча́стный	*And the unlucky one decided*
То́тчас умере́ть	*To end it right now*
Ри́нулся он стра́стный,	*He threw himself passionately,*
Ри́нулся он в сеть.	*He threw himself into the net.*

The murky Neva rolls on, but the little carp will never swim anywhere again.

Так шуми́ же му́тная	*So noisy and troubled*
Не́вская вода́!	*Are the Neva waters!*
Не поплы́ть кара́сику	*The carp will not swim*
Бо́льше никуда́.	*Anywhere evermore.*

I do not know a funnier or sadder Russian poem about fish. If you have any doubts about its significance, Dmitry Shostakovich wanted to compose an opera inspired by Oleynikov's "The Carp." But he never did. The famous maestro clearly had bigger fish to fry.

Lina Rozovskaya (March 2003)

Vegetarian Disses and Disguises

Long before advertisements anthropomorphized soft-drinks and candy into cartoon characters, people "animated" the food they grew by assigning it human qualities.

Take vegetables. If, out of the blue, a Russian acquaintance one day calls you a "cucumber," stay cool. You have just received a compliment. **Огурец** (cucumber) in colloquial Russian indicates a healthy, fresh-looking person. For example, **как огурчик** means "as fresh and in as good shape as a cucumber." It can also be used to approve of someone's condition or actions: "**А ты огурцом**" – ("You are looking great").

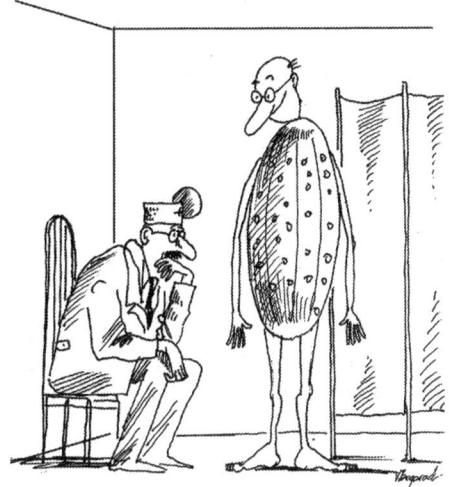

There are many problems and riddles associated with the cucumber, but most are outdated. Vladimir Dal, author of the famous 19th century dictionary of the Russian language, registered a perceptive one: **Где огурцы, тут и пьяницы.** (Where there are cucumbers, there will also be drunks.) Cucumbers, especially in their pickled form, are considered an excellent vodka appetizer.

At the other end of the vegetable scale is the radish (**редиска**), which can connote a bad, mean person. This meaning for an otherwise innocent-looking vegetable most likely came from the 1972 Soviet film **Джентльмены удачи** (*Gentlemen of Fortune*), where it is used as criminal cant. Vladimir Yelistratov, in his *Dictionary of Russian Argot* (Russkiye Slovari, 2000), registers a funny variation: **панкующая редиска**. Literally, it means a "punk radish," someone who is completely worthless, but puts on airs as if he were really cool.

Meanwhile, garlic (**чеснок**) is associated with two qualities: good health – **Чеснок семь недугов изводит** (Garlic cures seven ailments), and bad smell. The latter is spoken for in the almost biblical proverb from Vladimir Dal's dictionary: **Не ела душа чесноку, так и не воняет** (The soul has not eaten garlic, that is why it does not stink.). Dal also cites this gem, which reflects what the diet of the lower classes may have been like in his day: **Чеснок толчёный, да таракан печёный** (Crushed garlic and baked cockroach). In criminal argot **чеснок** can also be used to designate a **честный вор** (an upright thief).

Interestingly, Russians' "second bread" – the potato (**картошка**) – is not highly respected in colloquial speech. According to Yelistratov, "potato" can mean "trifles, nothing." **Не мешок картошки,** (not a bag of potatoes) means something is of no importance, and **это не картошка** means this is nothing to sneeze at. But what could underscore the potato's diminutive social status better than, **Ты мне друг или картошка?** (Are you a friend or a potato?)

Just as in English, cabbage (**капуста**) can be used to refer to money. Yelistratov notes that **капуста зелёная**, (green cabbage) is a rather specific reference to dollars.

Another basic food staple here is the turnip (**репа**). If something is **проще пареной репы** (simpler than stewed turnip), nothing could be easier. The turnip is also used to describe a face. Thus, **начи́стить ре́пу** (to polish a turnip) means to punch someone in the face (while **изруби́ть в капу́сту** means "to beat to a pulp").

Other vegetables have bodily connotations: a pumpkin (**ты́ква**) can be colloquial for a head (e.g. **дать по ты́кве**, to hit someone in the head), while a person who has gone bald can (at your own risk) be called an onion (**лу́ковица**).

But the most prolific plant in Russian slang is surely the horseradish (**хрен**). This is because **хрен** has the same first letter as the most common Russian obscenity (a vulgarity for "penis") and thus can tone down a tirade just as "shoot," "darn" or "heck" do in English. There are hundreds of **хрен**-based idioms, and we will leave the student to discover these on her own. But beware that even seemingly benign usages – **хре́н с ним** (to horseradish with him/that), **На́ хрен мне э́то** (Why the horseradish would I need this?), **посыла́ть на хрен** (to send someone to horseradish) – are all considered rude in polite society.

As a verb ("to horseradish" – **охрене́ть**), this vegetable indicates surprise, strong feelings or excitement, or simply the fact that someone has gone nuts. As a noun ("horseradish thing" – **хрено́вина, хреноте́нь, хрень**), it is used to name any object, particularly a troublesome one. In adjectival form (**хрено́вый**), it means something is spoiled, bad, or unfit for the purpose intended.

There is, however, an old, widely used proverb, where horseradish is used in its literal meaning, without the above connotations: **хрен ре́дьки не сла́ще**. Literally, it means "horseradish is no sweeter than a radish," but the idiomatic meaning is that both options are equally bad.

Vegetable idioms are absurd and exploit some unique quality of the item. You can experiment and create your own blends, but why worry your pretty pumpkin? The garden is full of choices ripe for the picking.

Lina Rozovskaya (September 2003)

Moscow
&
St. Petersburg

Moscow in Sunshine and Tears

Что ни го́род – то но́ров.
So many cities, so many customs.

Russians would surely not refrain from applying the above saying to their capital, referred to as "my dear capital, my golden Moscow" (**Золота́я моя́ столи́ца, дорога́я моя́ Москва́**) in a famous song written in the 1950s. The City on the Seven Hills – **го́род на семи́ холма́х**, i.e. Moscow, is not only famous for its nights (e.g., the famous song *Evenings near Moscow* – **Подмоско́вные вечера́**) but also has its own customs and habits.

Muscovites are very proud of their city, some reckon presumptuously so. Russian rulers used to say **"Москва́ – тре́тий Рим, а четвёртого не бу́дет"** ("Moscow is the Third Rome, and there won't be a fourth"). Visitors from the provinces like to take their Moscow cousins down a peg or two by calling them spoiled and arrogant. In return, Muscovites have christened such detractors **лими́тчики** (from the word "limit," for these visitors could only obtain temporary – or limited – employment and had to get a registration permit within a limited period of time). So, the **лими́тчики** would come to work in Moscow, in search of that much-coveted **Моско́вская пропи́ска** (Moscow registration permit).

Another Moscow saying stemming from local snobbery is "not to believe in tears," as you probably know from the movie title, **Москва́ слеза́м не ве́рит** (*Moscow Doesn't Believe in Tears*). Which means that you have to prove yourself to make it in Moscow; simple tears or whining won't cut it.

Another proverb (echoing a similar one about the first Rome) has it that "Moscow was not built overnight" – **Москва́ не сра́зу стро́илась**, which is quite true. After all, it took some 850 years to build everything that today's tourists marvel at. However, when you look at what Moscow Mayor Yuri Luzhkov has achieved just over the first five years of his tenure, it seems that every great proverb has its exceptions. Luzhkov has built many monuments practically "overnight" – the cathedral of Christ the Savior, the memorial at Poklonnaya Hills, and Manezh Square, to name just a few. Hence, his tremendous popularity with his electorate. By the way, the mayor's home district in Moscow –

Zamoskvorechye (**Замоскворе́чье**) (literally "behind the Moscow River") also has the word "Moscow" as its root.

Learning Moscow-related idioms may prove both instructive and enlightening. One such proverb reminds us that one can never take too many precautions – **От копе́ечной свечи́ Москва́ сгоре́ла** (Moscow was razed by a penny candle). In other words, a small act of carelessness can trigger a great disaster.

Inventive Muscovites, known for their sharp sense of humor, never missed their chance to poke fun at the ever-present Marxist-Leninist names given to the city's streets, squares and even metro stations. Thus, the once-famous subway station **Проспе́кт Ма́ркса** (Marx Avenue) was irreverently dubbed **Конспе́кт Ма́ркса** (the gist of Marx), a reference to the mandatory dull summaries of Marx's works that students were forced to write. But it was the metro station "Lenin's Library" (**Библиоте́ка и́мени Ле́нина**) that stole the show. Even though the Beatles never performed in Soviet Russia, students of the late 1970s and early 1980s baptized this station "John Lennon's Disco" (**Дискоте́ка и́мени Ле́ннона**), using perfect rhyme and assonance with the original name.

If you really want to be taken for a native Muscovite, it pays to remember some other funny slang names. The famous **лу́жа** (puddle), for example, refers to Luzhniki stadium, while the "cannon" (**пу́шка**) is slang for the centrally-located **Пу́шкинская пло́щадь** (Pushkin square).

While you're at it, why not learn a great street-related idiom – the beautiful **Бу́дет и на на́шей у́лице пра́здник** ("the sun will shine on our street too," i.e. we, too, will have our day). This is what Muscovites – and for that matter all Russians – tell themselves in hard times. Even though sometimes the **пра́здник** (holiday) is far away, it's better to anticipate it, rather than "shedding tears in Russia's capital." What's the point? It does not believe in them anyway.

Mikhail Ivanov (August 1997)

Dueling Capitals

There are practically no examples of Russian urban folklore that contain the names of both Moscow and St. Petersburg without emphasizing their opposition. Moscow's mercantile arrogance, kneaded on centuries of traditions and grandfathered principles, is counterposed with the aristocratic maximalism of a neophyte, destroying stereotypes with aplomb.

Barely one hundred years after Petersburg was founded, Vladimir Dal recorded the following proverb: **Москва́ со́здана века́ми, Пи́тер миллио́нами.** (Moscow was created by centuries, Piter by millions.) Later, this proverb was transformed into **Пи́тер стро́ился рубля́ми, Москва́ – века́ми.** (Piter was built with rubles, Moscow over centuries.) Another proverb speaks of the same controversy in even bolder terms: **Москва́ вы́росла, Петербу́рг вы́ращен.** (Moscow grew, Petersburg was grown.)

Moscow could not forgive the young *parvenu* who sprung from the marshes so suddenly and was now claiming leadership. In the middle of the 19th century, 150 years after Petersburg was founded, Muscovites still cherished secret hopes that Petersburg "was destined to end its days by sinking back into the Finnish swamps" (**Петербу́ргу суждено́ око́нчить свои́ дни, уйдя́ в фи́нское боло́то**). Slavophiles, one of the two major voices of

19th century Russian philosophy, proclaimed the following war-cry: **Да здра́вствует Москва́ и да поги́бнет Петербу́рг!** (Long live Moscow and let Petersburg die!)

For their part, Petersburgers called Moscow **больша́я дере́вня** (a big village); its residents were christened **пролета́рии** (proles). Muscovites responded by laughing: "**Что за петербу́ржство?,**" ("What sort of Peterbourgeois-ism is that?"), and added the insulting **аристокра́ты,** (aristocrats).

Dandyish, active, aristocratic Petersburg, arrayed in a gorgeous tail-coat or a dazzling military uniform, is portrayed as the masculine, while decorous and thorough merchant Moscow is female. When, in 1712, Peter married Catherine in Petersburg, a proverb was born: **Пи́тер же́нится, Москву́ за́муж берёт** (Piter gets married, Moscow is taken as a wife). In Russian there are two verbs for marriage: **выходи́ть (идти́) за́муж** is used for women and **жени́ться (брать кого́-то в жёны)** for men. In one hundred years time, Vladimir Dal precised: **"Пи́тер же́нится, Москва́ за́муж идёт."** Moscow is no longer "taken" as a wife; it gets married voluntarily.

In the 19th century, Petersburg was in fact a largely male-dominated city, inhabited by bureaucrats, officers, university and cadet college students, factory workers. Over two thirds of Petersburg's population was male. Even though by the 1970s this difference between Moscow and Petersburg had long vanished, the proverb still resonated: **"В Ленингра́де женихи́, в Москве́ неве́сты."** ("Leningrad has grooms, Moscow has brides.") The proverb spoke probably not of a quantitative, but of a qualitative difference. Young men from Leningrad were highly valued as partners for their education and good manners, while Moscow's beauties were praised for their thriftiness.

A popular joke, obviously born in Petersburg, speaks of other alleged qualities of Petersburg's men and Moscow's women. A woman gets on a tram. A young man gets up from his seat and lets the lady have it. "Are you from Leningrad?" asks the woman. "Yes, I am. But how did you know?" the man replies. "A Muscovite would not let me have his seat," she replied. "Are you from Moscow?" the young man asked. "Yes," she said, "but how did you know?" "You did not say 'thank you.'"

When, in the 1930s, Moscow was again ascendant over Petersburg, new proverbs came to the fore, emphasizing the northern city's dependence on the capital: **В Москве́ чихну́т, в Ленингра́де аспири́н принима́ют.** (When they sneeze in Moscow, in Leningrad they take aspirin.) Or: **В Москве́ игра́ют, в Ленингра́де пля́шут.** (In Moscow they play music, in Leningrad they dance [to Moscow's tune].)

The situation started changing again in the middle of the 1990s. Petersburg started being perceived as not yet the capital, but still not quite Russia's "second city." The media spoke increasingly of the "two capitals." The following joke (a weather forecast) spoke of Petersburg's reemerging self-respect and independence: **Завтра в Москве ожидается один градус. В Петербурге – совершенно другой.** (Tomorrow it will be one degree in Moscow. In Petersburg it will be something completely different.)

Today, various jokes speak of Moscow's newly acquired riches and persistent ignorance, as opposed to Petersburg's higher culture and lower incomes: А **москаль** (pejorative for Muscovite) comes to Petersburg. A Petersburger asks him a question: "Tell me, do you have palaces and park ensembles in Moscow?" "What do you mean, palaces and parks?" "Well, we've got Petergof, Oranienbaum, Tsarskoye Selo, Pavlovsk, Gatchina. What about you?" The Muscovite thinks for a long time and then says with uncertainty: "Barvikha!" [The location for Kremlin leaders' *dachas*.]

Today, richer and quicker Muscovites come to Petersburg to do business, while slower and poorer Petersburgers often move to Moscow to seek higher salaries than the city on the Neva can offer. In this respect, natives of the two capitals have become colleagues. But deep in their souls they are bound by stronger and more complex, almost familial ties. The stormy relationship is perhaps best summed up by the following joke: "Who are **москали** to Petersburgers – brothers or friends?" "Brothers, of course. You choose your friends!"

Naum Sindalovsky (May 2003)

Life & Death

How Do We Feel, Doctor?

Здоро́вья в апте́ке не ку́пишь
You can't buy health at the pharmacy

This popular Russian saying got a second meaning and a new lease of life in the late 1980s. In those years, Soviet citizens would search empty-shelved pharmacies for the most elementary drugs, like aspirin or nose drops. The only consolation was lyrics from a popular Soviet song in vogue in the 30s – **от всех боле́зней нам поле́зней со́лнце, во́здух и вода́** (sun, fresh air and water can heal any disease).

Another Russian folk saying sets a slightly different mood – **кто не ку́рит и не пьёт, тот здоро́веньким помрёт** ("he who doesn't smoke and drink will die healthy" – i.e. you'll die anyway so why bother trying to be healthy?).

If you've decided not to die healthy, please read on. Sooner or later you will end up seeing a doctor. If the closest one at hand is a Russian, brace yourself. With male life expectancy here falling to 57 years, it's not surprising that Russians don't think very highly of their health care system. Hence the incisive wordplay attributed to the famous surgeon Nikolai Amosov: **лечи́ться да́ром – да́ром лечи́ться** (a free doctor will "free" you from treatment).

No wonder then that Amosov, now in his 80s, jogs every morning and doe not smoke or drink. If you do, you'll end up saying **мне нездоро́вится, я себя́ нева́жно/парши́во/пога́но чу́вствую** (I'm not well / I don't feel well / I feel bad/ dreadful).

These words may come in handy if you catch that typically Russian disease, the **похме́лье** (hangover). And if a Russian friend catches you gulping down gallons of water in the morning, he may give you a knowing look and say: "**Что, тру́бы горя́т?**" ("Your tubes are burning, are they?" – see page 157)

A good subterfuge (if you don't feel like admitting you had a night of partying) is to reply to your Russian friend that you spent the day in a stuffy place (**в ду́шном помеще́нии**) and that's why you have a headache (**головна́я боль**). If you're really in agony you could say: "**У меня́ голова́ раска́лывается**" or "**Башка́ боли́т**" ("My head's splitting").

Conditions like diarrhea are also hard to own up to. So, instead of going for the easiest word, **поно́с**, use the euphemistic **расстро́йство желу́дка** (indigestion).

If you have something straightforward like a runny nose (**на́сморк**), Russians will probably advise you not to call the doctor but use folk or homemade remedies (**обойти́сь** наро́дными / дома́шними реце́птами / сре́дствами). These include **чай с мали́ной** (tea with raspberry jam) or **молоко́ с мёдом** (milk and honey).

One word of warning: not all colds are what they seem. If someone tells you they have a **гуса́рский на́сморк** (hussar's cold) give them a very wide berth. This is none other than a very magnificent euphemism for syphilis.

Suppose the worst comes to the worst, and you have to call a doctor? The first question you will probably hear from him is **"Как мы себя́ чу́вствуем?"** ("How are we feeling?") Or, **"На что жа́луемся?"** ("What is our problem?") Don't think the doctor's being patronizing – this is simply a form of address known as the "doctor's we" – **до́кторское мы**).

If you have aches and pains, there are several ways you can answer. You could say **"Поба́ливает"** ("It hurts a bit") or **"Терпе́ть мо́жно"** ("It's tolerable"). If it's not tolerable, say **"Мо́чи нет терпе́ть"** ("I can't take it any more"), or even stronger – **"Хоть на сте́нку лезь"** ("I'm about to climb the wall from pain").

Pain is a common feature of dental lexicon, though God forbid that you should personally experience this particular branch of Russian medicine. Note these phrases for domestic use only – **"Зуб дёргает"** ("I have a throbbing pain in my tooth"), **"Зуб но́ет"** ("I've got toothache"). Make sure there are no dentists within earshot when you say this, otherwise you might be offered a root canal – **пломбирова́ть кана́л** – a particularly unpleasant form of torture.

Finally, even people who stick to a healthy way of life (**здоро́вый о́браз жи́зни**) have accidents and need to see doctors. If you've had an accident at work, the Russian labor code calls it **произво́дственная тра́вма** (production trauma). If at home, then it's **бытова́я тра́вма** (domestic trauma), like a **синя́к под гла́зом** or, in slang, **финга́л** (black eye) from a quarrel with the neighbors. If your **синя́к** is an embarrassment, just say it was a **банди́тская пу́ля** (a bandit's bullet). This is a quote from a Soviet comedy film **Старики́-разбо́йники** (*Robber Lads*), where a wounded investigator keeps appearing with freshly broken limbs and repeating these words.

If you have just a minor scratch (**обыкнове́нная цара́пина**), forget the euphemisms. Show it proudly to everybody, because Russian women believe scars become a man (**шра́мы украша́ют мужчи́ну**).

On the other hand, if a Russian doctor sees your **цара́пина**, he or she will say: **до сва́дьбы заживёт** (it'll heal before your wedding). They like this formula, especially when talking to young men. In this context it means don't worry, there's plenty of time for the wound to heal. No ageism intended – words like these are just a friendly formula meant to put you at ease. So even if your **сва́дьба** is ancient history and you've no such new plans, rest assured that your scratch will heal anyway.

Mikhail Ivanov (August 1996)

Still Alive, Smoker?

> **Но дым отéчества нам слáдок и приятен.**
> *But the smoke of our native land is sweet and pleasant.*
> From Alexander Griboyedov's play, *Woe from Wit*

Okay, okay, we know that America is virtually a non-smoking country now, but not so Russia – here a pack of cigarettes is a vital accessory. Ever since Peter the Great started forcing tobacco on his countrymen, they've been unable to go without.

Indeed, plenty of Russian leaders, including Peter, have been turned into chain smokers by the pressure of office. Stalin is renowned for his famous pipe, filled with Gertsegovina Flor (Flowers of Herzegovina) tobacco, Brezhnev for his cheap and nasty Novost cigarettes, and now General Alexander Lebed with his world-famous cigarette holder (in Russian **мундштýк** – directly from the German, for "mouthpiece").

Of course, simple mortals here also smoke like crazy – to calm the nerves, to stay awake, and, of course, after eating. Some even recommend smoking as a remedy for toothache. It should therefore come as no surprise that smoking-related idioms are deeply rooted in the Russian language. So, even if you prefer to stick to an American, non-smoking lifestyle, you should learn some tobacco-laden proverbs and phrases if you are serious about your interest in all things Russian.

Most Russians over 30 have heard the famous lyrics from Klavdiya Shulzhenko's wartime ballad, "I'll remember the infantry and my beloved company, and you for sharing your tobacco with me" – "**Вспóмню я пехóту и роднýю рóту, и тебя за то, что дал мне закурить.**" Tobacco – or rather **махóрка** (the cheapest type) was precious in the army back then, so sharing your ration made you many friends.

A more contemporary bard, Vladimir Vysotsky, sang of smoking as a signal element of friendship and even existence: "**Друг, остáвь покурить, а в отвéт – тишинá, это он не вернýлся из бóя.**" "Friend, let me finish your cigarette, but no one answered – he was the one who didn't return from battle..."

Speaking of battles, writers and movie directors employ another tobacco idiom when recalling how the Soviets **дáли прикурить** (gave a light to) Hitler's troops near Stalingrad – even though the Nazis didn't necessarily ask for it... To give somebody a light in this sense means to give them a hard time.

Yet tobacco does not have only positive linguistic connotations. Even in today's press you may see the idiom **Де́ло – таба́к!** in a headline. It could be translated as "the deal is doomed."

Take note also of tobacco-oriented proverbs: when two friends argue over something – especially sharing profits or any other argument of a material nature, Russians say, "**Дру́жба дру́жбой, а табачо́к врозь**" (literally, "Friendship is friendship, but to each his own tobacco," i.e. friends can be friends and yet have different interests).

If you are one of those rare inveterate Western smokers, bear in mind some sacred formulae borrowed from Russian smokers' parlance. When they run out of cigarettes Russians say, "**ку́рево зако́нчилось**" ("the tobacco's gone"), stop passers by and ask, "**Закури́ть не найдётся?**" ("I don't suppose you would find a smoke on you?"). Fifteen-year-old Russian girls, though, might prefer the magic words, "**У Вас сигаре́точки не бу́дет?**" ("You don't happen to have a little cigarette, do you?")

During shortages, instead of finishing a cigarette, Russians would make a **бычо́к** (butt) out of it and finish it later. There's even a special verb – **забычкова́ть**. When smokers have no matches or their lighter (**зажига́лка**) is empty, they ask, "**У Вас не найдётся огонькy?**" or "**Разреши́те прикури́ть?**"

Anti-tobacco campaigns have had little impact on heavy smokers. It wasn't until the early 1980s that the Soviet Ministry of Health started putting its equivalent of the U.S. Surgeon General's warning on cigarette packs. It read: **Минздра́в СССР предупрежда́ет – куре́нье опа́сно для Ва́шего здоро́вья!** (The USSR Health Ministry warns – smoking is hazardous for your health). But cigarette brand names still encouraged people to go on smoking: e.g. **Друг** (friend) or **Дава́й закýрим** (let's have a smoke), a special brand produced for Victory Day.

So, most Russian smokers make fun of "say 'No' to cigarettes" campaigns. Sitting in a smoking room (**кури́лка** – the word originally meant a burning straw from a popular game) during a smoke break (**переку́р**), they might quote famous light verse like "**Куре́нье вред, а некуря́щих нет**" ("Smoking is mean but non-smokers are nowhere to be seen"). Another cliche slogan, "**Одна́ ка́пля никоти́на убива́ет ло́шадь**" ("One drop of nicotine can kill a horse") prompts the reply: "**Но мы то не ло́шади!**" ("But, we're not horses, are we?") A third: "**Куре́нье – ме́дленная смерть**" ("Smoking is a slow death") would prompt smokers to say "**А мы и не торо́пимся**" ("But then, we're in no hurry"). And so on...

Yet, not all Russians are so carefree about smoking. This is probably why sometimes they greet each other with the phrase: "**Жив кури́лка?**" (literally, "Still alive, smoker?") a version of the more traditional "How're things?" ("**Как дела́?**") This phrase is especially comforting for people who have had narrow escapes or been rescued after accidents. In fact, it may as well be applied to someone who has been smoking for years and just quit. It would not be a stretch to say he has just had a narrow escape.

Mikhail Ivanov (November 1996)

Matters of Life and Death

Regular readers of this column on linguistic survival may wonder what the Russian word for "survival" is and what Russians have to say about life and death more generally. In fact, survival-related vocabulary forms a substantial part of our lexicon, especially after recent market reforms pushed the overwhelming majority of Russians to the brink of poverty.

No sooner had Yegor Gaidar set prices free in 1992 than we Russians all began talking about how to **вы́жить** and how our life had become "a fight for survival" – **борьба́ за выжива́ние**. Indeed, many often confess their life is not a life but rather an existence: **Не жизнь, а существова́ние**, and that all they dream of is to live through these troubled times: **Пережи́ть э́то сму́тное вре́мя**.

In general, when Russians want to say they lead a tough life, they can say is it a fight **не на жизнь, а на смерть** (not for life, but to the death). In historical novels on the era of Peter the Great, we read how the Tsar-Reformer called on his soldiers and officers to wage the battle **не щадя́ живота́ своего́**. But no, this does not mean "without sparing one's belly," but rather "without sparing one's life." In old Russian, **живо́т** could simply mean "life."

Actually, Russian soldiers long had a reputation for fighting their enemies with bravery. Hence the popular Russian army proverb: **Двум смертя́м не быва́ть, а одно́й не минова́ть** (No one dies twice, but you can't avoid doing it once). Then there is the popular quote from a war song in which a soldier wishes, **Е́сли сме́рти, то мгнове́нной, е́сли ра́ны – небольшо́й** (If it is death, let it be swift, if it is a wound, let it be a small one).

But even in peaceful times many issues are considered to be a matter of life or death: **вопро́с жи́зни и́ли сме́рти**. This is especially true when one starts to compare the standard of living in Russia with that in other industrialized countries. Because, as the comic Mikhail Zhvanetsky said about the West – **"Их у́ровень сме́рти, э́то наш у́ровень жи́зни"** ("Their level of death is our level of life"). Indeed, the Russian minimal survival level – **Прожи́точный ми́нимум** – is simply nowhere near the minimum survival level in the West.

Such income discrepancies cannot but have an influence on life expectancy (**сре́дняя продолжи́тельность жи́зни**), which in 1994 plummetted to an all time low of 57.6 years for men, making Zhvanetsky's sardonic phrase all too true. According to the official state report "On the National Health in 1999" issued last fall, Russia's male life expectancy rose slightly, to 59.8, but is still two months short of the retirement age (**пенсио́нный во́зраст**).

But then not all is so gloomy in the sphere of life and survival in Mother Russia. Our women have a life expectancy of 72 – comparable to European levels, and enough to bring the overall Russian average to 65.5.

Of course, the verb **жить** does allow plenty of other relevant prefixes besides **пере** and **вы**. The wounds inflicted upon the nation in the first years of shock therapy have begun to heal (**зажива́ть**) and many Russians have learned to live with – **ужива́ться с** – the market economy. And each year more and more Russians are moving into new homes – **обжива́ть но́вое жильё**.

Worrying too much about the issues of **жи́зни и́ли сме́рти** is bound to send one's **сре́дняя продолжи́тельность жи́зни** plummetting. So why not use a philosophical approach preached by the winner of the last Moscow International Film Festival? Krzysztof Zanussi called his winning film: *Жизнь как смерте́льная боле́знь передаю́щаяся половы́м путём* (*Life as a Lethal, Sexually Transmitted Disease*)? That is why it is "vitally essential" (**жи́зненно ва́жно**) to be an optimist in life – **быть по жи́зни оптими́стом**.

Be aware that rampant use of the prefix **по** – as in the last example (e.g. **он по жи́зни ... он вообще́ тако́й по жи́зни**) – can get you in trouble with linguistic purists. Yet it is also true that it is better to use bad Russian and be an optimist than to speak flawlessly yet be a pessimist.

The perennial **"Как жизнь?"** ("How's life?") is usually answered with a simple **"норма́льно"** ("fine"), or, if your friend is in a great mood, **"лу́чше не быва́ет"** ("Things couldn't be better"). But there is also a quite funny (and now cliché) response that starts out: **"жизнь бьёт ключо́м"** ("life is spurting up like a spring"). Then at once you can add **"...по голове́"** ("on my head"). The addition is a wordplay based on a different meaning of the word **ключ** which means not only "spring" but also "wrench" (e.g. **га́ечный ключ**). Of course, such black humor is better than the other cliché response: **"Ра́зве э́то жизнь?!"** ("You call this life?!")

Mikhail Ivanov (January 2001)

Women
&
Men

Talking Man-to-Man

Just between us men, who among us has not dreamed of becoming a real macho man – what the Russians call a **настоящий мужик**? But what is a "real *muzhik*"? Some Russians think he should be able to drink anyone under the table, whereas some prefer sobriety, in order to show off their prowess at, say, a fitness center. As to qualities with which Survival Russian can be of help, it could reasonably be said that women all over the world value a *muzhik* with a good sense of humor. Didn't the French writer Stendhal say: "Oh, you made a woman laugh? It's as if you were already in her bed!" So, he who has many humorous idioms up his sleeve may be more likely to please the ladies.

To begin with, the title of this piece could be restated in a more humorous way. You will often hear Russian men saying, in fun, "Just between us girls" ("**Между нами, девочками, говоря**"). And this invariably draws smiles from all sides – of course, provided it is said amongst friends; amongst strangers, it may draw a negative reaction, political correctness knows no boundaries it seems...

As to manhood, there is an assortment of phrases to characterize a macho man. A **настоящий мужик** always behaves like a man (**по-мужски**), and, if he wants to urge someone to do the same, he might say "if you are a man" ("**если ты мужчина**") – which is also a good way to provoke a fight. Manhood (**мужественность**) can also be seen in someone's face, thus the phrase **мужественное лицо**. If two guys want to talk to each other man-to-man, they would have a **мужской разговор**. And men are supposed to speak like men. So, if someone says something juvenile (or simply says something you don't like) and then all of a sudden his words start making sense, you can condescendingly tell him, "**вот это речь не мáльчика, но мýжа**" ("now I hear a man talking, rather than a boy").

Athletes who show great endurance and character are said to have "shown themselves to be real men" (**показáли себя настоящими мужикáми**). And, prior to a sporting match, an underdog might tell the press that he came for a real fight and doesn't want to be treated "like a whipping boy" (**мáльчик для битья**).

Of course, for Russians, what's good for a **мужи́к** is no good for a woman. Hence, an exaggerated masculinity in the fairer sex is frowned upon here, and an iron lady (**желéзная лéди**) can be called a **мужи́к в юбке** (man in a skirt) – not a positive appellation. The adjective for such exaggerated masculinity is **мужеподóбная** (manlike or masculine). On the other hand, if a woman thinks her man is a wimp and really wants to humiliate him, all she needs to say is: "**ты не мужи́к, а тряпка**" (literally "you are not a man but a rag" – the Russian equivalent for being not a man but a mouse). And, call it gender segregation if you like, but in Russia there is still the notion of a "man's profession" (**мужскáя профéссия**) – serving in the army, piloting a plane, etc.

Needless to say, all boys dream of becoming a man (**стать мужчи́ной**) which, as in English, also implies a loss of virginity. And when you want to urge someone to behave in a more mature way, try: "**Ты ужé не мáльчик, юный барабáнщик**" ("You are no longer a boy, young drummer" – a cliché from an old song). Similarly, if someone thinks he is not being taken seriously, he might say in a vexed tone: "Are you taking me for a boy or what?" ("**Что я тебé, мáльчик?!**").

But not everything about boyhood is so bad. Otherwise, why would the Russians call a bachelor's party a **мальчи́шник** (this is exactly how Tom Hanks' movie *Bachelor Party* was translated here), though "bachelor" is more accurately translated into Russian as "**холостяк**." For instance, when someone's wife is away for a while, his friends might pat him on the back and say, with a conspiratorial look: "**Холостякýешь**" ("Bacheloring, eh?"). Which brings to mind the immortal phrase from the popular movie *Diamond Arm*: "**Нет такóго мýжа, котóрый не мечтáл бы хоть на час стать холостякóм**" ("There is no husband who wouldn't dream of becoming a bachelor, if only for an hour").

Comments on a lonely wife's situation take a more dramatic turn. If a wife stays without her husband for too long, the proverb has it that a woman without a man is twice as bad off as a widow (**женá без мýжа вдовы́ хýже**).

But don't even bother looking for an equivalent to the American exclamation "Oh boy!" – there isn't one ("**О! Мáльчик**" would be a stretch). Your best bet in this case is to sigh deeply and utter: "**Да, ребя́та ...**" ("Lemme tell ya, guys"). Or better yet: "**Ну, вообщé**," which means approximately the same thing. How do you tell the difference? Well, **спроси́те чегó полéгче** (ask me something simpler). **Мéжду нáми дéвочками говоря́**, sometimes I can't fathom this language myself. Just hang in there and keep learning the subtleties one-by-one. While it may or may not make a **настоящий мужи́к** out of you, it will help you speak **настоящий рýсский язы́к**.

Mikhail Ivanov (May 1998)

The Language of Love

With Russia becoming a Mecca for (mainly male) foreigners in search of a spouse, and as Russian marriage agencies proliferate like sidewalk kiosks in Moscow, a love-related vocabulary has become a vital topic.

The romantic-minded foreigner coming to Russia may be overwhelmed by the variety of vocabulary Russians use to express their feelings and plans vis-à-vis the opposite sex.

If you're looking for a marriage of convenience (**брак по расчёту**) then you can ignore linguistic subtleties and let your credit card talk instead. If, however, you want a true love match (**брак по любви**), then you must fall in love (**влюбиться**). Or, better still, "fall in love up to your ears" (**влюбиться по уши**), the ultimate in tender feelings.

Colloquial equivalents of "falling in love" range from **втюриться в кого-то** and **втрескаться в кого-то** (both of which make no sense in direct translation) to **запасть на кого-то** (to fall on someone).

Love at first sight (isn't that what you're looking for?) is **любовь с первого взгляда**. Then you can say about the object of your affections: **Она сводит меня с ума** (she drives me crazy). **Любовь с первого взгляда** can also be dangerous – remember the Russian proverb – Love is cruel, you may fall in love with a goat (**Любовь зла – полюбишь и козла**).

Once you made your choice, courtship begins. "To court someone" in Russian is **ухаживать за кем-то**. Needless to say, with the transition to the market economy, hit and run courtship has become more fashionable and the vocabulary has changed accordingly. **Ухаживать** has almost become a bookish expression applicable to *babushkas* from the old aristocracy.

Another colloquial verb for courting is **кадрить**, derived from the word **кадры** (personnel). So any potential object of courtship, both male or female, becomes a **кадр**. In this context, Russians of the older generation like to quote Stalin's famous slogan, **Кадры решают всё!** (The personnel decides everything). Any potential Russian partner over 50 understands the true meaning implied here.

The younger generation prefers **клеить** (to stick to someone). This word is a bit more relaxed in style, so when you say "**Я клею её**" ("I'm sticking to her"), it means you're courting without serious intentions.

The other way of saying it is **подкатывать к кому-нибудь** (to roll up to someone). This is even more relaxed in style, so you'd better not say it in front of a mid-40s intellectual with a Ph.D. in literature.

If your courtship has been successful, the time is ripe for "making an offer" (**сделать предложение**). In Pushkin's time, this meant **предложить руку и сердце** (to offer one's hand and heart).

Most native speakers would find this formula outdated and would just say "**Выходи́ за меня́ за́муж**" or "**Дава́й поже́нимся**" ("Marry me" or "Let's get married"). If you want to dazzle your in-laws with your level of education just pronounce these solemn words: "I ask for your daughter's hand in marriage" ("**Я прошу́ руки́ Ва́шей до́чери**"), which again, is perfect Russian, but not commonly used. Nowadays, people just don't ask their in-laws, at best they inform them of their intentions. So you can say something like, "**Мы с Ната́шей реши́ли пожени́ться**" ("Natasha and I decided to marry").

Try to memorize one more word if you plan to marry in Russia – **ЗАГС** (Z.A.G.S. – Marriage, Birth and Death Registry Agency). Apart from saying "**Да**" at the right moment, remember the formula used by the **ЗАГС** lady: "**Молоды́е, поздра́вьте друг дру́га!**" ("Newlyweds, congratulate one another" – i.e. kiss one another). Why there needs to be a euphemism here, nobody seems to know.

Afterwards, at the reception, you may hear another signal for kissing: "**Го́рько!**" ("Bitter!"), a call for the newly-weds to sweeten the bitter taste of vodka with their kisses. Whether you like this tradition or not, learn the word **го́рько** by heart. There's no way around it. You can expect your guests to shout it louder and louder with every toast.

What about words for more intimate relations, beyond gifts of flowers and phone calls? Since this aspect of relationships was taboo under the Soviets, the vocabulary was rather minimalist until recently. Surprisingly, it is the influx of foreign videos and literature that forced Russians to find an acceptable equivalent for it – **занима́ться любо́вью** – which still sounds a bit awkward (in English it sounds something like "to be occupied with love"). There has also grown an entire vocabulary of slang words that probably would not help to further the search for true love.

Getting back to marriage, make sure your wife has no **любо́вник** (lover) and don't look for a **любо́вница** (mistress) yourself. Like women anywhere in the world, Russian wives won't accommodate a womanizer (**ба́бник**) who likes to **ходи́ть по ба́бам** (chase women).

So find something else to do – for example try to become a **ма́стер на все ру́ки** (a jack of all trades) who can fix a TV set or fridge, or repair a broken chair in a matter of minutes Russian wives like to feel as secure with their husbands **как за ка́менной стено́й** (as if behind a stone wall).

If you can live up to this, your honeymoon with your Russian spouse could last longer than prescribed by the Russian language (the Russian equivalent for honeymoon – **медо́вый ме́сяц** – literally means "honey month"). Moreover, if you follow these love-related linguistic tips, you could even turn your honey **ме́сяц** into a honey **пятиле́тка** (five year plan) and, to use another ex-socialist cliche, end up with a **брак без бра́ка*** (a marriage without defect) – otherwise so hard to attain.

Mikhail Ivanov (October 1995)

***брак** in Russian has a dual meaning: (1) a marriage, and (2) a defect, a flaw.

Fishing for Tenderness

Valentine's Day is not far off, so it is a perfect time to help men learn some impressive Russian terms of endearment. In other words, what is the Russian equivalent of the English "honey" or "hon," or "dear"?

It varies, actually. The most standard endearment for one's wifey (**жёнушка**) is **дорогáя** or **дорогýша**. **Ми́лая** is equally popular with Russian men.

Right next to it stand all sorts of nicknames from the animal world. Feline formulas are the undisputed leaders. Enamored men call their "belle" **ки́са** (pussy-cat), **кисýль** or **кóтя** (from **кот**, cat). These sweet and sugary derivations are used to death and frankly make me cringe. But they must work for some.

Hares are not just the slang term for ticketless passengers (see page 36) but, perhaps because they are cute, furry little creatures, are also *apropos* for sweet-talking your sweetheart. The most popular nickname is the bile-inducing **зáйка** (little bunny). But, again, it's in use. Wide use. The king of Russian *popsa*, Filip Kirkorov (something like a déclassé Russian version of Julio Iglesias) even dedicated a song to his ageing ex-**жёнушка**, the pop Queen Alla Pugacheva, and titled it "**Зáйка моя́.**" Not that she resembles a bunny, but, well, "love is blind" as they say, so let her be a "little bunny" if the king of Russian *popsa* sees her this way (perhaps, had he been a bit more inventive with his endearments, she might not be his ex-bunny).

Russian beaux also call their belles **голýбка** (little dove) or **кýрочка** (little hen). But some might say these terms are only used by henpecked husbands – the one who, as someone once put it, "wears the pants in the house – under his apron," or, in more flamboyant Russian, the **подкаблýчный муж**, or, for short: **подкаблýчник** (literally, "the one under his wife's heel").

Then there are the fish. In a fit of tenderness, sometimes a Russian **мужи́к** might call his wife **ры́бка** or even **ры́бонька** (little fish). **Зóлотко** (goldie) or **сóлнышко моё** (my little sun) will work too. The creative type may call their honey **мой слáдкий** (my sweetie), using the masculine adjectival form. It somehow sounds less cliché this way. And the classic **лáпа – лапýля** (paw, little paw) is also available for those who have no imagination.

Not surprisingly, Russians are even more linguistically resourceful when it comes to pejoratives. When they fall out of love or their marriage falls into a boring rut, no holds are barred. The wife can become a **швáбра** (push broom) or a **клю́шка** (hockey stick). Also a **гры́мза** (untranslatable and quite vulgar), a **мегéра** (wet hen), а **гадю́ка** (viper), а **кóбра** (cobra) – you name it. A friend of mine calls his wife "**бли́зкая рóдственница по ли́нии сы́на**" ("a close relative on my son's side"). A friend of this friend simply calls his wife "**э́та**" (that). Pushkin-like, men may also call their partners **бáба моя́**. This is from the fairy tale

About a Fisherman and the Fish (**Сказка о рыбаке и рыбке**), whose main protagonist, a fisherman has a difficult time satisfying the rather expensive whims of his greedy **баба**.

But, of course, this is not something one should strive for in marital life. The happily married couples live **душа в душу** (literally "like one soul"), and, like all happy people, do not notice the passing of time – **счастливые часов не наблюдают** (from Griboyedov's play, *Woe from Wit*). And, while they may not necessarily call their loved ones little hares, little fish or pussy-cats, a diminutive derived from a lover's first name is *de rigeur*. **Лёночка, Наташенька, Машуля** are most pleasing options.

I personally call my **Надежда Надюша**. And she even does not take offense at the occasional use of **баба**. It is standard and (depending on the tone, of course) fine with loved ones. After all, my **баба** occasionally calls me **мужик**. And I know that, from her, it is a compliment. Perhaps it is simply because we share a loathing for all this animalia – **зайка, киса** and **рыбка**, *et al*. But then linguistic tastes differ. And the most important thing to remember is that nothing is too sweet for Valentine's Day, **рыбоньки мой**. (Just don't forget the chocolate!)

Mikhail Ivanov (January 2006)

Flirting and Courting

The 8th of March (**Восьмое марта**), known as International Women's Day, is the Russian equivalent of St. Valentine's Day (**День Святого Валентина**), except that presents (**подарки**) and compliments (**комплименты**) go only one way – from the citizens of Mars (**Марс**) to those of Venus (**Венера**).

Actually, for men, March 8 is a good day to appease the notorious heroine of Russian jokes – the **тёща** (a husband's mother-in-law), along with other Venetians, by lavishing them with your attentions (**оказывать знаки внимания**). But interacting with the opposite sex (**противоположный пол**) in a foreign language can be tricky. So here's a crib sheet for interplanetary communication.

On March 8, Russian men take their sweethearts on a date (**свидание**). Be careful, however, when transculturating the more direct English invitation, "Do you want to go on a date?" Russians tend to be more obtuse and avoid the word "date" by using invitation patterns such as: "**Пойдём куда-нибудь сегодня вечером?**" ("Shall we go somewhere tonight?") "**Ты пойдёшь со мной на вечеринку?**" ("Would you like to come to a party with me?"), "**Я хотел (хотела) пригласить тебя в кино.**" ("I would like to invite you to the movies"), etc.

In fact, the expression "to go out" does not have an exact Russian equivalent. Depending on the purpose of going out, it can be translated as **развлечься** (seek entertainment), **тусоваться** (hang out), **поужинать в ресторане** (dine out), etc. A cousin of mine who moved to Derby, England two years ago recently surprised me with her emigrant slang: "**Мы идём в аут**" ("We are going into out") and the even the more bizarre: "**Она в ауте**" ("She is in out"). Needless to say, use of either of these expressions is sure to under-impress your Russian teacher and probably confuse Russian friends.

Once you get to a party (**вечеринка**), also sometimes referred to as a **тусовка** (a slang word for a gathering of people who hang out together), you might decide to start hitting on someone. Men can do it in a gentlemanly fashion (**ухаживать за кем-то**), saying things like "**Разрешите за вами поухаживать?**" ("May I get you some food?"), "**Разрешите вас пригласи́ть" ("Allow me to invite you to dance.") or, more casually, "Потанцу́ем?" ("Shall we dance?"). The more direct manner of hitting on someone is denoted by the verbs подъе́хать (literally "to drive up to"), подкати́ть ("to roll up to") and пристава́ть ("to nag"). Thus, Он к ней пристаёт means he is making a pass at her, in a very pushy, irritating way.

One who pushes his пристава́ния too far risks being labeled an arrogant jerk (наха́л) or even getting a slap across the face (пощёчина) from the object of one's advances. It can be said about a spurned admirer that "Его отши́ли" (literally, "He was sewn off"), or, more rudely, "Его посла́ли ..." ("He was sent off to...").

To flirt is кадри́ть, while the perfective form, закадри́ть, implies that someone has already fallen under a flirter's spell (Она́ его́ закадри́ла). This can be achieved by making eyes at someone (Она́ стро́ит ему́ гла́зки). By the way, Он положи́л на неё глаз (He has put his eye on her) means he has fallen for her.

Before you start hitting on someone, you might want to check whether the person is already "taken," by asking the question, "У тебя́ есть де́вушка / молодо́й челове́к?" ("Do you have a girlfriend/ boyfriend?"). To brush off an unwanted admirer, you might say, "У меня́ есть де́вушка" ("I have a girlfriend"). From this, you can see that there is no universal word for girlfriend or boyfriend in Russian. While in English these words can be used to refer to men and women of all ages, the Russian де́вушка (young girl) and молодо́й челове́к (young man) or the more colloquial па́рень (guy) are generally reserved for those under 30. Older people might use же́нщина (woman) or мужчи́на (man), but should avoid любо́вница/любо́вник (mistress/lover), as these words usually connote sex and sometimes adultery. The phrase, "We are together" should be rendered in Russian as "Мы встреча́емся" ("We meet").

Unless it is любо́вь с пе́рвого взгля́да (love at first sight), the road from пе́рвое свида́ние (the first date) to the мы встреча́емся stage can be long and thorny. In Russia, which many still consider a sexist society (try using the borrowed term секси́стское о́бщество and your Russian interlocutor may enthuiastically say, "Yes, we have a very sexy society"), the way to a woman's heart is still usually strewn with flowers, compliments and "gentlemanly behavior" (вести́ себя́ как джентльме́н), which is usually applied only to the courting stage). Meanwhile, the path to a man's heart is said to run through his stomach (путь к се́рдцу мужчи́ны лежи́т че́рез желу́док), meaning that good cuisine will break down any resistance.

Such conservative views are still prevalent in Russia, but not universal, so be sure to tailor your approach to your situation, or who knows where you might get sent ...

Lina Rozovskaya (March 2004)

Figures & Measures

Better Than a Hundred Rubles

Alexander Druz, a famous Russian **знато́к** (expert) and long-time participant on the TV quiz program **Что? Где? Когда?** *(What, Where, When?)*, once bet a friend that he could tell a joke about any subject. His friend took the bet and then lost soundly when Druz proceeded to regale him with jokes for hours, on all his chosen subjects. While I would never pretend to Druz's level of erudition, after writing this column for five years I sometimes feel it would be possible to write a Survival Russian column on almost any topic. For this, we probably have the richness of the Russian language to thank.

Take for instance **"сто"** (100), the magic number of Young Russians which *Russian Life* selected for its year-long series of profiles (published in 2001-2002). There are so many "hundred-related" things that they cannot fit into this space. But let's get down to the basic ones.

The first is simple and quite mundane: it is the figure on our banknotes. Russians have many names for their 100 ruble note: from the old-fashioned and obsolete **ка́тенька** (little Katya), to the rather neutral yet colloquial **со́тня, со́тенная**, the rude **сотня́га**, and the contemporary **сто́льник** or the tender and cajoling **сто́льничек**. Whatever you call it, it always gives one pleasure to know that *"У меня́ в карма́не че́стная со́тня ..."* ("I have an honest hundred in my pocket") – as Lyube lead singer Nikolai Rastorguyev sings, anticipating a rowdy, weekend party.

Proverbs? Well, there is of course **Не име́й сто рубле́й, а име́й сто друзе́й** (Don't have a hundred rubles, but a hundred friends), or the rather universal **Лу́чше оди́н раз уви́деть, чем сто раз услы́шать.** It's better to see once than hear a hundred times.

It is not a proverb, but most Russian (and American, I suspect) parents say it enough to their kids that it should perhaps qualify as one: **Ну что мне, сто раз на́до повторя́ть?!** ("What do I have to do, repeat myself 100 times?")

As this example suggests, 100 is a standard bearer for idiomatic exaggeration and emphasis. If a Russian wants to emphasize that he does not need something (or someone) he might say **сто лет он мне не ну́жен**, (I wouldn't need it in a hundred years.) or, better yet, **сто лет он мне не присни́лся** (I wouldn't dream of it in a hundred years.).

One hundred is also a number near and dear to the hearts of war veterans. For there is a long tradition of distributing to soldiers a **фронтовы́е сто грамм** (100 grams at the front) of vodka or spirits before a battle.

In an interesting twist of old and new lexicon, young Russians (i.e. 25 and under) have combined the old weight measurement **пуд** (a pood, 16 kilos), with 100 to mean "sure thing" or "ironclad." Thus, a response to "Are you sure?" could be "**Сто пудо́в!**" An adverb has grown out of this: **стопудо́во,** a synonym of **то́чно** or **желе́зно**. And the Russian press has coined a special musical phrase: **стопудо́вый хит** meaning a "huge hit."

As these examples show, hundred-related words and expressions tend to have positive connotations – for instance the famous **со́тки** (one *sotok* equals 1000 m² – one-tenth of a hectare) – private plots where Russians grow their own vegetables and/or have a *dacha* (on a **шесть со́ток** – six hundredths – size plot). An exception to this is, of course, the infamous **Чёрная со́тня** (the "black hundred" known as **черносо́тинцы,** which, among other things, perpetrated *pogroms* during the tsarist era.

It is hard, when discussing 100, for the mind not to wander to that other important figure in Russian culture – 150. This, of course, is the common measurement (in grams) for a shot of vodka as served in a Russian restaurant. In times of war they may have passed out vodka in 100 gram allotments, but in times of peace, it is usually "**по сто пятьдеся́т**." But do not take my word for it: next time you are in a typical Russian cafe, order "**Два ра́за по сто пятьдеся́т!**" ("two at 150"). Even if you have a thick American accent in Russian, you will win the waiter over. **Сто пудо́в!** (Especially if, at the end of the meal, you leave behind a crisp, neat **сто́льничек** – about $3 – as a tip.

Mikhail Ivanov (March 2001)

The Power of Seven

Numeric idioms, as the above column indicates, have a special place in the Russian lexicon. And certainly the number seven is a first among equals in this regard.

If you need any proof of this, suffice it to note that seven is current Russian President Vladimir Putin's favorite number. Perhaps this had some bearing on Vladimir Vladimirovich's division of Russia into seven new federal districts. And it may have been one reason why he reportedly sought to make the presidency a seven-year post instead of a four-year one. But this is just idle speculation.

What we do know is that Putin's love for seven is shared by his fellow Russians – perhaps even contributing to his high approval ratings.

Семь раз отме́рь – оди́н раз отре́жь (Measure seven times before you cut.), Russians love to say when it comes time to make a crucial decision. And when a group of Russians are tired of waiting for someone who is late, they may quip that "seven don't wait for one" (**Се́меро одного́ не ждут**). While a Russian diplomat might find the former proverb useful in discussions with his American counterpart about the inadviseability of breaching the 1972 ABM treaty, he is advised to avoid the latter one, as it might get miscontrued in the context of the G-7, to which Russia is a "late" partner number eight.

But perhaps Russians and Americans can broach their differences by remembering what they share in common. Like the idiom used to express joy: **Я был на седьмо́м не́бе от сча́стья.** (I was in Seventh Heaven from happiness.)

Perhaps the number seven's popularity can be traced to Moscow, long renowned for being located on seven hills (**на семи холмах**). Whatever the reason, proverbs featuring this magic number abound: **Один с сошкой, а семеро с ложкой** (One with a plough, seven with a spoon – meaning one man does the work, but seven take the pickings), or how about the beautiful **Для милого дружка и семь верст не околица** (Even seven versts is not too far to travel for a dear friend.)

Of course, Russian students, like those the world over, study the **семь чудес света** (seven wonders of the world) and here as everywhere, it is common to call something miraculous or extraordinary the **восьмое чудо света** (eighth wonder of the world).

Seven has even worked its way into the titles of popular Russian movies. Hence the two comedies **Семь стариков и одна девушка** (*Seven Old Men and One Young Girl*) **Семь невест Ефрейтора Збруева** (*The Seven Brides of Private First Class Zbruyev*).

In history, seven had an important, often ominous meaning. Take the notorious period known as **семибоярщина** – when seven boyars were calling the tunes. So, in the Yeltsin era, when seven oligarchs were pulling the Kremlin strings, witty journalists renamed this period the **семибанкирщина** – the reign of the seven bankers.

But as is often the case in management, seven proved too many for poor Mother Russia. As the proverb has it: **У семи нянек дитя без глазу** (When there are seven nurses looking after one child, the child ends up losing his eye).

Partly in response to the mess wrought by the **семибанкирщина,** Tsar Boris picked his successor from the ranks of the organization once headed by a man named **Семичастный** (literally, "Mr. Seven Parts"): former KGB agent Vladimir Putin.

Putin, the lover of the number seven, quickly earned a reputation as a man of few words. So it was not long before the oligarchs began to feel the change in mood from words to deeds. For Putin, it was a case of **семь бед – один ответ** (literally, "seven crimes, one punishment," which, in this context, means to take the same sort of decisive action against all the different things that ail you, not fearing the consequences). Or, as courageous Russians say, **семи смертям не бывать, одной не миновать** (you only die once, not seven times).

In a matter of months, one by one, the seven banker-oligarchs either disappeared from the political scene of their own volition or found themselves far away from Russia. Or, as we say –**за семью морями** (beyond the Seven Seas).

Two of the most "notorious" oligarchs have taken up residence in Europe. Boris Berezovsky reportedly likes it in London, while Vladimir Gusinsky fought extradition from Spain (and even traveled to the U.S., where he was not touched, despite the fact that Pavel Borodin was arrested in the U.S. and extradited to Switzerland on the same sorts of charges for which Gusinsky is wanted in Russia).

But Russia's law enforcement bodies are nothing if not determined to bring the oligarchs back to Russia to face charges. Foiled in their first extradition request to Spain for Gusinsky, they are filing yet another. After all, there is no limit to the distance one would go to see a friend again...

Mikhail Ivanov (July 2001)

Just a Minute...

So you think a minute consists of 60 seconds? Hah! If you're thinking in Russian, think again. Russian and American time concepts are as different as the words **время** and "time." Time in the United States is a linear progression of specific units, a strictly regulated frame for behavior. Russian time is more elastic, a vaguely flowing continuum that defies definition. In American, "Just a minute, I'm coming" means exactly that. In Russian, **минуточку** (a little minute), **сию минуту** (this minute) or **сейчас** (right away) can mean ten or fifteen minutes or longer. "Time is money," goes the American saying; **Поспешишь, людей насмешишь** ("Hurry and you'll make people laugh") replies the Russian proverb.

"Let's have lunch three weeks from Tuesday at one-thirty at that Italian place on the corner" would be, for an American, a perfectly normal invitation to a friend. But to a Russian it would sound outlandish. Three weeks ahead? Who knows what **судьба** (fate) may have in store for him that far in the future? If the date is not for the next day or the day after, he will suggest that you and he could **созвониться** (call each other), a highly puzzling verb for English speakers, since it is perfectly unclear as to who is to call whom.

"**Момент – сейчас приду**" ("Just a minute/moment, I'll be there right away") can imply a point in time or a period of unspecified length. And **момент** can be much longer than a moment. With the Russian word's several meanings, a **важный момент в докладе** is an "important point in a report," **момент в жизни** is an "event" or "stage" in someone's life, and **нужно учесть этот момент** means the matter must be taken into account. And if something is done **оперативно** it is not done operationally but quickly or efficiently.

Apart from the elastic words, there are the flexible concepts. **Во второй половине дня** means "the second half of the day," but *when* in the afternoon – suppose someone is to call you – is left to the workings of fate and the mood of the caller. **После обеда** means not simply "after lunch," but the entire postlunch period. How long a period? An American couple living in Moscow were nonplussed when their four-year-old son's Russian **няня** (nurse) told them she was worried, since "**после обеда Джонни ничего не ел**" ("Johnny didn't eat anything after lunch"). Why in the world, thought the parents, should the kid eat something right after a big lunch?

To avoid being hours late some place you've been invited, it is well to remember that **вечернее заседание** (evening meeting) or **вечерний сеанс** (evening showing) may refer to an event set for the afternoon. And if you are wondering why your Russian guests are so often late, reflect on how reversing the order of "**в шесть часов**" to "**часов в шесть**" changes the meaning from "at six o'clock" to "around" or "approximately" six.

And the expression **уже седьмой час** – (literally "It's already the seventh hour") means "It's already past six." It could be be 6:01 or 6:30. So much for the souffle you had in the oven for your dinner guests.

Then there is that truly Janus-faced expression, **на днях**. It could mean "a few days ago," or it could mean "in a few days." "**Я об этом узнал на днях**" means "I found out about it a few days ago," while "**На днях он Вам даст ответ**" tells you that "He'll answer you in the next few days."

So, if you find yourself still waiting, past the hour, for friends who'd told you they'd be arriving **часов в восемь** or that they'd call you **во второй половине дня**, just wait a **минуточку**, resist the urge to **созвониться** and remember that your American 60 seconds may well stretch out to a Russian sixty minutes, more or less.

Lynn Visson (January 2004)

50 and Counting

I know, I know, **дорого яичко к Христову дню** (things are best on time). I was late with this Survival Russian piece, which would have been a much better fit for *Russian Life*'s 50th anniversary issue (September/October 2006). But then we Russians tend to stretch the celebration of round anniversaries out into year-round affairs. So, in any event, in honor of the jubilee, let us look at the number 50.

Fifty is actually quite a venerated figure in Mother Russia. The 50th anniversary – **50-я годовщина** – is always marked here *en grande pompe*. When someone turns 50 – in simple Russian, **полтинник** (from the 50 kopek coin's face value, it can also mean 50 kopeks, 50 rubles, or 50,000 rubles), this is nothing to sneeze at. Only a centenary – **столетие** – can beat it.

When, for example, Soviet Russia was celebrating the **пятидесятилетие Великой Октябрьской Социалистической Революции** in 1967, it was quite an event. And, had Russian President Vladimir Putin sent *Russian Life* a letter of congratulation, it might have sounded something like: "**От всей души поздравляю коллектив редакции журнала Russian Life с юбилейным, пятидесятым годом. Желаю всем журналистам этого славного журнала, который несёт американцам правду о России, крепкого**

здорóвья, твóрческих успéхов и журналúстских удáч." ("From the bottom of my heart, I congratulate the editorial staff of Russian Life magazine on the occasion of its 50th anniversary. I wish all journalists of this glorious magazine, which brings Americans the truth about Russia, good health, many creative successes and journalistic achievements.")

While I cannot predict the future, it is likely that Russian Life has more than a **пятьдесят на пятьдесят** (or as we say, **фúфти-фúфти**) chance of publishing into its 100th year. After all, not many magazines have 50 years under their belt (or, as we say, "behind their shoulders" – **за плечáми**).

Our generation of Russian Life writers could well be called **пятидесятники** – most of us are well over forty, or, as we

say in Russia, **нам хорошó за сóрок.** And hopefully our generation is not so fitness-obsessed that we shy from having our **пятьдесят грамм** (50 grams) of vodka on such occasions (or maybe even **два рáза по пятьдесят**, "two times 50"). The occasion is certainly worth it.

The peripatetic linguist Vladimir Dal worked on his dictionary of Russian for almost 50 years. In it, he cited at least one 50-esque proverb for those who might not be inclined to celebrate this occasion: **Не дал Бог ста рублéй, а пятьдесят не деньги.** It means, "God did not bless us with 100 rubles, and fifty rubles is not the kind of money you should be sitting on, so spend it." And, mind you, 50 rubles in Dal's time bought quite a gala-dinner and many, many times 50 grams.

But some may continue to object to celebrations, thinking only of the costs, of the morning after, of what might go wrong. They may retort: **расхóдов на полтúнник, а пóльзы на грош** (literally: "it costs 50 kopeks, and is worth but a penny"). It means that something is too much hassle, with too little benefit.

Of course, there is no arguing with such people. And why bother? Life, as the swift passage of 50 years shows, is too short. Best to simply not invite such ascetic types to one's **пятидесятилéтие**.

Mikhail Ivanov (November 2006)

Music & Art

Can I Sip on Your Tchaikovsky?

There is hardly a more venerated composer in Russia than Pyotr Ilyich Tchaikovsky. Which doesn't stop irreverent domestic jokers from using his name in situations much more mundane than a classic music recital. If you hear someone saying: "How about some Tchaikovsky?" ("**Мо́жет, Чайко́вского?**") he is not inviting you to listen to an excerpt from *Sleeping Beauty* or *Swan Lake*. He is simply offering you a cup of tea. For the composer's eminent family name – **Чайко́вский** – contains the word **чай** (tea).

The idiom was not in use during Tchaikovsky's lifetime. But now, in informal banter and in the right context, "Let's have some Tchaikovsky" means only "Let's have some tea." To which Tchaikovsky's contemporary and colleague, Modest Mussorgsky, might well have replied with the famous proverb: "**Чай не во́дка–мно́го не вы́пьешь.**" ("You can't drink as much tea as you can vodka.") The two composers certainly had their differences, and, in terms of beverages, Mussorgsky, as is plain to see from Ilya Repin's famous portrait of him (which we have somewhat irreverently pasted into our cartoon, below), was known to prefer vodka to "tchaikovsky."

Little could the great composer have imagined: in our time some inventive foreign distillers have launched a new premium vodka brand named after Pyotr Ilyich. It's a wonder Tchaikovsky's heirs have not sued the vodka-makers for abusing his name. Or, if copyright laws are not applicable to 19th century composers, at least for selling this otherwise quite ordinary vodka at exhorbitant prices.

Of course, Tchaikovsky does not stand alone in having his name "abused" by his countrymen a century removed. In the 1970s, when a short course in music history was required in all secondary schools, students compiled a whole short story based on funny connotations in the names of some composers, domestic and foreign: "**Вы́шел на Дво́ржак, круго́м оди́н Му́соргский, вы́пил Чайко́вского, в животе́–Пучи́ни.**" ("I went out in the courtyard [Dvorak], there was trash [Mussorgsky] all over the place, drank some tea [Tchaikovsky], and had gas [Puccini] in my stomach.") The last is from the phrase, **у меня́ пучи́т живо́т** (I have a mess in my stomach).

Ignoramuses amongst the New Rich know about Tchaikovsky as a beverage, and some may even have heard he wrote some music. That they have no clue about which music he wrote is the subject of a fresh new joke making the rounds here:

A New Russian is bragging about his recent visit to the Moscow conservatory:
"You know, **братáн** (brother), my wife told me I gotta become more cultured. So we've just been at a concert of classical music and heard some Tchaikovsky. I kinda liked him."
"Oh, cool! And who is this Tchaikovsky?"
"Shame on you! He wrote the music for our mobile phones."

Since the language of music is international, some English and Russian musical idioms often sound virtually the same. E.g. to call the tune: **задавáть тон**; to strike a chord: **задéть струнý**. Yet, if you want to say in a business context, "we will play it by ear," don't use the Russian **подбирáть на слух**. Although it is proper for the musical context, it is limited to that. For the wider meaning use another musical idiom: **игрáть с листá** (to sightread). A musician who plays **с листá** is someone who can play a piece well at the first sitting, never having seen the music before.

Music indeed adds charm to our language. Compare the plain **он дéйствует мне на нéрвы** (he is getting on my nerves) with the elegant **он игрáет у меня на нéрвах** (he is playing on my nerves). When you are pleasantly surprised by something that was obviously well-prepared in advance, you can say: **в кустáх случáйно оказáлся роя́ль** (and then, by chance, there was a piano in the bushes). Indeed, a piano doesn't belong in the bushes unless somebody had taken the trouble to put it there well in advance.

Of course, musical idioms have long invaded the political lexicon (and have direct equivalents in English). For example: The press smear campaign against Moscow Mayor Yuri Luzhkov was **оркестрúрована** (orchestrated) by the Kremlin. First TV channel anchor Sergei Dorenko **игрáл пéрвую скрúпку** (played the first violin) and was believed to be saying on air whatever his master, Boris Berezovsky (a major shareholder in the TV channel), wanted him to. But then, **Кто плáтит, тот и закáзывает мýзыку** ("He who pays, calls the tune").

The anti-Luzhkovian campaign was indeed **разы́грана как по нóтам** ("played by the notes," well-orchestrated), so much so that Luzhkov's ratings plummeted, forcing him to abandon his run for the presidency. After Luzhkov's party, Fatherland, did poorly in the December 1999 parliamentary elections, you could tell from Luzhkov's face that he was **настрóен на минóрный лад** ("tuned to a minor chord," looking and feeling down). This contrasted with the much younger Vladimir Putin who, after Yeltsin made him acting president of Russia, ended 1999 **на мажóрной нóте** ("on a major note," upbeat). After his election, Putin became a true **человéк-оркéстр** ("man-orchestra"), which means a man who is very active and can do a lot of different things at once – we saw him skiing, co-piloting a Sukhoi-27 fighter, on board a nuclear submarine, practicing judo, etc. In fact, he was doing it all smoothly and rapidly, **в ритме вáльса** ("in waltz rhythm," i.e. to do something quickly – a good phrase to use when you are giving someone an order).

You may have heard of the now famous episode when Yeltsin forced first-vice-premier Sergei Stepashin to switch his seat at a cabinet meeting and move closer to the "tsar," leading some to cite a proverbial quote from a fable of Ivan Krylov: **"А вы, друзья́, как ни садúтесь, всё в музыкáнты не годúтесь."** ("No matter where you sit, friends, you're poor musicians anyway.") And poor musicians, as we know, often **играют мимо нот** ("miss the notes"). So Stepashin was fired by Yeltsin... in the rhythm of a waltz.

Perhaps one of Luzhkov's great strengths while mayor is that his government has never suffered from this sort of "musical chairs." And, despite his need to abbreviate his presidential ambitions, he probably has a long political life – at least regionally – ahead of him. First, he leads a rather healthy lifestyle and drinks only "tchaikovsky." Second, he can continue to count on votes from Muscovites, as long as he makes sure there is no "mussorgsky" in their "dvoraks."

Mikhail Ivanov (July 2000)

Who Shall Judge?

Well-educated Russians can't help quoting literary classics once in a while to spruce up their speech. Foreigners who can follow suit will score points on the **культурный** index.

The list of such allusions is endless, so we will focus on the most famous and frequent ones. One such allusion is in the headline above: "**А судьи кто?**" This comes from Alexander Griboyedov's famous play **Горе от ума** (*Woe from Wit*), whose hero, Alexander Chatsky, at odds with Moscow's conservative *beau-monde*, utters these words, meaning "who are they, to judge me?!" Griboyedov's play alone is a wealth of literary allusions – no other Russian literary work has given us so many tidbits, clichés and set-phrases. Regulars of this feature will remember his tobacco-related cliché, **Но дым отечества нам сладок и приятен** (see page 118).

Actually, the title of the comedy *Woe from Wit* has become a literary cliché as well – it refers to someone who is way too intelligent, a perfectionist too particular about details, who therefore suffers too much in life. Today it is also applicable in humorous terms to someone who worries too much, knows too much and therefore cannot be happy.

Another idiom, borrowed from a famous Chatsky monologue is "**с корабля на бал**" ("from the ship to a ball"), which means someone found himself in a completely different situation/entourage overnight – often after a long and tiresome trip or just after doing something different. E.g., if your flight arrives in Moscow at 1 p.m. and you have a meeting at, say, 5:30 p.m. the same day, you could well excuse yourself with style by saying: "**Я сегодня прямо с корабля – на бал.**" If your trip to Moscow does not come out quite the way you expected, you can quote Chatsky with: "I am leaving Moscow and will never come here again." ("**Вон из Москвы, сюда я больше не ездок**"). And then, on top of that, you can quote Chatsky's famous final phrase – "**Карету мне, карету!**" ("My chariot, my chariot!") which means today "That's it for me." Yet, before you engage in these literary allusions, make sure the educational level of your Russian business counterparts is adequate – not all **бизнесмены** read Griboyedov these days.

The words of Chatsky's would be father-in-law, Famusov, also survive in modern usage with his phrase: "**Что станет говорить княгиня Марья Алексеевна?**" ("What will countess Mariya Alexeevna say?" meaning "What will the neighbors think?") But, being a father of a daughter, I like this one better: "**Что за комиссия, Создатель, быть взрослой дочери отцом?!**" ("Why is it so tough, oh Creator, to be the father of a grown-up daughter?!") Famusov's daughter Sofia, who spurned Chatsky's offer, pronounces in her own famous phrase: "**Счастливые часов не наблюдают**" ("Happy people pay no attention to the time"). Today this is often said to someone who is late and does not bother looking at his watch.

The merits of Leo Tolstoy in the development of the Russian language are undeniable. He was also a pacifist, hence the noun "**толстовщина,**" used by the Bolsheviks (the perjorative suffix "shch" underlined the Bolsheviks' negative attitude to pacifism). Yet, strange as it may seem, there are not that many modern idiomatic phrases to be culled from Tolstoy's works. This is probably because he was not so good at short, cut-in-stone phrases. Yet some of his shortest quotations are famous: **Все счастливые семьи похожи друг на друга, каждая несчастливая семья несчастлива по-своему** (All happy families resemble one another, but each unhappy family is unhappy in its own way – the opening line of *Anna Karenina*); **Мы любим людей за то добро, которое им делаем и ненавидим их за то зло, которое им причиняем** (We love people for the good we do to them and hate them for the evil we do to them).

Yet, Tolstoy's contemporary, Anton Chekhov, was very good at literary *bon mots*. You may already know his remark about "tainted sturgeon": **а осетрина-то с душком** (to indicate a non-sequitor). And what about his famous **краткость – сестра таланта** (brevity is the sister of talent)? You can use this Chekhovian phrase as an apt excuse for writing too short an essay in high school, or when, say, proposing a very short toast. The title of Chekhov's short story **Человек в футляре** (*A Man in a Case*) became an epithet for someone who lives only by strict regulations, never does anything on his own, and is afraid of showing initiative.

The title of Nikolai Gogol's famous novel **Мёртвые души** (*Dead Souls*) is still used today to characterize different types of illegal schemes, e.g. whenever someone registers a firm under a non-existent name. A character in the novel, Manilov, loved to devise unrealistic projects which never came to fruition, hence the modern name for such schemes – **маниловщина**. In the play **Ревизор** (*The Inspector General*), one of Gogol's heroes excuses himself for his corruption with the phrase: "**Я беру взятки, но борзыми щенками**" ("I take bribes, but in Borzoi puppies"). Today it is still said about corrupt *apparatchiks* who are embarrassed to take cash that they take bribes **борзыми щенками**, i.e. in kind.

In the Soviet era, they used to take food packages, bottles of cognac or perfumes in lieu of puppies. Today's equivalent of **борзые щенки** would be gorgeous apartments and *dachas*, cars or stocks. To rephrase the famous saying, corruption is the mother of invention – witness the recent case of the "Union of Writers," which drew the attention of Russia's

Prosecutor General for receiving sizeable "literary honorariums," paid as advances, for a book on privatization that few expect to ever be written. And ex-St. Petersburg Mayor Anatoly Sobchak stands accused of having secured apartments for his relatives.

But, frankly, for all the brouhaha around such scandals, none among Russia's rulers seems ready to prosecute the "writers" or St. Petersburg's ex-mayor. First, because, as Gogol used to say, bribes in puppies is a whole different ball game. But, most importantly, because any schemes to put an end to corruption in Russia, unfortunately, look at best like **маниловщина.** Who would be fit to judge such things anyway?

Mikhail Ivanov (August 1998)

Lights, Camera...

It is hard to underestimate the role of the arts in Russian speech. Consider film, which, to reluctantly quote Josef Stalin, was, for communists "the most important art form" (**"Важнейшим из всех искусств для нас является кино"**), because it reached such a broad audience. Actually, in my school days, the most important thing about films was that going to the **кинóшка** (little movie) was a great excuse for skipping school. Today, our kids can get anything they want on video (**на видеке/на видаке**), but this is not to say school attendance has gotten any better.

So, when a Russian says **"Интерéсное кинó!"** ("Interesting movie!"), it is not necessarily a cinema critique. Pronounced with the right intonation and a slathering of sarcasm, it connotes indignation, disappointment or disagreeable surprise (or all three at once), i.e. a sarcastic "Excuse me!" or "Well-well-well!" For instance, this is what a creditor might say to a debtor when the latter refuses to repay a debt.

Along these lines, if certain members of the Russian government had wanted to be more inventive when they announced the August 17, 1998, default, they could have simply said: **"Кина не будет – электричество кончилось!"** ("Sorry, no movie, we ran out of power!") This is a now idiomatic phrase from the film **Джентльмены удачи.** (*Gentlemen of Fortune*, 1971). Savely Kramarov (who actually ended his career as an émigré actor in the U.S.), starring as an escaped convict, uttered these words when he was caught by the militia. So, "no movie ..." means "the jig is up" or "oops, it didn't come off."

Cinema audiences, for their part, whenever there is a disruption in a movie projection on the screen, will still call the projectionist a **сапо́жник** (shoemaker), meaning they don't think highly of his skills. Interestingly, this phrase dates back to *kolkhoz* times, when a film in a local club was about the only distraction available, and when cinema equipment was far from perfect.

The spiciest movie-oriented phrase is apt when you lose your patience with someone who is being indecisive: "Мы бу́дем снима́ть кино́ и́ли мы не бу́дем снима́ть кино́?!" ("Are we going to shoot the movie or not?") This is the Russian equivalent for "fish or cut bait."

It is interesting that Stalin didn't rank the circus above the cinema, because Russian reality constantly seems to reflect life under the Big Top. Actually, *The Circus* was a famous anti-racist movie in the 1950s, starring megastar (and Stalin favorite) Lyubov Orlova as a U.S. circus star who sought refuge with her black son in an anti-racist and internationalist Soviet Union.

A couple of decades after Stalin's passing, in the 1970s, circus parlance was the basis of a potentially dangerous political rumor. Russian rock fans whispered that their idol – lead-singer of **Маши́на Вре́мени** (Time Machine) Andrei Makarevich – had in mind the attendees of the 25th Congress of the Communist Party of Russia (1977) when he wrote the lyrics of his then semi-underground song *Puppets*:

**Арлеки́ны и пира́ты, циркачи́ и акроба́ты
И факи́р,чей вид внуша́ет страх
Волк и за́яц, ти́гры в кле́тке – все они марионе́тки
В ло́вких и нату́женных рука́х**

*Harlequins and pirates
Circus performers and acrobats
and the conjurer whose looks arouse fear
Wolf and hare, tigers in a cage
They are all just puppets in adroit and savvy hands.*

Another two decades on, with the arrival of the August 1998 crisis, political events could be summed up by the phrase: "**Цирк – да и то́лько**" (meaning "What a circus!" or "What a joke!"). You can make the insult more personal by saying "**Ну ты цирка́ч!**" ("What a circus performer you are!")

Indeed, when, in 1998, bank accounts were frozen or annihilated in a matter of hours, the "brilliant" young Prime Minister Sergei Kiriyenko was exposed to be just a **факи́р на час** (magician for an hour). Someone who is a **факи́р на час** is a person who enjoys success or recognition for a short time and then is doomed to oblivion. But then Kiriyenko was merely the heir to the Yeltsin government's five years of **акробати́ческие трю́ки** (acrobatic tricks) with privatization and T-bills. The ruble had been performing a high-wire act without a net (**без страхо́вки**), and the fall was as inevitable as it was messy.

Others might compare the government's actions in the August crisis to that of a pickpocket or a master of the sleight of hand (**фо́кусник**). Such performers like to exclaim the cliche phrase: "**Ло́вкость рук – и никако́го мошенни́чества!**" ("Sleight of hand and no swindling!") A popular **фо́кус-по́кус** (hocus-pocus) of a **фо́кусник** is to pick a spectator, ask him for a R10 bill, burn it in front of him, then take a R10 bill from his ear. But sometimes, for comic effect, they will burn the bill and then tell the hapless spectator: "**Факи́р был пьян – фо́кус не уда́лся**" ("the magician was drunk, the trick didn't work"). This is what you can tell someone who has been expecting the world from you, but whom you have just disappointed. Come to think of it, this is what President Yeltsin may, in effect, tell the electorate after he leaves office in 2000. His movie was really interesting, but at some point he simply ran out of power.

Mikhail Ivanov (April 1999)

Drag Yourself to This!

What do plywood and the infamous U.S. duet Milli-Vanilli have in common? No, the duet didn't start a plywood business after they were stripped of their Grammy a few years ago for lip-synching. The answer is that the group lost their Grammy for singing "to the accompaniment of plywood" (**пе́ли под фане́ру**).

Since plywood is a veneer over compressed wood, whether in furniture or other wood products, it is considered a cheap surrogate for the real thing. Which is why it became a popular slang word for lip-synching, vs. singing live – **петь вживу́ю**. Someone guilty of "plywood singing" becomes a **фане́рщик**.

In Russian practice, it is singers of cheap pop songs who are most often guilty of **фане́ра**. So lovers of true live performances, those who like to hear **жива́я му́зыка** have coined a pejorative name for cheap pop: **попса́**. Singers of **попса́** are called **попсовики́**. Heavy metal fans, meanwhile, are called **металли́сты**, and are the arch-enemies of **попсовики́** – the two often get into ferocious brouhahas after concerts.

If you want to learn or practice music-related Russian vocabulary, there is no better place than Moscow's **Горбу́шка** (named after the local Gorbunov House of Culture, which often hosts live rock or pop concerts). Interestingly, **горбу́шка** literally means "end crust" – the heel of the bread that devotees insist is the tastiest part of a loaf.

The Gorbushka is famous for its tastelessly cheap CD market. Lovers of good **музо́н** (slang for music) flock to the Gorbushka to buy pirated CDs (**сидюки́**; old vinyl records were **диски́**) made in Bulgaria and Ukraine.

"What are you looking for – **медляки́?**" a vendor might ask you. Don't be surprised: **медля́к** derives from the simple word **ме́дленный** ("slow") and means a rock ballad a la Guns & Roses' *Don't Cry Tonight*. A good heart-breaking **медля́к**, like perhaps George Harrison's poignant *While My Guitar Gently Weeps*, is "plagued," i.e. **чумово́й медля́к** (**чумово́й** is Russian slang for "great," usually applied to music).

A **чумово́й медля́к** is something which can make a young audience experience the feeling of **тащи́ться** – literally "to drag oneself along," which is slang for enjoying something. Synonyms include **отрыва́ться**, and **балде́ть**.

A lead-guitarist like Jimmy Page or, say, Richie Blackmore, can make their audience "drag itself along" over long "**соляки́**" or "**запи́лы**" (slang for long, poignant and breathtaking solo-guitar pieces). The former is not to be mixed-up with **со́льник**, the informal term for "solo-album."

Jazz lovers might have come across the term **лаба́ть** – to play a musical instrument. So, whenever President Bill Clinton feels like playing his saxophone, he would **лаба́ть на** са́ксе. Though it is unclear if afficionados would call him a true ла́бух (musician).

Indeed, public opinion in the U.S. seems to have been split over his virtuoso соля́к (or was it a медля́к?) with Monica Lewinsky. Especially when Clinton, like a true попсови́к, didn't give his testimony вживу́ю, but sort of под фане́ру, as it was recorded first on a вида́к (video).

But long before the U.S. Congress had acquitted Clinton, Russia's women had forgiven him this – many have long тащи́ться от Кли́нтона. Local men in turn were dying to see Monica Lewinsky вживу́ю, after Vagrius publishers invited her to Russia to promote her book *Monica's Story*. But then the trip was canceled by the Russian publisher over NATO's bombing of Belgrade. For the Russians didn't seem to тащи́ться about this U.S.-orchestrated NATO соля́к. In our view, not the best piece of сакс Bill Clinton ever лаба́л.

Mikhail Ivanov (August 1999)

Painting in Bedroom Tones

French has many idioms derived from the world of painting. For example, instead of "hobby" the French often say *"violin d'Ingres"* (Ingres' violin) – apparently Dominique Ingres loved to play the violin. But then this is not a Survival French column, and we can certainly come up with some colorful idioms from the Russian world of painting.

Those who revere the splendid colors of Ivan Aivazovsky's canvasses (see Russian Life, July 1997) will understand the idiom – досто́йно ки́сти Айвазо́вского (worthy of Aivazovsky's hand). The phrase is widely applied to picturesque scenes or landscapes. But, of late, it has been used to express admiration (or amazement) over almost anything, often in the ironical sense.

At the other end of the spectrum, a poor or mediocre canvas may be called a мазня́ or пачкотня́ (daub) – terms used often by socialist realists to denigrate the work of abstract painters.

If you roam the halls of the Tretyakov or the Hermitage long enough, you are bound to overhear plenty of useful expressions to help make you sound like a true lover of the arts: игра́ свето-те́ни (the play of light and shadow), Это полотно́ принадлежи́т (this canvass was painted by), пасте́льные тона́ (pastel tones), портрети́ст (portrait artist), пейзажи́ст (landscape artist), батали́ст (painter of battle pieces), марини́ст (seascape painter), анимали́ст (animal painter). Oh, and don't forget about нату́рщица / нату́рщик – the feminine and masculine for "model." Because without a carefully chosen нату́рщица, the world's art would be short of many a шеде́вр (masterpiece).

Similarly, acquaint yourself with the useful terms **этю́д** (sketch), **натюрмо́рт** (still life), **панора́ма, диора́ма** and **три́птих** (panorama, diorama and triptych, respectively). But don't translate "nude" as **го́лая** (naked). The proper translation is **обнажённая**, or, rarely, **нага́я**. The term **передви́жники** can also trip up the best of translators, who will call this group of 19th century realists "Ambulants" or "Wanderers." The accepted term is "Itinerants."

Misinformed and misanthropic museum guides slipping on terms such as these are good grist for the humor mill. Comedian Efim Shifrin (see *Russian Life*, April 1996) made his comic debut with his now famous stand-up sketch **Ка́ющаяся Магдали́на** (Repentant Magdalena). In the sketch, Shifrin mimics a museum guide who points out the contradictory character of Magdalena's repentance (El Greco painted her nude...) and keeps repeating that the canvas was executed in "bedroom tones" – in Russian pronunciation, **пасте́льные** (pastel) and **посте́льные** (bedroom) are homonyms.

Returning to more serious notes, there are a number of Russian artists whose styles are so distinctive they have acquired adjectival status. For instance, there is something we have come to call a **ши́шкинский лес** (a forest like those in the paintings of Ivan Shishkin), and there is the incomparable beauty of **левита́новская о́сень** (an autumn landscape in the style of painter Isaac Levitan). But, most notably, there is the cliche **кусто́диевские же́нщины** (Kustodiev-like women). This refers to the buxom subjects of Boris Kustodiev, who liked to portray Russian women as creatures of flesh and blood, enjoying all the pleasures of life, be it a gorgeous meal or a steam bath.

Some, however, have criticized Kustodiev and the like of abusing of what we call **лубо́к** or **лубо́чность**, which derives from the word for "bast," but which can be approximately translated as "exaggerated, at times *kitschy* Russianness." Indeed, there are a lot of samovars, bliny, and "typical Russian colors" in Kustodiev's work. In the end, some like him, some don't.

Interestingly, Nikita Mikhalkov's recent film *Siberian Barber* has been criticized for such **лубо́чность**. Indeed, Mikhalkov confessed in TV interviews that he told his cameraman to think of Kustodiev paintings when shooting the film.

Many of the film's scenes shown in promo trailers are reminiscent of Kustodiev's bright paintings. These trailers actually dissuaded me from going to see Mikhalkov's three-hour-long canvass. Not that I don't like Boris Kustodiev or that I have anything against Russian **лубо́к**. Simply because, as they say in the world of art, **ко́пия всегда́ ху́же оригина́ла** – a copy is always worse than the original, or, throwing in the **лубо́к** is not enough to create a **шеде́вр**.

Mikhail Ivanov (January 2000)

Stomping on the Throat

Russians love clichés derived from poetry. After all, as Yevgeny Yevtushenko once wrote, **"поэ́т в Росси́и бо́льше, чем поэ́т"** ("a poet in Russia is more than a poet"). Public speeches, newspaper articles and even private speech are full of poetic phrases.

But, what is a cliché for a Russian, is a Chinese puzzle for even an educated foreign reader. Poetic clichés, complicated by word plays are often used in newspaper headlines, but frequently they are paraphrased or cut up in such a way that the unitiated will have a hard time tracing the etymology, much less grasping the hidden cultural meaning.

Examples abound. On the day this column was written, September 6, a headline in *Sevodnya* newspaper declared: **"Перо́ вновь приравня́ли к штыку́"** ("The plume once again has been equated with the bayonet"). This is in fact a wordplay on a famous quote by the poet Vladimir Mayakovsky: **Я хочу́, чтоб к штыку́ приравня́ли перо́** (I want the plume to be equated with the bayonet) – the poet was simply saying he wanted the poet's pen to become a powerful weapon. This quote has suffered from overuse, but it still works. The article cited above was criticising the government's intention to make "top secret" the line item in the state budget providing for mass media subsidies. The only other top secret line item in the budget is for the "state arms program," so the ironic Mayakovsky-related word play hit the mark.

Mayakovsky's art is an endless source of clichés, word plays and headlines. This is because, quite often to the detriment of his own gift as a lyricist, Mayakovsky was compelled to write propaganda poems, full of slogans. He voiced regret for this, confessing that he often had to **наступа́ть на го́рло со́бственной пе́сне** ("stomp on the throat of one's own song"). This line, in turn, became a cliché in its own right. It is very *en vogue* to say that one "has to stomp on the throat of one's song" in any situation – say, when a husband has to keep silent in a conversation between friends, so as to let his wife speak.

Another Mayakovsky cliché that pops up often in the press is **близнецы́-бра́тья** (twin brothers). It comes from Mayakovsky's poem dedicated to Lenin, where he said "Lenin and the party are twin brothers." Now that Lenin (and communism) are dead, the cliché is used every now and then, always with a healthy layer of sarcasm. For example, if you say that the rival media magnates Vladimir Gusinsky and Boris Berezovsky are "in fact, on closer examination, really twin brothers," you will make a very strong point.

The poet Nikolai Nekrasov (1821-1877) lived and died well before the 1917 revolution. But he nonetheless had a few words to say in defense of revolutionary ideals. One such quote was his **к топору́ зови́те Русь** (call on Russia to take up the axe), i.e. incite it to revolt. Another is **поэ́том мо́жешь ты не быть, но граждани́ном быть обя́зан** (You don't have to be a poet, but you are obliged to be a citizen). In other words, you may lack poetic talent, but you have to take a social position in your work. This quote has been paraphrased *ad infinitum*, particularly by replacing the words "poet" and "citizen" with others. For example, a recent story on male-female relations bore the headline: **Мужчи́ной мо́жешь ты не быть, но джентльме́ном быть обя́зан** (You don't have to be a man, but you are obliged to be gentleman).

A third oft-used Nekrasov quote is more ironic: **Жаль то́лько жить в э́ту по́ру прекра́сную уж не придётся ни мне, ни тебе́** (Sadly, neither you nor I will live to see those wonderful times). He meant the era of social equity, of course, but now one can say this in any situation, especially whenever someone paints too bright a picture of the future.

What about Alexander Blok? His poetry is also fertile ground for headlines and quotes turned into clichés. In Russia's present political context, two come to mind:. The first is: **И невозмо́жное возмо́жно** (And the impossible is possible), a line which helps one hold on to hope in difficult times. Second, and even more suitable for the new era here, is **И ве́чный бой! Поко́й нам то́лько сни́тся** (And the battle never ends, we can only dream of rest). The second half of the quote – **поко́й нам то́лько сни́тся** – has been widely used in everything from epigraphs to headlines to the titles of books.

Of course, Pushkinian clichés abound in Russian. His work is full of many quotable, love-inspired phrases, e.g. **Чем ме́ньше же́нщину мы лю́бим, тем ле́гче нра́вимся мы ей** (The less we love a woman, the easier it is for her to like us). For, unlike Mayakovsky, Pushkin was concerned more with plumes than bayonets. Of course, that did not stop revolutionaries from coopting his poetic creations. His famous **Из и́скры возгори́тся пла́мя** (The flame rises from the spark) was printed on the masthead of Lenin's revolutionary newspaper, *Iskra* (*Spark*).

One might be tempted to try to explain the political twists and turns of the last decade with Fyodor Tyutchev's famous line, **Умо́м Росси́ю не поня́ть** (One cannot fathom Russia with the mind). But nowadays this would only come across as a banal truism – the phrase has been overused by journalists both domestic and foreign. Perhaps a more appropriate poetic evaluation would be one offered by Sergei Yesenin: **большо́е ви́дится на расстоя́нии** (big things are best viewed at a distance). In other words, the passage of time will help us better appreciate the big changes we have been through.

As Blok wrote (in *The Scythians*): **Да, ски́фы мы. Да, азиа́ты мы...** (Yes, we are Scythians, Yes, we are Asians) – to which we owe our **ве́чный бой**. And yet, one can hope that someday we Scythians/Russians will be able to have a suitably boring life, free of runs on the banks, underpass explosions and the like.

We don't have to be cynical, but we do have to be honest: at times, one can't help fearing that "neither you nor I will live to see those wonderful times."

Mikhail Ivanov (November 2000)

Food & Drink

When the Foam Goes Down...

None other than Russia's "baptizer prince" Vladimir reputedly said over 1000 years ago: "**Весе́лие Руси́ есть пи́ти – не мо́жем мы без того́ бы́ти**" (Russia's fun is in drinking – we can't do without it). Indeed, the influence of drinking (and vodka in particular) on the Russian tongue is vast and significant. Let us begin with the beer lexicon.

First, however, it is interesting to note how many ways Russians have to say "to get drunk." While we can't provide exact statistics, we can provide this short-list of current terms. **Напи́ться до положе́ния риз** refers to **ри́за**, which is the metal mounting of an icon, the connotation being to drink until one is in a very low position (morally). You can also drink **до бе́лой горя́чки**, literally to a "white fever" of delirium. When one is drunk, they are "on their eyebrows" – **на брови́х**, have poured it into their eye – **зали́ть глаза́**, or are simply emotionally high: **быть навеселе́**. There are also plenty of colloquial terms for boozing it up, including **назюзю́каться** (get soaked), **нализа́ться** (to lap it up), **надра́ться** or **набра́ться** (to get loaded). Among cruder synonyms from the folk lexicon are **нажра́ться/нае́сться** (eat it up), **напи́ться в дрези́ну, в лом, в дрибода́н** (all untranslatable), **в хла́м** (to rubbish), **в соси́ску** (sausage-style), **в си́ську** (breast-style), **в ды́м** (to smoke). And of course there are plenty of unprintable synonyms...

Russians, however, consider it difficult to drink oneself into a white fever or icon mounting with beer, which is considered here as a sort of "warm up" drink – hence the famous, popular idiom, **пивка́ для рывка́** (let's have a beer to speed it up). The word play here is humorous, because **рыво́к** in Russian means both a final decisive effort and a "dash" or "acceleration," which comes from its use in relation to sporting events, particularly running and sprinting.

In Vladimir Dal's famous dictionary, one finds a myriad of beautiful proverbs and sayings about beer. But unfortunately most of them have gone out of use. Still, we coul not help picking up these two: **Сказа́л бы словцо́ – да уж вы́пито пивцо́** ("I would say a little word, but the beer has already been drunk," meaning it's too late to say something), and **Гля́дя на пи́во – хорошо́ и пляса́ть** (looking at beer makes you feel like dancing).

The only idioms which have survived into the popular lexicon from Dal's times are borrowed from folk stories and fairy tales. Russians say someone has "a head like a beer vat," ("**голова́ как пивно́й коте́л**") meaning a big and also usually stupid head. And a typical fairy tale's happy ending is: **И я там был, мёд-пи́во пил, по у́сам текло́, а в рот не попа́ло** (And I was there, I drank honey and beer, down my moustache it dripped, but never got to my lips).

The most recent idiom is the saying from the popular movie, *Specific Traits of Russian National Hunting*: **Во́дка без пи́ва - де́ньги на ве́тер** (Vodka without beer is money to the wind). The meaning is that beer is a great "hair of the dog" (**опохмели́ться**). But some Russians prefer to mix beer and vodka – i.e make a **ёрш** ("wire brush" or ruff), a Russian version of a boilermaker. The allusion here is to the drink's thorny/prickly character, comparable to the thorny fish and utensil.

Since Russians think beer innocuous, you may hear the refrain of the famous 1960s humorous song, **гу́бит люде́й не пи́во, гу́бит люде́й вода́** ("it's not beer but water which is harms people" – implying that natural disasters and water reservoirs claim more lives than beer consumption). Another amusing idiom is the "polite" folklore invitation/marketing slogan: "drink foamy beer and your muzzle will be unbelievable": **пе́йте, лю́ди, пи́во пе́нное - бу́дет мо́рда обалде́нная** (or **здорове́нная/офиге́нная**). This usually goes together with the somewhat rude but equally funny warning to a beer lover: **от пи́ва бу́дешь пи́сать кри́во** (beer will make you pee crooked). Which could be said to the hero of Vladimir Vysotsky's song: **ме́ры в же́нщинах и в пи́ве он не знал и не хоте́л** (he would not observe any limits, not in women, not in beer).

One popular saying comes from signs posted in old Soviet bars and especially in street kiosks: **тре́буйте доли́ва по́сле отсто́я пе́ны** (ask to be topped off after the foam goes down). This was, of course an impossible mission back then, given the rudeness of Soviet beer vendors, who skimmed cash by watering down or pouring out tall heads on the **осли́ная моча́** (donkey urine) they sold. The Soviet era and its beer deficits gave birth to a "punchy" joke. Someone would punch a beer lover in the kidney from behind and then say, "one blow to the kidney replaces one mug of beer" (**оди́н уда́р по по́чкам заменя́ет кру́жку пи́ва**), meaning it does the same damage...

But our favorite is the discreet formula for giving a low rating to a lousy movie, song or play: **с пи́вом/под пи́во сойдёт** (It would have been better with beer). Yet, I hope that reading these lines is okay for you as is.

Mikhail Ivanov (October 1997)

To Tula, Samovar Optional

Peter the Great tried to impose coffee on *boyar*-dominated Russia, but tea would not give way. This, however, did not stop coffee from having some linguistic influence here. In fact, a Russian's pronunciation of the word coffee (**ко́фе**) may help you discern their provenance: provincials often pronounce the final syllable with a hard "f," making it sound like "**фэ**," while the correct pronunciation sounds like "**фе**."

The incorrect pronunciation can be heard in a scene from the classic film, *Diamond Arm*. The smuggler Lyolik, at pains to cure his accomplice Gena's hangover, tries waking him with promises of "a bath, coffee, and even chocolate with tea." ("**Бу́дет тебе́ там и ва́нна, и ко́фе, бу́дет и кака́о с ча́ем!**")

But tea is king here, and the process of tea drinking is rich in protocol and etiquette. Even the least hospitable housewife, when admitting a guest or visitor into her home, is expected to offer him a cup of tea. This practice actually ends up giving a visitor an "out"–a way to escape an unwanted meal. "If only for a cup of tea," can be the polite reply to the invitation. ("**Ну, если только на чашку чаю**.")

This etiquette inspired humorist Leon Izmaylov's joke about a mother-in-law (**тёща**) who comes for an extended visit. "I won't be staying that long, don't worry," says the **тёща** upon her arrival. "**Что, даже чаю не попьёте?**" ("What, you mean you won't even have tea with us?"), responds the son-in-law, in a voice filled with hope.

In general, an offer of tea is always welcome. This gave birth to the proverb, "**Чай пить – не дрова рубить**" ("Drinking tea is not like cutting wood."), often used as a joking reply to an invitation to have tea. Indeed, tea is seen to be the very antithesis of work, as in the popular Soviet-era marketing slogan which has become ubiquitous in recent years, often imprinted on hotpads and aprons: **Выпьешь чайку – позабудешь тоску** (Have a little tea and you will forget your anguish).

If you tire of the normal "**пить чай**" ("drink tea"), you can mine old Russian for some more colorful expressions with which to lace your invitations. In the 19th century, Russians would offer graciously, "**Не угодно ли чаю откушать**" (literally, "Would it not be pleasant for you to taste some tea?") There is also the elegant verb **чаёвничать** (**Вы не будете чаёвничать?**)–perhaps best translated as "to tea." This is still used by middle-aged and

older Russians, as is the colloquial **чай гонять** (literally, "to drive tea," as in down one's gullet).

Not all tea-driven idioms are about tea *per se*. Some are about the famous **самова́р**, that very Russian appliance for brewing tea. Usually made of copper, when polished, samovars have a beautiful shine. Thus, if someone is irrepressibly happy, one may ask: "**Что ты сия́ешь как самова́р?**" ("Why are you shining like a samovar") And when someone brings something to a place which that locale already has plenty of (say, bringing maple syrup to Vermont), you may hear the proverb: "**В Ту́лу со свои́м самова́ром не е́здят.**" ("You don't bring your own samovar to Tula"). Thus, in Rogovoy's short story *Victoria*, we read: "Someone asked in a bass voice: 'Is that your wife you're with?' To which a lively tenor voice in the dark chimed in: 'You don't go to Tula with your own samovar!'" (Why bother taking one's wife to a town where there are plenty of other dates?)

But Tula is famous not only for its samovars, but also for its cookies: the **Ту́льский пря́ник** (Tula *pryanik*). A **пря́ник** is a dense, cake-like cookie typically filled with a layer of jam. Additionally, the dough often has honey in it. This makes for a sweet treat that has actually given the cookie a "political dimension." The Russian equivalent of "a carrot and stick policy" is **поли́тика кнута́ и пря́ника** (literally: "a whip and cookie policy"). Not surprisingly, Soviet political scientists often used this political idiom to describe U.S. foreign policies toward other countries.

Of late, this idiom seems to have fallen into disuse. Perhaps because both U.S. and Russian leaders want to find common ground (which Bush and Putin did in Slovenia: it turns out both named their two daughters after the girls' two grandmothers).

So the ice may be broken on the personal front, but both leaders still have plenty to disagree about on policy matters, which they will take up at a summit in the U.S. this fall.

To that end, Bush's team is advised to prepare a hospitable reception for his Russian counterpart, promising (perhaps in a rich, southern accent) that Putin will find in Texas **и ва́нна, и ко́фе, и кака́о с ча́ем.**

Mikhail Ivanov (September 2001)

A Tale of Three Sandpipers

In any language, there are plenty of ways to talk about drinking and getting drunk. Not surprisingly, this is a particularly "rich" vein in the Russian linguistic mine.

Some of the most common words that, in an appropriate context, can mean drinking without excess are **вы́пить** (drink), **приня́ть** (take in) and **подда́ть** (add, increase). A typical rhymed invitation to have a drink is: **Что-то ста́ло холода́ть – не пора́ ли нам подда́ть?** (It's getting kind of cold; isn't it time we added a bit?)

Dozens of drinking words start with the prefix **на-**. All usually signify not light, social drinking, but really getting hammered. One can **нажра́ться** (get gobbled up), **накача́ться** (get pumped full), **набра́ться** (gather it up), **нализа́ться** ("over-lick" it), **налака́ться** (lap it up), **наква́ситься** (get fermented), or **наклю́каться**, which probably derives from the archaic word **кулю́кать**. **Кули́к** is a sandpiper, but also, according to Vladimir Dal, used to signify a drunkard. So **кули́кать** meant both crying like a sandpiper and getting drunk. In Dostoyevsky's *Dvoynik* (*The Double*), Golyadkin cajoles his servant Petrusha with: "**ну,**

клю́кнул, мерза́вец, мале́нько... на гри́венник, что ли, клю́кнул?" ("come on, you had a nip, you scoundrel ... you drank up a *grivennik* [ten kopek piece], did you?")

Drinking euphemisms hint that booze can be replaced with everything from kerosene (**накероси́ниться**), to rosin (**наканифо́литься**). The word **налимо́ниться** (get lemoned) leaves one at loss – what has this citrus fruit got to do with it? Dal suggests that it might be because lemon was added to punch.

The cute-sounding **назюзю́каться** is a classic word, encountered often in 19th century Russian literature. It derives from an archaic noun **зю́зя**, meaning a man soaked by rain or, alternatively, soaked with booze. In Chekhov's play, *The Three Sisters*, Kulygin teases Chebutykin: "**Назюзю́кался, Ива́н Рома́ныч! Молоде́ц! In vino veritas, говори́ли дре́вние.**" ("You've been hitting the bottle, Ivan Romanich! Congratulations! *In vino veritas*, as the ancients said.")

Most of the above, if used without the perfecting prefix **на**, connote the process of drinking rather than the sloshed result. For instance, **ква́сить** designates a prolonged drinking session, not just taking a shot or two.

The notion of getting drunk on a more or less regular basis can be expressed by a neutral **выпива́ть** But why not use the more colorful **поддава́ть** (imperfective form of **подда́ть**), or **закла́дывать за воротни́к** (to stow it behind one's collar). Alternatively, booze can be put behind one's necktie (**га́лстук**) or trunk (**хо́бот**).

Interestingly, many drinking words seem to share the rattling consonant pair **др**, which makes them easily associated with the English "drink." Thus, one can be drunk **вдры́зг** (to smithereens) or **надры́згаться** (get plastered), **надра́ться** (get thrashed), or, if words fail, **надри́нькатся** (from the English). The words **дёрнуть** or the onomatopoetic **деря́бнуть** and **колдырну́ть** all imply sloshing.

The degree of drunkenness can be emphasized by different adverbs. To the adjective **пья́ный** (drunk) can be added: **в дугу́** (arch-drunk), **в до́ску** (as a board), **в сте́льку** (as the sole of a shoe), **в ло́скут** (like a rag), **в дыми́ну** (smoked) and **в хлам** (trashed), to offer almost too much subtlety to the idea of "very drunk."

In Russia, cheap, unceremonious drinking is traditionally done in groups of three. A bottle of liquor is easily divided by three and so is its cost. Thus **сообрази́ть на трои́х** (figure it out for three) means to drink in a company of three. "**Тре́тьим бу́дешь?**" ("Wanna be our third?") is how a couple of drunks might ask you to join their pointless party of dissipation. Not that this is the company you might fall into, but the phrase could be used in a funny, non-serious way among more temperate friends.

A bender lasting for days or weeks is referred to as a **запо́й**. When you depart on such a journey you **уйти́ в запо́й**, or simply **запи́ть** (start [long-term] drinking), or **загуде́ть** (hoot away).

Most all drinking ends the same way, with a hangover. The most neutral word for this morning-after disease is **похме́лье**, but it has more colorful synonyms, such as **похмелю́га** or **буду́н**. The origin of the latter is unknown, although it might have some connection to the word **бода́ть** (to butt, gore). One's state at this time is referred to as **с похме́лья** or **с буду́на**.

The morning after, of course, is when, discussing one's exploits with some of the vocabulary above, one remembers too late the trenchant warning of the Health Ministry: **Чрезме́рное употребле́ние алкого́ля вреди́т ва́шему здоро́вью!** (Drinking to excess is bad for your health.)

Lina Rozovskaya (November 2003)

Here's to You and Us...

Toasting is essential to socializing in Russia. If you are good at it, then you are almost guaranteed to win attention and respect. So it will pay off at least to be familiar with Russian toasting manners. This piece of Russian poetry makes for a good introduction to the etiquette and ceremony of drinking:

Для пья́нства есть таки́е по́воды:	*Pretexts are different for drinking*
Поми́нки, пра́здник, встре́ча, про́воды,	*Feats, funerals, new kids, a sinking*
Кристи́ны, сва́дьба и развод,	*New meetings, weddings and divorce*
Моро́з, охо́та, Но́вый Год,	*Hard frosts, New Year's, deep remorse*
Выздоровле́нье, новосе́лье,	*Recovering, repentance, joy*
Печа́ль, раска́янье, весе́лье,	*Success, rewarding, a new toy,*
Успе́х, награ́да, но́вый чин	*Promotion, friendship, a good whit*
И про́сто пья́нство – БЕЗ ПРИЧИ́Н!	*And, drinking for the sake of it*

The most typical introductory toast is **за знако́мство** or **со свида́нием** (literally, "to our meeting"). This may be shortly followed by: **по́сле пе́рвой не заку́сывают.** (no snacking after the first drink) or **ме́жду пе́рвой и второ́й переры́вчик небольшо́й** (the pause is/should be short between the first and the second toasts). Or, in the Cossack version, **ме́жду пе́рвой и второ́й пу́ля не пролете́ла** (a bullet should not pass between the first and second toasts)

In the middle of the meal, toasting may take different forms, depending on the initiative and wit of your companions.

If your are at a wedding party, you will hear loud cries of "**го́рько**" ("bitter") all night long. The reason for this is that the drink is considered to be "bitter" if not sweetened by the newlyweds kissing in front of the gathered guests (the first toast is always to the newlyweds, and the second to their parents, by the way). The one who proposes toasts should also remember this proverb: **тосту́ющий пьёт до дна** ("the toaster drinks to the bottom" – i.e. don't make a toast you can't drink down), so beware. It is the job of the **тамада́** (the word for "toastmaster," derived from the Georgian) to make everyone drink and to, himself, remain more or less sober – that is, he should be able to **перепи́ть любо́го** (to drink anybody under the table). Good *tamadas* usually have a good stock of toasts where word

plays and rhymes abound. If you ever need to interrupt the toastmaster, the classic cry is "**алаверды́**" another word borrowed from the Georgian.

If you are at a wake, on the other hand, the first toast is made in honor of the deceased. And never, never should glasses be clinked – apparently this is seen to be disrespectful of the dead.

Needless to say, Russians are fond of the familiar Georgian toast which goes: "There is a girl standing on one riverbank and a **джиги́т** (young Georgian warrior) on the other. Let's drink to the possibilities (**за перспекти́ву** – also a word play on the word *perspektiv*, which in Russian can mean "view" as well as "possibilities, potential").

But Russians certainly have a rich toasting tradition all their own. Drinking **на брудерша́фт** is an important example tradition. This dates back to the pre-revolutionary Russian army, when two hussars would interlock their arms at the elbow. with glasses in hand, and sip their drinks in this position. After this quite significant ceremony, the two partners may call one another **на ты** – the second person singular in Russian – marking a closer type of relationship.

Another good, general toast that is: **За нас с Ва́ми и за чёрт с ни́ми!** (To you and us and the hell with them!)

Here are some more examples to bolster your repertoire:

• **Мы собра́лись здесь, что́бы вы́пить, так дава́йте же вы́пьем за то, что мы здесь собрали́сь!** (We got together here to drink, so let's drink to our getting together.)

• **Говоря́т, 'Е́сли хо́чешь приня́ть пра́вильное реше́ние – спроси́ сове́та у жены́ и сде́лай наоборо́т.' Так вы́пьем же за на́ших жён, кото́рые помога́ют нам приня́ть пра́вильное реше́ние в тру́дной ситуа́ции.** (It is said, 'If you want to make the right decision, get your wife's advice and then do the opposite.' So, I raise my glass to our wives who make it possible for us to make the right decision in a difficult situation.)

- A toast to a young man: **На вопрóс: 'Когó вы предпочитáете – блондúнок или брюнéток,' настоя́щий мужчúн отвéтит, 'Да!' Так, вы́пьем же за настоя́щих мужчúн.** (To the question: 'Which do you prefer, blondes or brunettes,' a real man will answer, 'Yes!' So let's drink to real men.)

- A toast to a young woman: **Желáю Вам имéть четырёх живóтных: сóболя на плечáх, 'Ягуáра' в гарáже, льва в постéли, и ослá, котóрый бы за всё это платúл.** (I wish you four animals: a sable on your shoulders, a Jaguar in your garage, a lion in your bed and a donkey who would pay for it all.)

And finally, the shot concluding toasts for the evening is called the toast **на посошóк** (for the road). This derives from the Russian word **посóх**, a sort of long staff used by Russian pilgrims on a long journey. This toast has Cossack origins, and, upon declaring **на посошóк**, further toasting (or compulsory drinking) is off limits. So, such a toast is surely a must, even if it might be easy to forget if the toasts have been flying fast and furious for many an hour, as they are wont to do at Russian dinner parties.

Mikhail Ivanov (December 1997)

Cooling Off the Tubes

Okay, it's the morning after a hard night of drinking and you are recovering from the well-deserved **похмéлье** (hangover). The appropriate refrain in this instance is **упúлся медáми, опохмеля́лся слезáми** (got drunk on honey but recovered through tears).

At this time, it won't do much good to console yourself with the Russian folk wisdom that **вóдка бывáет хорóшей и óчень хорóшей** (there are only two types of vodka, good and very good). If the vodka was very good, but in excess, simply tell your household **я вчерá перебрáл** (I overdid it yesterday) by way of an excuse. And if you really overdo it, you probably deserve it if you are "teasing the loo" (**дразнúть унитáз** – perhaps the best Russian equivalent for "worshiping the porcelain god").

The satirist Mikhail Zhvanetsky, in his famous monologue on hangovers described this phenomenon in more sophisticated terms: "The body rejects any position... Got up in the morning... saw some knees on my hands... then I came to realize that these were my knees... When I went out on the balcony, two doves died on the spot, but then, I did yell at them to move awhaaaay...." ("Органúзм не приéмлет никакóго положéния... У́тром проснýлся – смотрю́ в рукáх чьи-то колéнки, оказáлось – мой... Вы́шел на балкóн – два гóлубя ýмерли срáзу, а ведь я кричáл им – отойдúте-е-е!")

In Soviet times, doves were better protected. Most drunkards were coercively taken to a sobering-up station (**вытрезвúтель**), where they were mistreated but made sober overnight, be it by kicks in the ribs or cold showers. Then, the next day a bill, along with a letter, would notify the drunkard's employer that the former was found **в нетрéзвом состоя́нии** (in a state of drunkenness). So drunkards would do their best to avoid these *vytrezvitels*. Now there are many fewer of these stations (thanks to the market economy). And the tab is higher at those that remain...

Okay, back to the morning after. Perhaps it is not so bad. You look alright, and there was no **вытрезвúтель**. But the vodka is more than wreaking its revenge and you are desperate for several glasses of water (the cause of a hangover largely being dehydration brought on by the excessive alcohol in your blood). The "People's Diagnosis" for this is to

say your "tubes are burning" (**тру́бы горя́т**). This sympton, by the way, is a sure way for an employer to find out about your personal drinking habits. In the "good old days," when a **характери́стика** (resume or reference) could either help someone's career skyrocket or send it dribbling down the drain, humorists came up with this great bureaucratic cliche: **в пья́нстве заме́чен не был, но по утра́м пил холо́дную во́ду** (never caught drunk, but did drink cold water in the mornings).

Water is one step towards rehabilitation. But there is the danger that, if you have drunk a lot of vodka the night before, this water can chemically interact with the remnants of yesterday's vodka, prolonging a hangover. So don't rush to fight your **обезво́живание** (dehydration) with water alone. A more serious remedy to **опохмели́ться** or, as Russians affectionally call it, **полечи́ться** (to have a little cure), is the notorious **рассо́л** (pickle juice). Not that brave? Well, in Russia as in the U.S., beer is an approved "hair of the dog." But keep in mind this great folk warning: "a poorly organized hair of the dog easily turns into a drinking binge" (**Пло́хо организо́ванное похме́лье перехо́дит в запо́й.**) So, go easy on beer or any other alcoholic hair of the dog.

Obviously, after 600 years with **во́дочка** (our affectionate term for vodka), Russians can go on and on about the best means for curing a hangover. One point worth bearing in mind, however, is that **похме́лье** is often used in the figurative sense – meaning some negative costs or consequences of ill-considered actions. Thus, when Russians say, "**А мне в чужо́м пиру́ похме́лье**" ("I have someone else's hangover"), they mean they are unjustly bearing the cost of someone else's mistakes. And, as everyone knows, if you have to suffer through a **похме́лье**, you should at least be entitled to the previous night's fun.

Mikhail Ivanov (April 1998)

Etiquette & Deceptions

It's the Little Things That Count

It is hard to say what Russians like more – to give or receive gifts. Probably the former. After all, Russia is known for its hospitality. Surely you have heard that you should never compliment a Russian on any item in his or her home, otherwise they will do their utmost to make you a gift of it. Such is the unwritten code of Russian largesse. Which, as this column attests, has overflowed into the Russian language itself.

To begin with, here is a practical hint: when you have decided on what type of gift the occasion requires, do not waste any time. Run right out and buy the gift before it's too late. For, as the Russians say: **Дорого яичко к Христову дню** ("An egg is dearest at Easter," or, That which is most appreciated is given when needed).

Upon receiving a gift, Russians do not usually unwrap the gift at once, preferring to put it aside for a more private moment, unless, of course, the gift giver insists. Russians share the English belief that one should never look a gift horse in the mouth (**дарёному коню в зубы не смотрят**).

But, what if you do not have any idea what to give? In that case, bear in mind the fact that Russia still considers itself to be "the most literate nation in the world," (**самая читающая нация в мире**). So, when shopping, remember this bit of folk wisdom – a book is the best gift: **книга – лучший подарок**. But take care when selecting presents for New Russians: reading is not their favorite activity. Hence the famous joke about two *nouveaux-riches* arguing over what gift to buy their mutual friend: "Let's give him a book," says one to the other. But the second differs, "Why? He's already got one." ("**Давай подарим ему книгу.**" "**Зачем? Ведь у него уже есть одна?!**")

In principle, Russians consider selecting the right gift a special talent: **дар Божий.** Many Russians are quite particular about the gifts they give. They carefully choose their gift, have it wrapped elaborately, and then heighten the overall effect by a thoughtful inscription – **дарственная надпись** – to the one receiving the present. Take note of the most typical dedications: **Дорогому Ивану Ивановну в день 60-летия... в день свадьбы... на добрую память... в знак нашей дружбы... на память о нашей встрече** (To dear Ivan Ivanovich on the occasion of his 60th birthday... on his wedding day... as a souvenir... as a token of our friendship... in memory of our first meeting).

Well-educated Russians also consider it an art in itself to correctly receive gifts. Learn how to be appreciative upon receiving a gift. Say: "**Вот угодил-так угодил**" ("This guy really knows how to please."), or: "**Я об этом мечтал всю свою жизнь, подарок моей мечты**" ("I've been dreaming all my life about a gift like this, it's my wildest fantasy!"). If the gift is expensive and you feel embarrassed (or are just pretending to be so out of politeness), say "**Мне да́же неудо́бно**" ("I feel kind of embarrassed.").

But even if the gift was not what you wanted, or maybe if you already have something like it, don't try to fob it off onto someone else, as Russians consider this a bad omen, besides being simply rude. So, next time you get another tie, keep this saying in mind: **дарёное не да́рят** (a gift once received is not to be given again).

What to give and what not to give could be the subject of another column altogether, but, briefly, you should always apply different criteria to women and men, in order not to "mix up God's gift with fried eggs" (**не пу́тать бо́жий дар с яи́чницей**), or, in other words, not to get confused. The best choices for men are the traditional Western ones like razors, cologne and ties. For women worrying about what to give their men, Russians are fond of saying that the best gift a woman can give is a son, and, especially upon the birth of their first son, Russian men proudly say "She gifted me a son" (**Она́ подари́ла мне сы́на**).

As for the Russian woman, when you ask her what sort of gift she wants, she might, out of coquetry, tell you "**Да́же не зна́ю**" ("I don't even know."). If she won't say anything else, don't forget that most women like perfume, flowers and small, pretty knickknacks (**духи́, цветы́ и ра́зные безделу́шки**).

Chances are, though, that upon reflection, she will utter these common phrases: "**Что-нибу́дь из оде́жды**" ("some item of clothing"), or "**Что-нибу́дь из косме́тики**" ("some kind of make-up"). Or, even, "**каки́е-нибудь ча́сики**" ("a little watch"). If you can't afford clothing, expensive make-up, or a "little watch," just make sure you come up with something nice. For, as the saying goes, "it's the thought which counts, not the gift itself" (**до́рог не пода́рок – до́рого внима́ние**). However, if you are serious about your relationship with this or any woman, don't abuse this linguistic ruse!

Mikhail Ivanov (March 1997)

A Little Filler, You Know, Goes a Long Way

Everybody frowns upon the nonsense phrase and the filler. But only the highest of the high-brow seem to avoid either in everyday language. Russian, has a rich arsenal of filler words. And for the foreigner searching desperately for the right word or phrase, these fillers can provide relief, humor, and even escape.

Let's start with the direct Russian equivalent for the ubiquitous English "you know." Russians say this, but rarely and in a different way: "**Зна́ете ли?**" For example, "**А я, зна́ете ли, предпочита́ю...**" ("You know, I prefer...").

This is perfect Russian, but very few native speakers would use it today – you will most likely hear it in a Chekhov play or in TV interviews with film and theater critics.

A synonym for this phrase is **ви́дите ли** (you see), which, stylistically, sounds the same. The most common and stylistically neutral phrase is **так сказа́ть** (so to say). This one can be heard on TV, radio, and on the street. Another set phrase is **бу́дем говори́ть** ("let me put it this way" or "shall I say").

If you want to sound like President Yeltsin in his impromptu (i.e. unwritten) speeches, use **понима́ешь** (you understand). Otherwise, this turn of phrase seems to be owned by the older generation of Soviet-style *apparatchiks*. It's an ideal device for say, the head of a former collective farm reprimanding his fellow *kolkhozniki* for low milk production.

Yeltsin and other highly-placed personages use **понима́ешь** when they are getting tough with somebody. Mind you, none of them studied their Russian in Tsarskoye Selo (an imperial lyceum where many a Russian poet, including Pushkin, were educated).

The most common filler used by all generations in Russia is **зна́чит** (so). For example: "**Я ему́, зна́чит, говорю́..**" ("So, I told him...").

The most fashionable filler, mainly used by the younger generation, is the now-famous **коро́че** (in short). However, it doesn't make the story any shorter. For example: "**Коро́че, пришли́ мы туда́, и я ему́, коро́че, говорю́...**" This story will, for sure, contain several dozen *koroches* ("In short, we came there, and I said, in short, to him...")

Use **коро́че** occasionally, but don't abuse it. While it is very colloquial, it's not the ideal way of rendering your thoughts in Russian.

Apart from fillers, Russian is "full of" senseless phrases, mostly inherited from the Soviet era. Some are worth knowing about in order to avoid them.

Until the winds of change began to blow, Russians would say "we fight for..." in any situation, e.g. "we fight for quality," "we fight for ecology," "we fight for the harvest" (there was even a set phrase, **би́тва за урожа́й** (the battle for the harvest). Ilf and Petrov, authors of the famous satirical novel *The Twelve Chairs*, started the satire rolling: "Let's not fight for cleanliness," they wrote, "let's just mop the floor."

Mikhail Gorbachev was famous for using the phrase **проце́сс пошёл** (the process is under way). In fact he used it so often that every Russian now knows it by heart.

"Mikhail Sergeyevitch," the correspondent asks, "how would you assess the early results of *perestroika* in economic terms?"

"**Проце́сс пошёл**," the General Secretary would reply.

Russians now love to exploit the irony of using this deliberately vague phrase in concrete situations. For example:

"How is it going with Natasha?" one Russian asks a friend who is courting Natasha.

"**Проце́сс пошёл**," comes the reply.

Another archetype of Soviet-style phraseology is "to solve the question of..." Or "to raise the question of..."

"Where do we stand with our customs clearance?" a business colleague queries.

"**Этот вопро́с реша́ется.**" (This question is being solved).

But the phrase also has a problematic quality, in that it carries a dual meaning. "We need to solve the question of the bookkeeper" ("**Надо реши́ть вопро́с с бухга́лтером**") in normal language could mean either "we need to hire a bookkeeper," or "we should fire the bookkeeper," depending on the context. (Thus, while the problem of customs clearance might be being solved, it is not clear from the context given by whom or to what effect.)

Коро́че, the sooner you, **так сказа́ть**, are able to **реши́ть вопро́с** of fillers and senseless phrases, the easier your spoken Russian is going to be. The important thing, **зна́ете ли**, is that the **проце́сс пошёл**.

Mikhail Ivanov (July 1995)

The Enobling Deception

Cheating, deceit and lies are vices as familiar to Russia as its folklore and culture. Of course, no one likes to be cheated, but there is cheating, and then there is cheating. As Pushkin once proclaimed, "Тьмы низких истин нам дороже нас возвышающий обман." ("The ennobling deception is more dear to us than the dark, base truths.")

In Alexei Tolstoy's fairytale *Buratino*, a translation of *Pinnochio*, the heroes Fox Alisa and Cat Bazilio cheat the hapless wooden puppet Buratino after luring him into the Field of Miracles in the Country of Fools (**Поле чудес в стране дураков**). The two rascals have advised Buratino to bury his golden coins under a tree, and then water the buried treasure so that it will grow to an even greater treasure. Buratino falls for the scheme and Bazilio and Alisa sing, while digging up Buratino's money after he has gone, "**На дурака не нужен нож, ему с три короба соврёшь и делай с ним что хошь**" ("You don't need a knife to rob a fool – just tell a big lie and do whatever you want with him.")

Given this cultural "heritage," it should be no surprise that we have many derivations for the word **хитрый** (cunning, perfidy, guile). The noun is **хитрость** (ruse, cunning, ingenuity) and there is even a proverb praising this "virtue": **Хитрость – второй ум** (Cunning is your second mind). There are also some useful diminutive suffixes (-**ец** and -**инк**), with which you can declare that someone's eyes are **с хитрецой** (have a little ruse in them) or **с хитринкой**.

Other slang words for cheating abound. There is the ubiquitous phrase **крутить динамо** (to turn Dinamo). It derives from the Dinamo machine of the 1920-1930s and came into modern usage in the 1960s and 1970s, when **крутить динамо** meant cheating taxi drivers by asking them to wait while you ran in to get your billfold, only to run out the back door, stiffing the driver. A general synonym is **продинамить кого-то** (to cheat or fool someone). The crook who is "turning Dinamo" is known as a **динамист**. Of late, the phrase's usage has expanded widely – today, when a date fails to show-up at a rendezvous, you can say: **он/она меня продинамил/а.**

The more contemporary word **кидать** (**кинуть**, in the perfective) is not quite *comme il faut*, but useful nonetheless. The verb means to dump or cheat someone for money (**кинуть кого-то на деньги**), to not pay what's promised or overdue. Of late, **кинуть** has also been applied to relationships between the sexes, and could be used as a synonym for "**она меня продинамила**" (thus the current pop song by Lyapis Trubetskoy: "**Ты, ты-ты кинула, ты**"). The slang noun for a failure to pay what is promised or due is **кидалово**.

The Buratinos in this world are often called a **лох** – an unhappy combination of a naive fool and a simpleton. The word also serves as the root for the recent addition to the Russian language – **лохотрон**, which is a word play on the word **лототрон** (lottery drum), and means a con or scam. Con artists are called **лохотро́нщики**, and, legally-speaking, **лохотро́н** is classified as **моше́нничество** (fraud). The person engaging in fraud is a **моше́нник** (swindler).

The victim of a **лохотро́нщик** – the **лох** – after realizing he has been fooled might ask himself, "**Как я мог так лохану́ться?!**" ("How could I have been swindled so?!") The reflexive nature of the verb underlines that the **лох** had a hand in his own undoing.

Cheating in Russia, when it all comes down to it, hinges on the passion bequeathed us from Soviet times: a desire to get everything **на халя́ву** (for free). Without working for it, that is, no matter the risk. But, as the more **хи́трый** guys are fond of saying: **беспла́тный сыр быва́ет то́лько в мышело́вке** (free cheese is only found in mousetraps).

Mikhail Ivanov (July 2002)

Promises, Promises

Whenever I start to feel that this column will some day run out of material, I soon stumble over yet another untapped theme. This is not to say this space is guided (entirely) by whimsy, but there is a grain of truth to the joke about the Chukchi song of quiet contemplation: "**что ви́жу, то и пою́**" ("I sing about what I see").

But, unlike in the Chukchi joke, what one sees or experiences is just our launching-off point. For instance, all of this talk about the ABM treaty has gotten me thinking about the word **обеща́ния** (promises), which of course is often paired with **ожида́ния** (expectations). A typical dialogue between two Russians might be: "**Но ты же обеща́л!**" ("But you promised?!") To which the other replies: "**Обе́щанного три го́да ждут.**" ("There's a three year wait on all promised items.")

When I translated that popular Russian proverb for American friends, they came to love it, and even began to **применя́ть его́ на пра́ктике** (apply it in practice) with solicitors.

Of course, anyone who hears this proverb feels a bit frustrated and may start to talk of "deceptive expectations" (**обма́нутые ожида́ния**). He may even say "you have led me astray" (**ввёл меня́ в заблужде́ние**). To which the deceiver could respond with the joke about the folk hero Ivan Susanin (who led Polish invaders astray after promising to lead them to Moscow). The joke goes:

"**Куда́ ты привёл нас, Суса́нин Ива́н?**" *"Where have you led us, Ivan Susanin?"*
"**Иди́те вы на́ фиг, я сам заблуди́лся!**" *"Go to hell, I'm lost myself!"*

Of course, the word "promise" also brings to mind **Звезда́ плени́тельного сча́стья** (*The Star of Tempting Happiness*), a poignant film directed by Vladimir Motyl about the Decembrists. A lyric from the soundtrack is now a cliché: "**Не обеща́йте де́ве ю́ной любо́ви ве́чной на земле́...**" ("Don't promise a young lady eternal love on earth.")

A more contemporary musical reference to promises and expectations comes from Zemfira (see *Russian Life*, Jan/Feb 2001): "**Ожида́ния – са́мый ску́чный по́вод.**" ("Expectations are the most boring pretext.") This line has now become as famous in Russian as the American standard: "I never promised you a rose garden." And it is the perfect response to those who say they expected something you did not deliver.

Etiquette & Deceptions

While it seems universally accepted that Russians are extremely patient in waiting out promises (i.e. waiting 70 years for communism or 10 years for an apartment), we do in fact have a popular proverb which contradicts this conventional wisdom: "**ху́же нет, чем жда́ть и догоня́ть**" ("there is nothing worse than waiting about and then having to catch up"). Few of our proverbs could be more *apropos* of our waiting for prosperity during the last century.

Of course, there are plenty of things to say to those who break promises (of prosperity, missile defense, what have you). For example, you could recite: "**Береги́ пла́тье сно́ву, а честь смо́лоду**" ("Take care of your dress when it is new, but your honor from your youth.") The meaning is simple: a good name is sooner lost than won. Or you could use the criticism: "**У тебя́ вообще́ со́весть есть и́ли нет?**" ("Do you have a conscience or not?") Beware, however. A quick-witted person could well respond by quoting from Maxim Gorky's play *The Lower Depths*: "**Заче́м мне со́весть? Я не бога́тый.**" ("What do I need a conscience for? I am not rich.")

Not only are we Russians famous for waiting patiently for promises, I think perhaps there is something in us that likes to believe in something, despite "objective" realities to the contrary. Like Alexander Pushkin's lyrical hero who confessed that "I myself am glad to be deceived" ("**Я сам обма́нываться рад.**"). As another Russian proverb has it (by the way, it became the name of a play by Nikolai Ostrovsky): "**Пра́вда - хорошо́, а сча́стье - лу́чше**" ("Truth is good but happiness is better").

Mikhail Ivanov (January 2002)

All Play and No Work

When I was a little girl, I got my fair share of Russian **сказки** (fairy tales) at bedtime. While they rarely succeeded in putting me to sleep, they did teach me the Russian philosophy of life... while likely negatively affecting my impressionable personality.

Contrary to Soviet mythology, **сказки** taught that the world is a cruel place, where one's morality has no influence upon one's fortune. The **сказки** swarmed with young fools (**дураки**) and lazybones (**лентяи**) who always got the biggest piece of pie at the end of the story.

Take a **неудачник** ("loser," today anglicized simply as **лузер**) named **Емеля** (Yemelya). The youngest son of the prototypical **старик со старухой** (an old man and his wife), Yemelya was also the stupidest **дурак** his village ever knew. All he would do was lie on the **печь** (stove) all day **пальцем не пошевелит** (not lifting a finger). Then, one day, his family somehow manages to coax him into going down to the river to get water.

As luck would have it, Yemelya catches a miraculous **щука** (pike) in his bucket. It will grant his every wish. All he has to do is say **"по щучьему веленью, по моему хотенью"** ("by the pike's command, by my desire") and any whim is realized. Yemelya started by having the water-filled buckets walk home on their own and finished his wishing spree by marrying the local tsarevna. Somewhere in the middle of the fairy tale, he made his stove drive him all the way to the tsar's palace. The image of a lazy **лузер** lying on a **печь** and getting whatever his heart desires firmly imprinted itself in my mind.

This getting everything for nothing is summarized by one of Russia's most untranslatable words – **халява**. It is a word with such a broad semantic field that a single column cannot hope to accommodate all the shadows of its meaning. **Халява** means a freebie, something someone gets for free or without making much effort – **на халяву,** e.g. the way Yemelya got himself a tsarevna for a wife. This is not to say that **халява** only applies to things of great value. After all, as modern Russian wisdom has it, **на халяву и уксус сладок** ("Even vinegar is sweet when it is *khalyava*").

Халява also means an easy, low-effort (**халявный**) job, something that requires little effort and is compensated well. And it means moonlighting too. A person who is good at getting such jobs and at doing the least work possible is called a **халявщик**. This is a person who is good at dumping his workload on others, or eating in restaurants at others' expense – a freeloader. The verb is **халявить**.

An easy job or moonlighting can also be referred to as **халту́ра**. The person who works carelessly, a hack or potboiler who works without due diligence, follow through or dotting his i's (the verb being **халту́рить**) is called a **халту́рщик**.

In November, as it turns out, the Russian State Duma indulged the national **халя́ва** habit by passing a bill that considerably extends Russia's most celebrated national holiday. Deputies stretched the official New Year holiday from January 1 to 5, giving Russians five consecutive days to **пра́здновать**. This is not to imply, of course, that, before the bill came into effect, the Russian workforce was universally to be found in offices at 9 am sharp on January 2 or the first working day (**рабо́чий день**) after the official New Year's break. It is just that now the New Year's **халя́ва** has been made official.

National traditions must be enshrined in law, after all. Work, as we know, can wait. Or, as the familiar Russian adage has it: **Рабо́та не волк, в лес не убежи́т.** (Work is not a wolf, it won't run off into the woods.)

Lina Rozovskaya (January 2005)

The Discreet Charm of Avos

Fatalism (**фатали́зм**) is widely considered one of the most indispensable Russian character traits. Human lives are geared in one direction or other by fate (**судьба́**), chance (**слу́чай**), luck (**уда́ча**) and other mysterious, supernatural (**сверхъесте́ственный**) forces. A person is not responsible for her own actions; she can only watch life take unpredictable (**непредсказу́емый**) twists and turns and either exclaim blissfully "**Как мне повезло́!**" ("How lucky I am!") or sigh with regret, "**Как меня́ угора́здило!**" ("How could I have ended up this way!").

Note the use of the impersonal, passive voice here: the pronoun is not **я** (I), but **меня́** (me).

You could say, "I lost my wallet" ("**Я потеря́л кошелёк**"). But why take the blame for the wallet's disappearance? There is always a safer way to put it. The wallet was lost ("**Кошелёк потеря́лся**"). Fate should have it this way: "**Так получи́лось.**"

Our friends got married but soon they divorced. Why? "**У них не сложи́лось**" ("It didn't work out between them"). A mysterious something brought them apart.

"Why didn't you come to the party last night? We were waiting for you." "**Я собира́лся, но не получи́лось**" ("I was planning to come, but it did not work out"). "**Ка́к-то не сложи́лось**" ("Somehow it just didn't work out").

But, beyond the passive voice, the fatalist's key verbal talisman is the untranslateable **аво́сь**.

You have health problems and need to see the doctor. Why bother? "**Аво́сь, само́ пройдёт**" ("It could be that, the problem will cure itself").

You are carrying some antiques through customs at Sheremetyevo, but decide to take the green corridor to save yourself the trouble of dealing with officials. "**Аво́сь, проскочу́.**" ("Hopefully, I will slip though.")

There have been SARS cases in Russia. But, hopefully, not in our town. "**Аво́сь, пронесёт.**" ("With luck, it may pass us by.")

I just had some mushrooms that may have been poisonous. But they might not have been. "**Аво́сь, обойдётся.**" ("God-willing, the worst won't happen.")

To do something **на аво́сь** usually means to do something very risky or outright insane, on the assumption that some mysterious force will deter the inevitable failure or harm.

The essence of the word **аво́сь** is perhaps best explained by the following archaic saying, **Не во вся́кой ту́че гром; а и гром да не гря́нет; а и гря́нет, да не по нас; а и по нас – аво́сь не убьёт.** (There is not thunder in every cloud, and even if there is thunder, it may not strike, and even if it does strike, then it won't hit us, and even if it does hit us, hopefully it won't kill us.) And if you get the sense of **аво́сь** from this, you can learn this archaic tongue-twister: "**Поаво́ськаем: аво́сь, до чего́-нибудь доаво́ськаемся.**" ("Lets **аво́сь** a bit: **аво́сь**, we will **аво́сь** something out of it.")

In Soviet times, **аво́сь** produced a neologism – **аво́ська** – a folding string-bag carried in one's bag or purse just in case (**на вся́кий слу́чай**) a deficit item turned up on sale (see Survival Russian in *Russian Life*, Sept/Oct 2004).

An expression synonymous with **аво́сь** is **крива́я вы́везет** (literally, "a curve shall carry one through"). Linguists suggest that the expression originally meant that, by setting out on a journey on a lame horse, one is taking a chance, acting on an **аво́сь**.

While the word **аво́сь** is not used very frequently in contemporary speech, all the impersonal verb-forms associated with it are quite common: **пронесло́** (Trouble passed by) **обошло́сь** (It turned out all right).

As for **аво́сь**, it is often used sarcastically, to mock the fatalist mentality. "**Понаде́ялся на ру́сский аво́сь**" ("He put his stock in Russian *avos*"). Russians or those here long-term may voice skepticism about our national **аво́сь**, but deep inside they worship this deity of chance. As Vladimir Dal points out in his dictionary:

"**Аво́сь не бог, а полбо́га есть.**" "*Avos* is not god, but it is a demigod."

Lina Rozovskaya (November 2004)

He Who Laughs Last...

Смеяться, право, не грешно над всем, что кажется смешно.
It's not a sin, of course, to laugh at everything that seems funny.
Nikolai Karamzin, 1796

Russians have long believed that laughter is the best remedy for whatever ails you: **смех – лучшее лекарство**. But somehow it seems that Russians don't always practice what they preach. Could it be that Russians are corrupting their own medicine with the bitter pill of tears? Hence, another laughter-related idiom, "laughing through your tears" **смех сквозь слёзы**. This is an apt expression, for in Russia, the comic usually borders on the tragic, and vice versa. Therefore, for many of Russia's most celebrated artists, tragicomedy (**трагикомедия**) is the most popular genre. When they encounter a tragicomedy in everyday life, Russians say: **и смех, и грех** (it's fun, it's a sin).

But no matter how they may love to laugh, Russians are suspicious of those who laugh without a reason. That is why (Americans take note), Russians, aghast at someone who is always smiling, may say: **у него рот до ушей** (his mouth has stretched to his ears). Sometimes, they even repeat this perfectly rhymed idiom: **смех без причины – признак дурачины** (laughter without any reason is a sign of the fool). Anyone who finds himself labeled as such has no choice but to tell his accuser that he "caught a little laughter in his mouth" (**смешинка в рот попала**). Those who suffer from this problem are called **хохотун/хохотунья**. To help them quit giggling, you may be forced to order them to "stop doing he-hes and ha-has" (**хватит разводить хиханьки да хаханьки**).

Russians describe a good eye-watering laugh, as "laughing from the bottom of their heart" (**смеяться от всей души**), or they say they "laughed until they dropped"(**смеялись до упаду**), or even "blew up from laughter" (**лопнуть от смеха**).

The best time for laughing until you drop is April Fool's Day. Since Russians love to play an April Fool's Day joke (**первоапрельская шутка**) on friends, colleagues or even relatives, it is wise to heed the warning to "never believe anyone on April first," – **Первого апреля никому не верь.**

For those of you planning your own April Fool's Day jokes, be sure to think twice before involving your superior in any way if she or he happens to be a former communist *apparatchik*. Don't forget how Russians rephrase the famous saying **хорошо смеётся тот, кто смеётся последним** (he who laughs last, laughs best): **хорошо**

смеётся тот, кто смеётся без послéдствий (he who laughs without consequences, laughs best.) The tens of thousands of innocent people who served up to 10 years in Stalinist labor camps for making puns on the Leader's name or his thick Georgian accent, testify to the expression's bitter accuracy.

Sadly, Russia's rulers have never let the **хи́ханьки** and **ха́ханьки** laugh without consequences. The idea of the ruler's invincibility to satire stems from historic times, when, except for court jesters and clowns, most Russians were never allowed to "he he and ha ha" at the Russian rulers' expense. Even after the 1917 Revolution, poking fun at the Soviet regime could have deadly repercussions. Hence, the famously macabre wordplay: **ю́мор – э́то когда́ стра́шно хо́чется смея́ться; а сати́ра – э́то когда́ хо́чется смея́ться, а стра́шно**, which could be translated as "humor is when you want to laugh terribly, satire is when you want to laugh, but it is too terrible." Or, as the Russian comics like to say **"сме́ха бои́тся да́же тот, кто ничего́ не бои́тся**" ("laughter scares even those who fear nothing").

Mikhail Ivanov (April 1997)

Linguistics
&
Ephemera

Fishing With Dried Pasta

There are thousands of Russian idioms, proverbs and aphorisms. Many are explained in language textbooks and dictionaries, yet most rarely find their way into everyday speech. Some are so archaic as to be meaningless, others so overused as to become boring. As old folkloric wisdom is discredited, language users fracture old idioms into new ones. These usually pop up in colloquial speech or on the Internet, yet they cannot be ignored, for they tell us a lot about the language and the creativity of those using it.

Russian provides endless opportunities for wordplay. Consider the following idiomatic centaurs: **У вас ещё лапша на ушах не обсохла** (The noodles on your ears are not dry yet). It is a hybrid of two idiomatic expressions: **вешать лапшу на уши** ("to hang noodles on someone's ears," meaning to dupe someone) and **у тебя ещё молоко на губах не обсохло** ("the mother's milk has not dried on your lips," meaning you are still green). Another pseudo-idiom reads: **А вы и ухом не моргнули** (you didn't even bat an ear). This is a mix of **и глазом не моргнул** (didn't bat an eyelid) and **и ухом не повёл** ("didn't twitch an ear," meaning paid no heed to).

Pseudo-proverbs are often made by slightly altering one word, as in the English witticism, "Chaste makes waste." **Что посмеешь, то и пожнёшь** (You reap what you risk), reads the anti-proverb, contradicting the time-honored **Что посеешь, то и пожнёшь** (You reap what you sow).

Or there is this nonsensical remake: **Не йоги горшки обжигают** (Yogis don't fire jugs). The original reads **Не боги горшки обжигают** (Gods don't fire jugs), which means "It can't be that hard, you'll manage."

Anti-proverbs often rebel against the morals of the original, as in "If at first you don't succeed, you're average," or "Love is blind, but neighbors aren't." **Любишь кататься – люби и катайся** (If you like riding on the sledge, go ahead), proclaims the neo-proverb, reworking the concept that, if you like riding on a sledge, you also must pull it (**Любишь кататься – люби и саночки возить**). Another rejects the need to work hard to achieve something: **Без пруда не выловишь и рыбку из него** (You can't catch a fish without a pond). This is a parody on the well-known truth, **Без труда не выловишь и рыбки из пруда** (You can't catch a fish from the pond without work).

As we have seen, some anti-proverbs cross-pollinate two proverbs, often with bizarre results (and uncertain meanings). **И баба с возу, и волки сыты** (The woman is off the cart and the wolves are fed) derives from **И овцы целы, и волки сыты** ("The sheep are safe and the wolves are fed," meaning all parties are content) and **Баба с возу – кобыле легче** (The woman is off the cart and the mare's burden is lighter). **Не плюй в колодец, вылетит – не поймаешь** (Don't spit into the well – you won't catch it once it's out), advises another anti-proverb, a hybrid of the well-known **Слово – не воробей, вылетит – не поймаешь** (A word is not a sparrow, once it's out, you won't catch it) and **Не плюй в колодец** (Don't spit into the well).

Another way to make a pun on a proverb is to "retell" it, or throw it into an unfamiliar context. Thus, **Не по Хуану сомбреро** (Juan does not deserve such a sombrero) is a take-off on **Не по Сеньке шапка** (Senka is not worthy of such a *shapka*).

Popular slogans and song lyrics are also fair game for linguistic mutations. This is how the triumphant line from a Soviet song, **Мы рождены, чтоб сказку сделать былью** (We were born to make dreams into reality), was transformed into **Мы рождены, чтоб Кафку сделать былью.** (We were born to make Kafka into reality). The sarcastic **Брежнев умер, но тело его живёт** (Brezhnev is dead, but his body lives on) is an historically accurate pun on the popular Soviet slogan **Ленин умер, но дело его живёт** (Lenin is dead, but his work lives on).

Finally, some of the best neo-proverbs are born unintentionally. An expat friend who wanted to show off his knowledge of Russian made the following contribution to Russian folklore: **Милые бранятся – только чешутся.** The original reads: **Милые бранятся – только тешатся** (When lovers fight, it is just to amuse themselves). In my friend's version the verb **тешатся**, rarely used in contemporary speech, was replaced with the similar sounding **чешутся** (scratch themselves). It was a Freudian slip of almost Kafkaesque proportions.

Lina Rozovskaya (July 2003)

Getting the Endings Right

As anyone who has studied Russian knows, it is a language that hinges on endings. If you don't conjugate your Russian verbs and nouns properly, you risk being labeled **неграмотный**. And yet, the conjugation that flusters students of Russsian also helps make the language more poetic, more lyrical.

Less taxing than conjugation, but of no small importance in developing good, Survival Russian is mastering the use of colloquial noun suffixes. In Russian, these suffixes carry a lot of cultural baggage and convey volumes of linguistic awareness.

The most common suffixes are diminutives. These are used to connnote affection, love and familiarity. Thus, the famous phrase "Mother Russia" translates, in literal Russian, as "Little Mother Russia" – **Россия-Матушка**. The well-known **бабушка** (grandma) derives from "**баба**" (woman) plus the dimunutive suffixe -**ушк**.

But affectionate suffixes are by no means limited to persons or countries.

"**Бутылочку водочки и пару бутылочек пивка.**"

This modest request, overheard in a wine shop ("May I please have a little bottle of vodka and a couple of little bottles of beer") is by no means a way of asking for small portions. Rather, it is a way of softening up the request and showing a bit of affection for (or familiarity with) the object in question. The generic **бутылка** (bottle) is replaced with "little bottle."

Similarly, you might hear Russian drunks call their favourite cheap portwine **портвешок** (little portwine).

In some cases, diminutives play a more complicated role. Here is a price quote given by a local **таксист**: "**двадцаточку**" derived from **двадцать** (twenty). In this case, the suffix was being used to sweeten the price a bit (note that the word for "thousand" was also dropped).

Perhaps it is because money can be a touchy subject that it is a common recipient of diminutives: to lighten the tone a bit. The term **шту́ка**, for instance, which refers to one thousand rubles, easily becomes **шту́чка**. Similarly, a black market currency dealer might once have approached someone in an exchange point line and ask "**Сдаёте зелёненькие?**" ("Would you like to sell some greenbacks?") The **-енк** turns **зелёные** (greenbacks) into "tiny little greenbacks" and softens up an otherwise intrusive (or offensive) query.

"**Сигаре́точкой не угости́те?**"

"Could you offer me a little cigarette?" a 14-year-old girl asks a young man who is taking a smoke. The familiarizing suffix, aimed as much at the man as the cigarette, softens up the normal aversion to underage smoking and the girl's request is satisfied.

"**Почём Ма́рльборо, бабу́ля?**"

"How much for a pack of Marlboros dear lady?" asks the customer approaching a senior citizen working as a street vendor.

Normally, this gentle **-ля** suffix can melt a heart of ice. But the **бабу́ля** is not bested and, not batting an eyelid, retorts "**Как обы́чно, сыно́к.**" ("Same as always, sonny.") This dry, almost sarcastic **-ок** added to the generic **сын** tells the buyer not to push for a discount.

There are other suffixes imbued with cultural meaning, but not necessarily positive. The suffice **-щина** was often used in Soviet times to add perjorative meaning (one source translates the suffix to mean "the wicked deeds of"). Thus the word **штурмовщи́на**, the term to describe the end of the month, overtime production schedule wrought by centralized economic planning. Or **ежо́вщина**, to refer to the purges of the late 1930s overseen by Nikolai Yezhov (who himself fell victim to the purges of the 1930s). Or **дедовщи́на** to refer to the ruthless and now notorious hazing that takes place in the Russian military (seasoned recruits are referred to as **деды́**, or grampas).

Hearkening back to this era, current, Soviet-style publications like *Sovetskaya Rossiya* or *Zavtra* often lambast the increased presence of foreigners and foreign culture in Russia. These journals now frequently use the perjorative **иностра́нщина** to refer to things foreign.

And there are other perjorative suffixes. Like **-щи**, which can mean big and, when tacked on to the word **де́ньги**, makes **деньжи́щи** a negative term for New Russians, or those with "big money."

Черну́ха ("black stuff," from the word чёрный and the prefix -ха) is a colloquial name for blue literature and cheap movies often associated with иностра́нщина authored by Ба́ба Катя́ – Moscow street vendors' affectionate name for Barbara Cartland.

Of course, this is only an introduction to the huge number of noun suffixes available in Russian. And it is a subject well worth studying. If only because such richness means that a few letters can (purposely or accidentally) completely change the meaning of rather innocuous words. As was the case in Pushkin's story Ска́зка о рыбаке́ и ры́бке where a бабу́ля altered the rather innocuous дере́вня (village) to toss a sharp insult at her husband, calling him a деревéнщина (uncultivated, ignorant, uncultured).

Mikhail Ivanov (June 1995)

An Introduction to Russian Acronyms

Does your spouse often give you ЦУ? Have you ever had a ЧП in your private life? Do you know how many сексо́т worked for the ЧК? This installment of SR will help you to answer these and other questions, and to appreciate the flavor — and often the humor — that acronyms bring to the Russian language.

You may already know that ЧК (Cheka) is short for Чрезвыча́йная коми́ссия (emergency commission — predecessor to the KGB), but why would a сексо́т work there? Strange as it may seem, сексо́т has nothing to do with sex – it stands for секре́тный сотру́дник (a "secret employee," i.e. secret agent) recruited by the Cheka and its successor, the NKVD, in the 1930s. This acronym became known to ordinary Russians only with the publication of Anatoly Rybakov's late-1980s novel, *Children of the Arbat*, with its insights into the goings-on at the Lubyanka — Russia's inner sanctum of counterintelligence.

A more democratic acronym is the all-purpose ЧП (pronounced *che-pah*), which stands for чрезвыча́йное происше́ствие (emergency incident). Once used mainly by bureaucrats and law-enforcement bodies, ЧП is now utilized in every imaginable situation. For example, an army lieutenant who catches a drunk soldier in his platoon might term the incident a ЧП in his report. The recent launching of a grenade at the U.S. Embassy in Moscow is a definite ЧП in the diplomatic sense.

In the early 1970s, a meeting of young communists, debating the case of a long-haired student with flared jeans, would call it a ЧП in the life of the school. While a case of adultery might be described as a family ЧП. The recent State Duma scuffle between ultra-nationalist Vladimir Zhirinovsky and a female colleague was an example of a parliamentary ЧП.

One ill-conceived acronym even helped to foil a *coup d'etat*. The plotters of the 1991 attempt to overthrow Mikhail Gorbachev and restore Communist rule to Russia chose to call themselves the ГКЧП (State Emergency Committee). It didn't help their cause any that every news anchor in Russia was making fun of their name.

Another legacy of bureaucracy-speak is ЦУ, which stands for це́нное указа́ние ("valuable directive" – a bureaucratic euphemism meaning "advice"). So, if you ever hear "мне не ну́жны твои́ ЦУ," you can be sure that your advice isn't welcome.

The spasmodic distribution of the former command economy led to the widespread adoption of the military acronym НЗ (неприкоснове́нный запа́с, untouchable stock), which was used mostly to refer to stockpiled food or ammunition. Russians now use НЗ to

mean anything they are holding in reserve, whether food or money. For example, in Soviet times, when a chain smoker was sent to a *kolkhoz* (collective farm) to help bring in the potato harvest, he would always take along an **НЗ** of cigarettes, in anticipation of a tobacco shortage at the local stores.

Incidentally, *kolkhoz* (**колхо́з – коллекти́вное хозя́йство**, meaning "collective farm"), an acronym born of the now-defunct **СССР** (USSR), is now so integral a part of the language that nobody remembers that it is an acronym. Other such words include **совхо́з** (state farm), **комсомо́л** (**коммунисти́ческий сою́з молодёжи** – Union of Communist Youth), and **Политбюро́** (Politburo or political bureau). To say nothing of the ill-famed **НКВД**, or **КГБ** (*kah-ge-be*) or **КПСС** (*kah-pe-es-es*; CPSU, Soviet Communist Party).

One acronym that's hard to get past in Russia is the infamous **ГАИ**, or **Госуда́рственная автомоби́льная инспе́кция** ("State Automobile Inspection" – Russia's Highway Patrol*). A run-in with the notoriously corrupt **гаи́шники** (patrolmen) can at any time turn into a **ЧП**. Another public safety body that you should stay out of trouble with is the **ОМОН** (**отря́д мили́ции осо́бого назначе́ния**, an elite police unit, also known in the West by its acronym), renowned for its less-than-genteel methods.

On Moscow's streets, you might also be held up by a **бомж** (*bomzh*, bum) asking for small change. **Бомж** stands for **Без определённого ме́ста жи́тельства** (without a definite place of residence). With the transition to a market economy, you will see more and more of this category of people on the street.

If you are planning a trip to Russia in the near future, you should memorize these four letters — **СПИД** — Russian for AIDS. According to recently-passed legislation, foreigners going to Russia for more than three months will have to prove that they are free of **СПИД** by producing a certificate to this effect.

The regular traveler to Russia should also be familiar with the letters **УВИР** (**Управле́ние виз и регистра́ций** — Directorate of Visas and Registration). There's no way around these guys if you want to keep your travel papers in order, and they are specialists in the art of the **ЧП**.

Mikhail Ivanov (December 1995)

---

*A name that has since changed. See page 39-40.

A Small Crowd of Oxymorons

An oxymoron (**оксюмо́рон**) is an idiom that is, according to the original Greek, "pointedly foolish." It unites two incompatible notions or properties, usually in the form of an adjective plus a noun, and Russian is full of them. For example: **го́рькая сла́дость** (bitter sweetness), or **тёмное освеще́ние** (dark lightness). Speaking of lightness, there is the phrase **он испы́тывал лёгкую тя́жесть в нога́х** (he felt a light heaviness in his legs).

There are several which have perfect American counterparts, like **небольша́я толпа́**, which finds a parallel in the American oxymoron "small crowd." Another classic is the expression **секре́т полишине́ля** (literally "puppet's secret," but best translated as "open secret").

There are also some purely Russian oxymorons: **Я тебе́ по-хоро́шему зави́дую** (I envy you in a good way). The very notion that there could be **хоро́шая за́висть** (good envy) is an oxymoron by definition. It is kind of like a twist on that double oxymoron: "a bad peace is better than a good war."

But then, of course, in addition to more classic, literary oxymorons like these, there are those discovered by keen wits or invented by humorists. My U.S. colleagues, for instance, single out "Amtrak Schedule" or "military intelligence." I liked both, as I once rode Amtrak and also served in the military and sampled their "intelligence," like the Russian officer's command, "Hey, you three, both of you get over here" (see page 69).

Some such oxymorons depend perhaps on your political perspective. For instance, we used to call our leaders **"ми́лостивый госуда́рь"** ("merciful sovereign"). But even a superficial analysis of Russian history makes it clear that our sovereigns were never merciful.

Modern times offer still more riches, like the howlers **беспла́тное лече́ние** (free [medical] treatment), or **росси́йская эконо́мика** ("Russian economy") – not as funny a joke as it used to be when it was **сове́тская эконо́мика**. So it is with **госуда́рственный де́ятель**, sometimes translated as "state functionary," but more literally translated as "state doer," which is as oxymoronic as **росси́йские зако́ны** ("Russian laws").

From the communist era we have **культу́рная револю́ция** ("cultural revolution") and **желе́зный Фе́ликс** ("Iron Felix"), which referred to the statue of Felix Dzerzhinsky, which proved not so solid after it was toppled in 1991.

For those who do not like their mother-in-law, **до́брая тёща** (good-hearted mother-in-law) is a perfectly composed oxymoron. For me, I find **безалкого́льное пи́во** (non-alcoholic beer) to be one of the biggest offenders. It ranks right up there with **ую́тный тролле́йбус** (cozy trolleybus). Absurdity knows no bounds. As in the **вку́сный** гáмбургер (tasty hamburger) or полéзная пéпси-кóла (healthy PepsiCola) touted in ads. It makes this lover of what Americans call "slow food" shiver... And what a perfect oxymoron "fast food" is…

But to end this piece on a conciliatory note, perhaps we can construct some useful and truthful oxymorons of our own about "both our three" countries – Russia, the U.S. and France (the nations I know best). I think most would agree that these are oxymorons in the best tradition of the word: **негостеприи́мный ру́сский** (inhospitable Russian), **безала́берный америка́нец** (disorderly, lazy American) and **неопря́тный францу́з** ("sloppy Frenchman" – in appearance, not work habits, that is).

All these phenomena are quite hard to find, and, while there could be some exceptions, with your acquiescence, **ми́лостивые госуда́ри**, I will add these to my growing list of the best oxymorons.

Mikhail Ivanov (November 2002)

Virtual Russian

So there you are, sitting in front of your **компью́тер**, connected to the **Интернéт** with your **брáузер** program open to your favorite Web-**сайт**. After entering your **логи́н** and your **пассвóрд** (though the more "proper" Russian term is **парóль**), you enter a technical news **фóрум**. You **скрол** down the page (ignoring the **бáннеры** at the top) and read where one company is seeking a Flash-**дизáйнер**; another, a web**мáстер**. A third company has announced the release of a new program, a download-**мéнеджер**, implemented as a Java-**áпплет**. A **хáкер** in Asia has released a new **ви́рус**. While reading the new **пóсты**, you note that there are several **оффтóпик** messages, as well as some containing **спам**. Afterward, you visit an interesting **блог**, or maybe just do some **сéрфинг**.

As you may have noticed by now, a really important skill for understanding much of modern Russian computer-speak is the ability to transliterate. It wasn't always this way. Back at about the time when high-powered executives at companies like DEC and IBM estimated the total worldwide demand for computers to be – at most – several dozen units, the term **электрóнная вычисли́тельная маши́на** (electronic computing machine) was coined in Russian. This healthy mouthful was nearly always shortened to the time-saving **ЭВМ** (*eh-veh-em*), and as it became clear that computers would develop along fundamentally electronic lines, the first word (letter) atrophied and was often omitted.

When computers became personal, **вычисли́тельные маши́ны** became **персонáльные** until the early 90s, when **компью́тер** finally overwhelmed the old, bloated collocation, and Russians started using the **персонáльный компью́тер**, or **ПК**. In today's jargon, even **компью́тер** has given ground in everyday slang (and on the Web) to the shorter "**комп**." Terms used for "software" evolved in a roughly parallel manner. Originally, "software" was described by the term **прогрáммно-математи́ческое обеспéчение** (programmed mathematical support), abbreviated **ПМО**. Many manuals still refer to **прогрáммное обеспéчение, математи́ческое обеспéчение**, or just **обеспéчение**. Today, on the Internet, the single-syllable word **софт** (or less frequently, **прóга**, short for **прогрáмма**) rules.

One of the most remarkable phenomena of the past few years in Russian cities such as Moscow is the increasingly widespread mixing of Latin words and names with Cyrillic in print and broadcast media (I recently saw "Das ist fantastisch!" on a Moscow billboard for German beer, and thought: "It certainly is!"). The same mixing can be seen at a much more intense level over the extent of the entire Russian Internet (**Рунет**). The rules of expression are fairly simple. Names of companies (Toshiba, Dell), programs (Flash, Windows), hardware (Palm Tungsten, iPod), and abbreviations (HTML, ASP) generally remain Latinized. In addition, there is virtually no penalty for using English words for commonly used concepts (e.g., shareware, WYSIWYG, ftp) or for using English words in conjunction with Russian modifiers, e.g., CGI-**скрипт** (a program that generates a web page dynamically) and write-**доступ** (the ability to change – "write" in computerese – the contents of a **файл**).

This intermixing of Latin and Cyrillic in Russian computing has resulted in the curious neologism **лытдыбр**, often found online as a reference to an online journal entry. The etymology of this word turns on the fact that, if you type the Russian word **дневник** (journal) on a standard Russian keyboard but do so while the keyboard is toggled to type in Latin, the resulting characters typed spell "lytdybr" on the screen. Transliterating into Cyrillic completes the cycle and produces the neologism.

This is not to say that knowledge of a little Russian will not be useful in finding one's way around a computer or the Internet. A variety of closely-related words are used to describe downloading. These include **качать, скачивать, откачивать,** and **загружать**. Unless you have reliable access, you will probably use a **качалка**, or a download-**менеджер**, which is a program that permits you to download portions of a file at a time, for those times when your **модем** keeps dropping the connection. If you're using a **дайлап** connection, you'll probably use a **звонилка**, or a program that manages the dial-up process between your computer and the **сервер** used by your **Интернет-провайдер**.

If you're looking for a link to a site's home page, you should be on the lookout for either a **главная страница, первая страница**, or **домашняя страница** (although the first is used four times more often on the **Рунет** than the other two combined).

In keeping with the glorious tradition of never using more syllables when fewer will do, the word **хомяк** is gaining ground as the name for a site's home page (**хомяк** also means hamster).

If you see (or more likely, hear) a reference to **ася** or **аська**, know that the subject is ICQ, the instant messaging service. **Мыло** (soap) refers to e-mail. Sites that distribute **варез** (warez) should be avoided as they offer illegal copies of commercial software. When things don't work the way they are intended, or if your computer crashes, the problem can be said to be the result of a **глюк** (bug).

A network is a **сеть**, which is also used to refer to the Internet, unless the adjective **локáльный** (local) is used, thus referring to a LAN. And while most old-timers will understand what you mean if you refer to a **винчéстер** ("Winchester," referring to an early hard drive technology), you'll sound more up to date if you speak of a **жёсткий диск**, or even – surprise, surprise – a **хард драйв**.

Alex Lane (May 2003)

Repeat and Ye Shall Learn

Of all the pieces of "invaluable" advice the founder of the Soviet Union had to give to the younger generation, there was one he made a point to repeat thrice – "to learn, learn and learn" (**"учи́ться, учи́ться и учи́ться"**).

All the subsequent generations of Russian youth – whether communist or not – had no fundamental problem with this bit of Lenin's wisdom. After all, many years before Lenin said this, another famous Russian, Field Marshal Alexander Suvorov, had this to say: **"тяжело́ в уче́нье – легко́ в бою́"** ("training is tough, battle is easy").

Most prominent figures in Russian history from Peter the Great onward agreed on the need to learn. For, as the Russian saying goes – **уче́нье свет, а неуче́нье тьма** (learning is light and ignorance is darkness). So, don't be surprised to come across the word "learn" in many Russian idioms and sayings. And, since we all know that students always follow the advice of their ancestors religiously, it follows that students in Russia have developed a keen interest in learning, along with their own student parlance. It is in secondary school that students learn how to **спи́сывать** – to copy off of somebody (**сдува́ть, содра́ть**), how to skip classes (**прогу́ливать уро́ки**) and how to write a **шпарга́лка** (cheat-sheet).

Once you have a **шпарга́лка**, you need to make sure you sit in **Камча́тка** (reference is made to the distant Kamchatka peninsula), the row of tables farthest from the teacher, so you can copy from it undisturbed by her eagle eye. Kamchatka is also a great place to **подска́зывать** (whisper the answers) to the guy standing at the blackboard.

Secondary school students may call their teachers **учи́лка** (a pejorative form of **учи́тельница**). A female teacher of mathematics would be a **матема́тичка**, of Russian language, a **руси́чка**, and so on. The **учи́лка** gives Russian kids marks on a five-point system, ranging from the dismal **дво́йка** or **па́ра** (2), **тро́йка** (coll. **троя́к**) (3), and **четвёрка** (4), up to the laudable **пятёрка** (5). If the teacher were really angry, she would give a kid a **едини́ца** or **кол** (1). Someone who has too many *dvoykas* runs the risk of staying back a year and becoming a **второго́дник**.

At the college level, marks change from numbers to adverbs. Thus, after an exam, a professor would write not a 2, but rather the word **неудовлетвори́тельно** (unsatisfactory), in a student's **зачётная кни́жка / зачётка** (report card). Note the colloquial **поста́вить/ влепи́ть "не́уд"** – literally, to stick an unsatisfactory mark on a student. Accordingly, a 3 becomes **удовлетвори́тельно** (satisfactory), a 4 – **хорошо́** (good), and a 5 – **отли́чно** (excellent). Those who receive only *dvoykas* are called **дво́ечники,** *troykas* – **тро́ечники,** 4's – **хороши́сты,** and 5's – **отли́чники**. In order to give students incentive to earn high marks, institutes sometimes give a stipend (**стипе́ндия,** coll. **стипу́ха**) only to those who had just 4's and 5's in their **зачётка**.

However, real life tends to go way beyond textbooks, so many a student would not pay too much attention to marks and grades, figuring that social skills would prove equally, if not more, important in the future. This type of student would hang out a lot at the **общежитие** (dormitory) or **общага** (dorm). Take note of a popular student song on the subject: **Почему́ мой друг – да потому́, что я жизнь учи́л не по уче́бникам, про́сто я рабо́таю волше́бником.** (Why, my friend? Well, because I didn't learn about life from textbooks, I simply work as a magician.) These guys pretend to be savvy and knowledgeable. They usually go to institutes after the army and have in their arsenal such idioms as **я́йца ку́рицу не у́чат** (eggs don't teach the hen) or **не учи́ учёного** (don't teach the teacher). However, it is often these same "magicians" who flunk exams (**провали́ться на экза́мене**).

Another idiom related to magicians and studying sounds like this: **я не волше́бник, я ещё то́лько учу́сь** (I'm not a magician, I'm just learning), which means – don't ask too much from me, I just do what I can. This saying has by now become an idiom, but Russians over 40 will recall that it originated in the old Soviet movie *Cinderella*, where the fairy godmother had a young apprentice who kept repeating this sentence.

On the other hand, it is possible to keep learning for a century and still remain ignorant. As they say: **век живи́, век учи́сь** ("live a millemium, learn for a thousand years," the equivalent of live and learn). This is what members of the Russian *intelligentsia* repeat to themselves and their children. And since repetition is the mother of learning (**повторе́нье – мать уче́нья**), it might pay to take the advice of an old comrade and **учи́ться, учи́ться и учи́ться**. After all, with learning Russian, as with so much else, hard work tends to pay off.

Mikhail Ivanov (September 1997)

Study Guide & Indexes

Study Guide

This Study Guide is organized in keeping with the thematic sections of the book. Within each section (and across chapters), words are alphabetized. Russian words from each section are listed in the left column, along with a reference to the {page number} where the word or phrase can be found.

The student is to look up the words and phrases, then write the translations or meanings in the empty right hand column. Then, to quiz oneself and learn Russian → English or English → Russian, the student merely needs to cover one or the other column and work their way up or down the list.

Not all phrases and words from *Survival Russian* are listed in the Study Guide. It is assumed that the student has at least a full year of Russian study and thus simpler vocabulary has been left out.

Compliments & Insults

А сколько бы Вы мне дали? {11}
братва {14}
в принципе, да {14}
В сорок пять баба ягодка опять {11}
вешать лапшу на уши {14}
грамотей {16}
Доброе слово и кошке приятно {11}
дразнилка {12}
Его голыми руками не возмёшь {14}
Ему про Фому, а он – про Ерёму {13}
Если не секрет, сколько Вы получаете? {16}
За мной не заржавеет {17}
За что купил – за то и продал {17}
Иван, не помнящий родства {12}
катавасия {15}
классный {11}
козырнуть этими словами {16}
кондуит {16}
Конечно, это не моё дело... {16}
Кто его / её спрашивает? {10}
куда Макар телят не гонял {13}
Кузькину мать {12}
Мели Емеля – твоя неделя {12}
Михаил коров доил {13}
Мишка-Мишка, где твоя улыбка? {13}
Мне кажется, ты похудела {11}
Может так договоримся? {17}
На бедного Макара все шишки валятся {12}
Нас не объегоришь и нас не подкузьмишь {12}
Не в службу, а в дружбу {16}
Не сочтите за труд {16}
невежда {16}
объегорить {12}
она какая-то Маша {12}
Паша с уралмаша {12}
Перезвоню {14}
по Сеньке и шапка {13}
подкузьмить {12}
Показать Кузькину мать {12}
преступный мир {14}
прохиндей {15}
Прохиндиада {15}
разбираться {14}
разборка {14}

разгильдяй {15}
Сколько ты зарабатываешь? {10}
Сколько ты получаешь? {10}
Сколько у тебя выходит
  'грязными'? ...'чистыми'? {10}
Сколько у тебя выходит в месяц? {10}
словечки {16}
со смаком {16}
созвонимся {14}
Старик, ты сегодня в ударе {10}
Ты настоящий мужик / парень {10}
ты поправилась {11}
Ты сегодня выглядишь бесподобно /
  блестяще / восхитительно /
  сногсшибательно {11}
Ты сегодня выглядишь как
  огурец (огурчик) {10}
Ты сегодня выглядишь на 'пять с плюсом' {11}
Ты сегодня выглядишь на 100 рублей {11}
Ты сегодня превзошёл самого себя {10}
У вас тут такая катавасия! {15}
Федот – да не тот {13}
Федя-Бредя сьел медведя {12}
халдей {15}
хмырь {15}
хороша Маша – да не наша {12}
Это не телефонный разговор {10}
Это платье на тебе сидит, как влитое {11}
Это платье тебе очень идёт {11}
Я бы Вам столько не дал {11}
Я Вам сам позвоню {14}
Я с ребёнком {17}
Я бы с ним в разведку пошёл {10}
Я Вас отблагодарю {17}

FATHERS & SONS

баба, бабанька {21, 25}
бабка, бабки {25}
бабник {25}
бабские разговоры {24}
бабульки {25}
бабуля {25}
Бабушка надвое сказала {26}
бабье лето {25}
барышня {20, 23}
бесит меня {28}

бесполезняк {29}
бизнес-вуман {25}
братва {21}
бриллианты {23}
в кайф {29}
водопроводчик {25}
Вот тебе, бабушка, и Юрьев день {26}
впадали в детство {28}
Дама, вы мне все ноги оттоптали {23}
Дети – цветы жизни ... на могиле родителей {27}
Детская болезнь левизны в коммунизме {27}
домохозяйка {25}
думать так было бы ребячеством {27}
его заказали {23}
Женщина, вы выходите на следующей? {24}
Женщина, вы кошелёк уронили {24}
зарплата {25}
золотые дети {27}
и к бабке не ходи {26}
и к гадалке не ходи {26}
йога {24}
кайф {29}
клюшка {20}
коммуняки {22}
Кому 'товарищ' а тебе 'гражданин' {20}
конкретно / конкретный {28}
краснокоричневые {22}
Красный Пролетарий {21}
круто / крутой {28}
кулаки {21}
ленинец {21}
лох / лох педальный {29}
любезнейший {20}
маленькие детки – маленькие бедки, а вырастут
    велики – будут большие {27}
мартышка {20}
маршрутка {28}
меньшевик {21}
метаться {29}
милостивый государь {20}
мочалка {20}
Мы старый мир разрушим до основанья,
    а затем... а зачем... {22}
мэн {21}
надо сегодня оторваться не по-детски {29}
назло бабушке отморозить себе уши / отрезать себе
    ухо {26}

нам так по кайфу {29}
наши дети будут жить при коммунизме {28}
не бабье это дело {24}
не парься {28}
не по-детски {28}
незнакомый человек {23}
новарищи {23}
Ну спасибо тебе, бабанька! {25}
октябрь {22}
октябрята {21}
Он настоящий мужик {25}
он нашёл себе новую бабу {24}
оторваться {29}
париться {28}
плотник {25}
по кайфу {29}
поздняк {29}
понтово {28}
поставить на счётчик {23}
посуда {25}
прекрасный пол {24}
прикольно {28}
прихватизация {22}
прихватить {22}
продавщица {24}
раскулачивание {21}
расслабься {28}
реально, реальный {28}
ребята {22}
Революция пожирает своих детей {22}
с младых ногтей {27}
семибанкирщина {23}
со всей пролетарской ненавистью {22}
Собачье Сердце {22}
советы {21}
солидная {23}
старперы {29}
Сударыни, больше растяните подмышечные впадины! {24}
сударыня {20, 23, 24}
сударь {20}
Тамбовский волк тебе товарищ {20}
товарка {20}
Тоже мне девушку нашёл? {20}
У нас господ нет! {24}
у семи нянек дитя без глазу {27}
уборка {25}

феминистки {25}
хозяйка {25}
хотели как лучше, а получилось как всегда {22}
Хоть горшком назови, только в печку не ставь {20}
чем бы дитя не тешилось, лишь бы не плакало {27}
чёртовой бабушке {26}
Что ты ворчишь, как старая бабка {25}
чубайсизация страны {22}
чубайсята {22}
чувак {21, 29}
шуба {23}
Это всё ерунда / фигня по сравнению с мировой
 революцией {21}
Я тебе в матери гожусь! {20}
яблоко от яблочка недалеко падает {27}

Out & About

а Вы что рекомендуете? {33}
А я готовлюсь стать отцом {36}
абонентная книжечка {37}
аварийная ситуация {38}
авоська {40}
автолюбители {38}
Алло {35}
без очереди {41}
безбилетник {37}
бессознательное {40}
бомбить {39}
браток {33}
Будьте добры {33}
Бюро находок {38}
в итальянское посольство за визой {40}
В какой ресторан пойдём? {33}
В очередь, сукины дети, в очередь! {41}
Вас здесь не стояло {41}
Вас слушают {35}
водила {39}
водительские права {39}
водительское удостоверение {39}
вождение в нетрезвом состоянии {39}
встать в очередь {40}
второе {33}
Вы выходите / сходите на следующей? {37, 41}
Вы уже выбрали? {33}
гаишник {39}

Гони инспектору бабки и двигай дальше! {40}
Государственная Инспекция по Безопасности
 Дорожного Движения {40}
Давайте с Вами поменяемся {37}
дайте пройти {36}
двадцатку / двадцаточку {39}
десерт {33}
десятку / десяточку {39}
дефицит {40}
до свидания {36}
договориться {39}
Его нет и неизвестно, когда он будет {36}
ездят зайцем {37}
жалобная книга {33}
Желаете что-нибудь на десерт? {33}
женщина за рулём – что фашист на танке {38}
жетон {37}
за билетами на самолёт {40}
За двумя зайцами погонишься, ни одного не
 поймаешь. {36}
За чем стоим? {40}
закуски {33}
замена водительских прав {38}
занять очередь {40}
записки {35}
заяц {37}
здравствуйте {34}
Здравствуйте, можно Ивана Иванова? {34}
Иван Иванов на месте? {34}
Квитанция нужна? {39}
клиент всегда неправ {32}
коллективное {40}
командир {39}
контролёр {37}
Кто его спрашивает? {35}
Кто последний? {40}
кто-то теряет, кто-то находит {38}
лишение водительских прав сроком на год {39}
Мне не нужна квитанция {39}
мне то же самое {33}
Можно Вас на минуточку {33}
Молодой человек, как Вам не стыдно,
 уступите место женщине – она готовится стать
 матерью {36}
мотор {39}
на выставку {40}
На поезд посадки нет {37}

на приём к ветеринару {40}
нарушили правила дорожного движения {39}
не пихайтесь {36}
не толкайтесь {36}
недовешивать {32}
нет мест {32}
Новые Русские {34}
обсчитать {32}
Одну минуточку / минуту / секунду {35}
Он / она / я у телефона {35}
Он Вам перезвонит {35}
Он говорит по другому телефону,
    Вы подождёте или позвоните попозже? {35}
он меня не понял {33}
оставить записку {35}
остался только сороковой размер {40}
официант {32}
очередь {40}
пейджер {34}
Передайте ему, пожалуйста, трубку {34}
Передайте пожалуйста, что... {35}
Передайте, пожалуйста, на книжечку {37}
по телефону {34}
Подождите, пожалуйста {35}
подрезать {38}
подснежники {38}
Поезд дальше не идёт, просьба
    освободить вагоны {37}
Пожалуйста, господина Смита {34}
половой человек {32}
полтинник {39}
поменять пепельницу {33}
Попросите пожалуйста /
    Позовите Ивана Иванова {34}
Поставьте меня на лист ожидания {41}
превышение скорости {39}
предъявите Ваш билет {37}
приятного аппетита {33}
проезд на красный сигнал светофора {39}
Пройдёмте в милицию {37}
проныра {32}
прохиндей {32}
разбавить водой {32}
салфетки {33}
сбрось / скинь мне на пейджер {34}
Своевременно и правильно оплачивайте проезд {37}
связи {32}
сливки {40}

советский человек {40}
Созвонимся! {35}
сотовые / мобильные телефоны {34}
справочная {35}
стольник {39}
стоять в очереди {40}
Счёт, пожалуйста/посчитайте нам пожалуйста {33}
таксисты {39}
тачка {39}
телефонное право {34}
техосмотр {38}
трактир {32}
тридцатник {39}
Уважаемые пассажиры,
  не забывайте свой вещи {38}
удар ниже пейджера / пояса {34}
уступите место {36}
фирменное блюдо {33}
хамство {32}
чаевые {33}
чайник {38}
частники {39}
Чего желаете? {33}
четыре рулона в одни руки {40}
Что дают? {40}
Что ему передать? {35}
что-нибудь из напитков {33}
швейцар {32}
шеф {39}
штраф {37}
штраф {39}
это не телефонный разговор {34}
Я Вас выпущу {37}
Я за вами {40}
Я могу это убрать / унести? {33}
Я отойду на минутку {41}
Я плачу {33}
я полагаюсь на Ваш вкус {33}
Я приглашаю Вас в ресторан {33}
Я сегодня гуляю {33}
Я угощаю {33}

Euphemisms & Expletives

акулы пера {46}
белые пятна на карте {45}
белые страницы {45}
Блин! {48}
Бог подаст {49}
Боже мой! {49}
Болят мои раны {48}
в положении {46}
всё видит в розовом свете {45}
вторая половина {46}
выглядеть, как белая ворона {45}
голубая мечта {44}
Господь с тобой {50}
Дай Бог, чтобы твоя страна тебя не пнула
  сапожищем Дай Бог, чтобы твоя жена тебя
  любила даже нищим! {52}
дают зелёный свет {44}
Два сапога – пара {52}
до синевы выбрит {45}
до синевы пьян, слегка выбрит {45}
дурак любит красное {44}
Ё моё! {48}
желторотик {44}
женщины лёгкого поведения {46}
исполнять свои супружеские обязанности {47}
их деятельность несовместима с их официальным
  статусом {46}
каждое лыко в строку {51}
Каждый охотник желает знать,
  где сидит фазан. {44}
Карту купи, лапоть! {51}
кормилец {46}
красная девица {44}
Креста на тебе нет! {50}
Куплю жене сапоги! {52}
лапотная Россия {51}
лапоть / лапти {51}
Лапти, да лапти, да лапти мои! {51}
лучшая половина человечества {47}
лыко {51}
места весьма отдалённые {47}
места не столь отдалённые {47}
на блюдечке с голубой каёмочкой {44}

начать набело {45}
не дай Бог {49}
Не лаптем щи хлебаем {51}
Не так страшен чёрт, как его малюют {50}
Не упоминай имя Господа своего всуе {49}
нести свой крест {50}
нечист на руку {47}
ночные бабочки {48}
Он лыка не вяжет {51}
Он не лыком шит {51}
оранжевые мамы оранжевые песни оранжево
    поют {44}
паршивая овца в стаде {45}
побелеть от страха {45}
покраснеть от злости / стыда {44}
послать его к чёртовой матери / бабушке {50}
представительницы древнейшей профессии {46}
презренный металл {46}
приказал долго жить {46}
Прости Господи! {48}
проститутка {48}
пускаться во все тяжкие {46}
Пусть нас "лапотной Россией" называет Вашингтон,
   Мы недавно запустили лапоть
   в сорок тысяч тонн {51}
 ради Бога {49}
Ради Бога, перестань называть меня 'малыш'! {49}
ради Христа {49}
русский городовой {48}
рыцари плаща и кинжала {46}
сапоги {52}
Сапожник без сапог {52}
свести счёты с жизнью {47}
свят-свят {49}
серые кардиналы {45}
сильные мира сего {47}
сильный {47}
синий от холода {45}
слава Богу {49}
слегка пьян, до синевы выбрит {45}
смотрит на мир сквозь розовые очки {45}
стражи порядка {46}
характеристика {51}
Христа ради {49}
чёрная зависть {45}
чёрные дни в истории {45}
чёрный юмор {45}

чёрт побери {50}
чёрта лысого ты получишь вместо денег {50}
чертовски хороша {50}
чертяка {50}
Это чёрт знает что! {50}
Японский Бог {48}
Японский городовой! {48}

RUSSLISH & BEYOND

а ля мужик {63}
аккуратная фигурка {54}
аккуратно {54}
актуальный {54}
актуальный вопрос {55}
альковные страсти {63}
амикошонство {64}
амурные дела {63}
баксы {60}
батлы {62}
без пальта {57}
белый пиар {60}
бланманже {64}
блезир {64}
блицкриг {58}
ботлы {62}
бренди {63}
брют {63}
будировать этот вопрос {64}
Велика Россия, а отступать некуда –
 позади Москва! {58}
Великая Отечественная Война {59}
видик {62}
вискарь {62}
вложить {58}
ВОВ {59}
вольвушник {62}
всенародный праздник единения партии
 и народа {60}
Вставай, страна огромная... {58}
вторая мировая война {59}
высадка союзников в Нормандии {59}
высокая мода {64}
высокая точность {54}
гамбургер {61}
гаупт-штурмбанфюрер {59}

Давайте без сантиментов {64}
джинсы {62}
для блезиру {64}
добить фашистскую гадину в её логове {59}
Долг платежом красен {63}
дринкануть {62}
другая альтернатива {57}
знак качества {60}
извиняюсь {58}
имидж {61}
импичмент {62, 64}
имплоймент брендинг {61}
интеллигент {58}
интеллигентно {55}
интеллигентность {54}
интеллигентный {54}
ихний / ихние {58}
кадровик {61}
кадровые {61}
кадры решают всё {61}
кантри {62}
кантрушник {62}
карт-бланш {64}
квартал {57}
класть {57}
клише {64}
кокотки {63}
комильфо {63}
компьютер {62}
консенсус {57}
корректно {55}
корректный {54}
крейзануться {62}
культ личности {60}
куртизанки {63}
лейбл {62}
лентяи {55}
ловбургер {61}
ложить {58}
лузер {55}
ленд-лиз {59}
людские ресурсы {61}
манкировал своими супружескими
    обязанностями {64}
масло масляное {57}
мерс {62}
моветон {63}

Мои пэрентцы сегодня домой не придут – давайте
    устроим у меня сэйшн и позовём герлов. {62}
на брудершафт {59}
на самом деле {54}
на халяву и уксус сладок {56}
народное хозяйство {60}
настоящий мужик {63}
натуральный {54}
некорректное поведение {54}
неудачник {55}
от кутюр {64}
отдел кадров {61}
открытие второго фронта {59}
па-де-де {64}
пальцем не пошевелит {55}
пелетон {64}
пиар {60}
пиариться {61}
пиаровская статья {60}
пиаровский {61}
пиарщик {61}
писюк {62}
план Барбаросса {58}
пленум {61}
по ленд-лизу {59}
по щучьему веленью, по моему хотенью {55}
победитель социалистического соревнования {60}
положить {58}
потенциальные возможности {57}
праздновать {56}
принтер {62}
просторечие {58}
противотанковые ежи {58}
прочный {54}
пуанты {64}
пэрентцы {62}
пюре {64}
пять тысяч рублей {62}
Работа не волк, в лес не убежит {56}
реально {54}
реальный шёлк {54}
рейтинг {61}
рулет {64}
самопиар {61}
сантименты {64}
сидюк {62}
Слово – не воробей, вылетит – не поймаешь. {54}

согласие {57}
солидно {54}
солидный {54}
сохранить нынешний статус-кво {57}
специалист по эйчар {61}
старик со старухой {55}
стейтсовый {62}
стопроцентный {54}
телик {62}
тен {62}
Третий Рейх {59}
трузера шузы {62}
туше {64}
тушёнка {59}
умно {55}
файлец {62}
файфушник {62}
фактически {54}
факультативный {65}
форс-мажор {65}
форсмажорные обстоятельства {64}
фрицы {59}
фуэте {64}
фэйс {62}
халтура {56}
халтурить {56}
халтурщик {56}
халява {56}
халявить {56}
халявный {56}
халявщик {56}
чёрный пиар {60}
чувства {64}
шампанское {63}
шёлк {54}
шерамыжник {65}
шерочка с машерочкой {65}
шипучее вино {63}
шнапс {59}
Шнеллер! {59}
щука {55}
эйчаровец {61}
эскапады {64}
Это актуальный вопрос {54}
я очень / сильно извиняюсь {58}

WAR & COMPETITION

Ах война, война-война, дурная девка –
   стерва она. {71}
Ах война, что ж ты, подлая, сделала {71}
Без этого хоккей потерял бы едва ли не половину
   своей зрелищной привлекательности {72}
беспроигрышную серию {72}
в гостях {73}
Великая Отечественная Война {70}
вне игры {73}
во второй лиге {72}
военная выправка {70}
военные {70}
военный трибунал {68}
Война кровь любит {71}
Война не лечит, а калечит {70}
Воюй не числом, а уменьем {70}
время приёма пищи {68}
все средства хороши {70}
Всё, отвоевался {70}
Вы трое – оба ко мне {69}
выносливость {72}
высоко держать планку {75}
Главное не победа – главное участие {73}
грубая игра {73}
губа {68}
Да не посрамим земли Русские, но ляжем костьми,
   мёртвы ибо срама не имам {70}
двойные ошибки, невынужденные ошибки {72}
дедовщина {68}
деды {68}
дембель {68}
держать удар {72}
живая сила {68}
задрать планку до заоблачных высот {75}
закончился ничьей {72}
компьютеры спаму не имут {70}
Кому война, а кому мать родна {71}
Копать от забора и до обеда {69}
Королева спорта {74}
левое плечо вперёд {68}
лёгкая атлетика {74}
личный состав {68}
мёртвые срама не имут {70}
Мы ещё повоюем {70}

На войне, как на войне {70}
на своём любимом покрытии {72}
на своём поле {73}
на скамейке запасных {72}
на чужом поле {73}
нарушения правил {73}
Наступил на землю русскую, да оступился {70}
начать спуртовать {74}
Не делаете умное лицо – Вы же офицер {69}
неуставные отношения {68}
новобранец {68}
нокаутировал {71}
О спорт! Ты мир! {71}
обязательная программа {71}
определить победителя по системе "гол+пас" {72}
освистаны {73}
Отогрелся в Москве, да замёрз на Березине {70}
первым делом – самолёты,
    ну а девушки – потом {69}
передать эстафетную палочку {75}
перловая каша {68}
плох тот солдат, который не мечтает стать
    генералом {69}
по очкам {71}
Повоевали – и будет {71}
по-военному чётко {71}
поднять планку {75}
поймать второе дыхание {74}
политика выкручивания рук {73}
поражать живую силу противника {68}
порядок в танковых войсках {69}
Посмотрим, как ты обязательную откатаешь {71}
поторопись {69}
правое плечо вперёд {68}
президентский марафон {74}
приказ о демобилизации {68}
принимают пищу {68}
произвольная программа {71}
пройти отборочный турнир {72}
пропустить много мячей {72}
салабон {68}
салага {68}
самоволка {68}
сбить дыхалку {74}
сойти с дистанции {74}
солдат спит, а служба идёт {69}
Такой хоккей нам не нужен {72}

толчковая нога {75}
тяжёлая атлетика {74}
тянуть время {73}
У кого толчковая – левая, а у меня
    толчковая – правая! {75}
убивать людей {68}
удалён с поля {72}
удаление {72}
удары ниже пояса {71}
устав {68}
Учиться военному делу настоящим образом {70}
фальстарт {74}
фигурное катание {71}
финишный рывок {74}
черпак {68}
черпать {68}
Шайбу! Шайбу! {72}
шире шаг {69}
шрапнель {68}
эстафета поколений {75}
Я на десять тыщ рванул, как на пятьсот,
    и спёкся {74}

Weather & Seasons

белые мухи {76}
в осень и у воробья пиво {80}
весеннее настроение {78}
Весна пришла – щепка на щепку падает {78}
вступит в свои права {77}
где раки зимуют {80}
генерал Зима {79}
гололёд {77}
готовь сани летом, а телегу – зимой {77, 79}
грибной дождь {78}
гром не грянет – мужик не перекрестится {78}
день чудесный {79}
дождь стеной {79}
его как ветром сдуло {77}
Жду ответа, как соловей лета {79}
зима настоящая {80}
Зима прошла, настало лето –
    спасибо партии за это {77}
зима-красна {79}
зимовать {80}
зимовье {79}

зимой и летом одним цветом {76}
зимостойкий {79}
Зимушка-зима {79}
Зимы ждала, ждала природа! {76}
знает, где раки зимуют {80}
и в зной, и в стужу {77}
И рады мы проказам матушки зимы {79}
играть в снежки {77}
ищи ветра в поле {78}
Как гром среди ясного неба {78}
как кот мартовский {78}
как рыба об лёд {76}
как снег на голову {77}
Крещенские морозы {79}
Лёд тронулся, командовать парадом буду я {76}
лепить снежную бабу {77}
лето припаси-ка, а зима прибери-ка {80}
лето пролежишь, зимой с сумой побежишь {79}
ль рады мы {79}
льёт, как из ведра {78}
Люблю грозу в начале мая... {78}
Май холодный – год хлебородный {78}
метель {77}
Мороз и солнце, день чудесный {80}
На дворе марток, надевай трое порток {77}
не по образцам зима и лето бывает,
   по воле божьей {80}
Ничего, как-нибудь перезимуем {80}
перезимовать {80}
показать, где раки зимуют {80}
после дождичка в четверг {79}
растает как первый снег {77}
расти, как грибы после дождя {78}
русская кость тепло любит {79}
Сейчас я ему покажу, где раки зимуют {80}
Сколько лет, сколько зим! {76}
снежная буря {77}
снегоуборочная машина {77}
собака лает – ветер носит {78}
сугробы {77}
То ли дождь – то ли снег, то ли будет –
   то ли нет {76}
У него зимой снега не выпросишь {76}
узнать, где раки зимуют {80}
Щепка {78}

эффект снежного кома {77}

Power & Glory

ажиотажный спрос {87}
Алло, дорогой Леонид Ильич слушает... {82}
аортокоронарное шунтирование {90}
аппарат {88}
Ах, вот где собака зарыта {94}
бандитский капитализм {90}
без царя в голове {84}
беспредел {91}
Боже царя храни {84}
Борис, ты не прав! {89}
ботать по фени {85}
бродячая {93}
будет хлеб – будет и песня {82}
в сортире террористов замочим {90}
в чулке {87}
век воли не видать! {85}
верный ленинец {82}
Вертикаль не абсолют {92}
взять политический реванш {87}
Воры в законе {86}
времена царя-Гороха {85}
Всевышний {91}
всмятку {91}
встреча без галстуков {90}
Второй срок {92}
высшая мера наказания {87}
вышка {87}
Геракл {88}
геронтократии {88}
гиперинфляция {87}
Голосуй сердцем! {90}
Голосуй, а то проиграешь {90}
дефолт {88}
Джентльмены удачи {85}
дойная корова {91}
домушник {86}
его ушли {88}
Если бы молодость знала,
   если бы старость могла {89}
Если мозги утекают, значит они есть {92}
За большие заслуги... {82}
За царя, за Родину, за веру {84}
за чертой бедности {87}
завязать {87}

заживает как на собаке {93}
Зато мы делаем ракеты и покоряем Енисей,
    а также в области балета мы впереди
    планеты всей {83}
зона {86}
и лично {82}
их кинули {88}
Интеллигенция – г**, а надо дело делать {91}
как собака на сене {93}
как собаке пятая нога {94}
карманы Гусинского {91}
катить бочку {86}
кинуть {88}
козла {92}
контролируемая эмиссия {89}
крепкое слово {91}
куда царь пешком ходил {84}
легавая собака {86}
легавый {86}
лепить горбатого {86}
лучше рубль в руке, чем два в банке {87}
Люди простят все, кроме вранья {92}
маленькая собачка – до старости {93}
маньяки и шпионы {91}
медвежатник {86}
мелкий политический деятель
    эпохи Аллы Пугачёвой {82}
мент {86}
Место встречи изменить нельзя {86}
милостивый государь {84}
младогегельянцы {88}
младореформаторы {87}
мокрое дело {86}
мокрушник {86}
молодо – зелено {88}
молодым везде у нас дорога,
    старикам везде у нас почёт {88}
моргать {85}
мочить в сортире {91}
мусор {86}
наградил по-царски {84}
не царское это дело {84}
Не знаю, как там в Лондоне, не была.
    Может там собака друг человека.
    У нас – управдом друг человека. {93}
непереводимая игра слов {91}
Обижаешь, начальник! Мокрое дело шьёшь {87}

оленина по-царски {84}
олигархи {91}
олигархический капитализм {88}
он завязал {87}
от Ильича до Ильича {82}
отпущения {92}
паника в магазинах {87}
параша {86}
Пасть порву! Моргалы выколю! {85}
первый президент России {89}
Первый срок {91}
перо {86}
по бумажке {82}
под матрацем {87}
пока уляжется пыль {87}
преемник {90}
Президент работает с документами {89}
преступная халатность {83}
принципиальную оценку {83}
просвещённый чекист {91}
Проси больше, дадут, сколько нужно. {92}
Простите меня {90}
Путинки {91}
пушка {86}
пьяницы и матершинники {91}
пятая нога {94}
разборки {85}
расколоться {86}
раскрученный бренд {92}
редиска {85}
рейганомика должна быть рейганомной {83}
рецидивист {87}
розовая {87}
рокировочка {90}
рубль упал {88}
рукопожатие {91}
сбросить рубли {87}
сделать обрезание {91}
съедает рублёвые сбережения {87}
Слушай, что тебе царь говорит {84}
собака – друг человека {93}
собачья жизнь {93}
сосиски сраные {83}
социалистические страны {83}
срок мотать {87}
стоять на шухере {86}
стукачи {86}

Тяжела ты, шапка Мономаха! {85}
тяжеловес {88}
тянуть на себя одеяло {85}
У нас есть старинная русская
   забава – поиск виновных {92}
У нас такой умный пёсик... {94}
у президента крепкое рукопожатие {89}
халатность {83}
хозяин {93}
хочу – казню, хочу – милую {84}
Царская охота {84}
чифирь {86}
Шарик {93}
шариковщина {93}
шестёрка {86}
шить дело {86}
щенок на охоту ехать – собак кормить {93}
экономика должна быть экономной {83}
Это полная чушь, несуразица, сапоги всмятку. {91}
Я вообще не знаю, что там можно написать.
   Я бы лично про себя столько не смог
   написать {92}
я лягу на рельсы {89}
яйцо всмятку {91}

Flora & Fauna

А потому обычай мой: с волками иначе не делать
   мировой, как снявши шкуру с них долой {103}
А ты огурцом {107}
Антошка-Антошка – пойдём копать картошку {96}
Ах ты, поганка! {99}
белая смерть {100}
белуга {105}
белый гриб {98}
биться, как рыба об лёд {105}
бледная поганка {99}
блеять {102}
боровик {98}
В какой малинник ты попал! {97}
В огороде бузина–а в Киеве дядька {97}
водяной {99}
волк в овечьей шкуре {104}
Волка ноги кормят {103}
волчий аппетит {103}
воробей {102}

ворона {101}
всю малину испортил {97}
второй хлеб {96}
гав-гав {101}
Где огурцы, тут и пьяницы {107}
грибник {98}
грибница {98}
грибной дождь {98}
грибные места {98}
гудит как улей {100}
дать по тыкве {108}
Дед плачет, бабка плачет–а курочка кудахчет: "Не
    плачь дед, не плачь бабка, я снесу Вам другое
    яичко–не простое, а золотое {101}
детей находят в капусте {96}
Её можно трясти, как грушу {97}
ему медведь на ухо наступил {104}
Если бы да кабы, да во рту росли грибы (то был бы
    не рот, а целый огород {99}
есть и моя доля в бочке мёда {100}
Ешь пирог с грибами, а язык держи за зубами {99}
жало у пчёлки знаешь где? {101}
жало {101}
Жареная рыбка... {106}
Живу я, как поганка – а мне летать охота! {99}
жизнь – не сахар {100}
за грибами! {98}
змея {102}
знаем, проходили! {104}
и овцы целы – и волки сыты {104}
И решил несчастный... {106}
и-го-го {101}
изрубить в капусту {108}
каждая собака знает {104}
Каждому овощу – свой срок {96}
как медведь в берлоге {100}
как об стенку горох {96}
как огурчик {96}
как пчёлы на мёд {100}
как рыба в воде {105}
как рыбке зонтик {105}
как сельди в бочке {105}
как сморщенный гриб {99}
как собака на сене {104}
как собаке пятая нога {104}
Какой малинник {97}
Какой фрукт выискался. {96}

капуста зелёная {107}
карась {106}
кар-кар {101}
каркать {101}
картофельное поле {96}
картофельные бунты {96}
клубничка {97}
клюква {97}
коза {102}
кровь-морковь {96}
крякать {102}
кря-кря {102}
кудахтать {101}
кудах-тах-тах {101}
кукарекать {101}
ку-ка-ре-ку {101}
ку-ку {102}
кукушка {102}
Кукушка-кукушка, сколько мне жить? {102}
лаять на кого-то {102}
лаяться с кем-то {102}
Ловить рыбу в мутной воде {105}
ложка дёгтя в бочке мёда {100}
луковица {108}
Маленькая рыбка лучше большого таракана {105}
малина {97}
медведь на ухо наступил {100}
медвежья болезнь {100}
медвежья услуга {103}
медовый месяц {99}
м-е-е {102}
му-у-у {101}
мычать {101}
мяукать {101}
мяу-мяу {101}
на безрыбье и рак рыба {105}
На нём как на собаке всё заживает {104}
на халяву – и уксус сладок {100}
На хрен мне это {108}
назвался груздем–полезай в кузов {98}
накаркать {102}
начистить репу {108}
Не ела душа чесноку, так и не воняет {107}
не каркай {102}
Не мешок картошки {107}
Небось картошку все мы уважаем, если
    намять её с сольцой? {96}

ни рыба, не мясо {105}
Никто не водится со мной {99}
нос картошкой {96}
О, наши русские коалы! {103}
огород {97}
оказать медвежью услугу {100}
она всех щучит {105}
осетрина {105}
охренеть {108}
панкующая редиска {107}
петух {101}
Петя-петушок {101}
пить как сапожник {105}
По грибы! {98}
поганка {99}
подберёзовик {98}
подосиновик {98}
подсластить пилюлю {100}
покраснел, как помидор {96}
половина сахар – половина мёд {100}
посылать на хрен {108}
Прости, дяденька {103}
проще пареной репы {107}
раскудахталась! {102}
растут как грибы после дождя {98}
реветь белугой {105}
редиска {96}
репа {107}
ржать {101}
Рыба она так себе, толку от неё мало, а трески
   много. Как начнёт трещать – хоть вон беги {105}
с волками жить – по-волчьи выть {103}
с утра до ночи судачит {105}
селёдка {105}
сёмга {105}
Сиди–не кукарекай! {102}
сколько мёд ни говори – во рту слаще не станет {99}
Собака – друг человека! {104}
собака лает – ветер носит {104}
Собаке – собачья смерть {104}
собачья жизнь {104}
спелый персик {96}
Старичок Судачок {105}
старый гриб {99}
судак {105}
судачить {105}
Так шуми же мутная... {106}

таракан {106}
Таракан сидит в стакане... {106}
твоими устами да мёд пить {100}
треска {105}
трещать {105}
трудятся как пчёлки {99}
Ты мне друг или картошка? {107}
тыква {108}
У меня голова трещит {105}
уверенность в завтрашнем дне {102}
укутан как капуста {96}
утка {102}
участки {99}
Фефочка, скажи: ыыба {105}
форель {105}
ходить за грибами {98}
хрен редьки не слаще {108}
хрен с ним {108}
хреновина, хренотень, хрень {108}
хреновый {108}
хрюкать {102}
хрю-хрю {102}
цокать {101}
цок-цок {101}
цыплёнок {102}
цып-цып-цып {102}
Чеснок семь недугов изводит {107}
Чеснок толчёный, да таракан печёный {107}
честный вор {107}
чик-чирик {102}
чирикать {102}
чтобы жизнь мёдом не казалась {100}
шипеть {102}
шут гороховый {96}
ш-ш-ш {102}
щука {105}
щучить {105}
это камень в мой огород? {97}
это не картошка {107}
Эх, жизнь моя жестянка – ну её в болото {99}
Я водяной–я водяной {99}
Яблоко от яблони недалеко падает {96}

Moscow & St. Petersburg

аристократы {112}
Библиотека имени Ленина {111}
большая деревня, {112}
брать в жёны {112}
Будет и на нашей улице праздник {111}
В Ленинграде женихи, в Москве невесты. {112}
В Москве играют,
  в Ленинграде пляшут. {112}
В Москве чихнут,
  в Ленинграде аспирин принимают. {112}
выходить (идти) замуж {112}
город на семи холмах {110}
Да здравствует Москва и
  да погибнет Петербург! {112}
Дискотека имени Леннона {111}
жениться {112}
Завтра в Москве ожидается один градус.
  В Петербурге – совершенно другой {113}
Замоскворечье {111}
Золотая моя столица, дорогая моя Москва {110}
Конспект Маркса {111}
лимитчики {110}
лужа {111}
москаль {113}
Москва – третий Рим, а четвёртого не будет {110}
Москва выросла, Петербург выращен. {111}
Москва не сразу строилась {110}
Москва слезам не верит {110}
Москва создана веками, Питер миллионами {111}
Московская прописка {110}
От копеечной свечи Москва сгорела {111}
Петербургу суждено окончить
  свои дни, уйдя в финское болото. {111}
Питер женится, Москва замуж идёт / берёт. {112}
Питер строился рублями, Москва – веками {111}
Подмосковные вечера {110}
пушка {111}
Пушкинская площадь {111}
Что за петербуржство? {112}
Что ни город – то норов {110}

Life & Death

А мы и не торопимся {119}
бандитская пуля {117}
борьба за выживание {120}
бытовая травма {117}
быть по жизни оптимистом {120}
бычок {119}
в душном помещении {116}
вопрос жизни или смерти {120}
Вспомню я пехоту и родную роту,
    и тебя за то, что дал мне закурить. {118}
выжить {120}
гаечный ключ {121}
головная боль {116}
гусарский насморк {117}
Давай закурим {119}
дали прикурить {118}
Двум смертям не бывать,
    а одной не миновать {120}
Дело – табак! {119}
до свадьбы заживёт {117}
докторское 'мы' {117}
Друг, оставь покурить, а в ответ – тишина,
    это он не вернулся из боя. {118}
Дружба дружбой, а табачок врозь {119}
если смерти, то мгновенной,
    если раны – небольшой {120}
Жив курилка? {119}
живот {120}
жизненно важно {120}
жизни или смерти {120}
жизнь бьёт ключом {121}
Жизнь как смертельная болезнь
    передающаяся половым путём {120}
забычковать {119}
заживать {120}
зажигалка {119}
Закурить не найдётся? {119}
здоровый образ жизни {117}
Здоровья в аптеке не купишь {116}
зуб дёргает {117}
зуб ноет {117}
Их уровень смерти, это наш уровень жизни {120}
как мы себя чувствуем {117}

ключ {121}
кто не курит и не пьёт, тот
    здоровеньким помрёт {116}
курево закончилось {119}
Куренье – медленная смерть {119}
Куренье вред, а некурящих нет {119}
курилка {119}
лечиться даром – даром лечиться {116}
лучше не бывает {121}
махорка {118}
Минздрав СССР предупреждает
    – куренье опасно для Вашего здоровья {119}
мне нездоровится, я себя
    неважно/паршиво/погано чувствую {116}
мочи нет терпеть {117}
мундштук {118}
на что жалуемся {117}
Не жизнь, а существование {120}
не на жизнь, а на смерть {120}
не щадя живота своего {120}
Но дым Отечества нам сладок и приятен {118}
Но мы то не лошади! {119}
обживать новое жильё {120}
обойтись народными/домашними
    рецептами/средствами {116}
обыкновенная царапина {117}
Одна капля никотина убивает лошадь {119}
он по жизни ... он вообще такой по жизни {121}
от всех болезней нам полезней
    солнце, воздух и вода {116}
пенсионный возраст {120}
Пережить это смутное время. {120}
перекур {119}
пломбировать канал {117}
по голове {121}
побаливает {117}
понос {116}
похмелье {116}
Прожиточный минимум {120}
производственная травма {117}
Разве это жизнь?! {121}
Разрешите прикурить? {119}
расстройство желудка {116}
с мёдом {117}
синяк под глазом {117}
средняя продолжительность жизни {120}
терпеть можно {117}

У Вас не найдётся огоньку? {119}
У Вас сигареточки не будет? {119}
у меня голова раскалывается ог башка болит {116}
уживаться с {120}
фингал {117}
хоть на стенку лезь {117}
царапина {117}
чай с малиной {117}
что, трубы горят? {116}
шрамы украшают мужчину {117}

WOMEN & MEN

баба моя {128}
бабник {127}
близкая родственница по линии сына {128}
брак без брака {127}
брак по любви {126}
брак по расчёту {126}
Венера {129}
вести себя как джентльмен {130}
вечеринка {129}
влюбиться по уши {126}
Восьмое марта {129}
вот это речь не мальчика, но мужа {125}
втрескаться в кого-то {126}
втюриться в кого-то {126}
Выходи за меня замуж {127}
гадюка {128}
голубка {128}
Горько! {127}
грымза {128}
Да, ребята ... {125}
Давай поженимся {127}
День Святого Валентина {129}
дорогуша {128}
душа в душу {129}
Его послали ... {130}
если ты мужчина {124}
железная леди {125}
жена без мужа вдовы хуже {125}
жёнушка {128}
ЗАГС {127}
зайка {128}
закадрить {130}
заниматься любовью {127}

запасть на кого-то {126}
Золотко {128}
кадр {126}
кадрить {126, 130}
Кадры решают всё! {126}
как за каменной стеной {127}
киса {128}
кисуль {128}
клеить {126}
клюшка {128}
кобра {128}
комплименты {129}
котя {128}
курочка {128}
лапа – лапуля {128}
Леночка, Наташенька, Машуля {129}
любовница / любовник {127, 130}
Любовь зла – полюбишь и козла {126}
любовь с первого взгляда {126, 130}
мальчик для битья {125}
мальчишник {125}
Марс {129}
мастер на все руки {127}
мегера {128}
медовый месяц {127}
между нами, девочками, говоря {124}
мой сладкий {128}
Молодые, поздравьте друг друга! {127}
мужеподобная {125}
мужественное лицо {124}
мужественность {124}
мужик в юбке {125}
мужская профессия {125}
мужской разговор {124}
мы встречаемся {130}
Мы с Наташей решили пожениться {127}
Надюша {129}
настоящий мужик {124}
настоящий русский язык {125}
нахал {130}
Нет такого мужа, который не
   мечтал бы хоть на час стать холостяком {125}
Ну, вообще {125}
О! Мальчик {125}
оказывать знаки внимания {129}
Он к ней пристаёт {130}
Он положил на неё глаз {130}

Она его закадрила {130}
Она сводит меня с ума {126}
Она строит ему глазки {130}
отшили {130}
парень {130}
первое свидание {130}
подарки {129}
подъехать {130}
подкаблучник {128}
подкаблучный муж {128}
подкатывать / подкатить к кому-нибудь {126}
Пойдём куда-нибудь сегодня вечером? {129}
показали себя настоящими мужиками {125}
по-мужски {124}
Потанцуем? {130}
поужинать в ресторане {129}
пощёчина {130}
предложить руку и сердце {126}
приставания {130}
приставать {130}
противоположный пол {129}
путь к сердцу мужчины лежит через желудок {130}
пятилетка {127}
развлечься {129}
Разрешите вас пригласить {129}
Разрешите за вами поухаживать? {129}
рыбка {128}
рыбонька {128}
свидание {129}
сделать предложение {126}
сексистское общество {130}
Сказка о рыбаке и рыбке {129}
солнышко моё {128}
спросите чего полегче {125}
стать мужчиной {125}
счастливые часов не наблюдают {129}
тёща {129}
тусоваться {129}
тусовка {129}
ты не мужик, а тряпка {125}
Ты пойдёшь со мной на вечеринку? {129}
Ты уже не мальчик, юный барабанщик {125}
У тебя есть девушка/ молодой человек? {130}
ухаживать за кем-то {126, 129}
ходить по бабам {127}
холостяк {125}
Холостякуешь {125}

человек {130}
Что я тебе, мальчик?! {125}
швабра {128}
Я клею её {126}
Я прошу руки Вашей дочери {127}
Я хотел / хотела пригласить тебя в кино {129}

Figures & Measures

50-я годовщина {136}
в шесть часов {136}
важный момент в докладе {135}
Великой Октябрьской Социалистической... {136}
вечернее заседание {136}
вечерний сеанс {136}
во второй половине дня {136}
восьмое чудо света {134}
два раза по пятьдесят / сто пятьдесят! {133, 137}
Для милого дружка и
   семь вёрст не околица {134}
дорого яичко к Христову дню {136}
железно {133}
за плечами {137}
за семью морями {134}
знаток {132}
катенька {132}
Лучше один раз увидеть,
   чем сто раз услышать {132}
минуточку {135}
Момент – сейчас приду {135}
момент в жизни {135}
на днях {136}
На днях он Вам даст ответ {136}
на семи холмах {134}
нам хорошо за сорок {137}
Не дал Бог ста рублей, а пятьдесят не деньги {137}
Не имей сто рублей, а имей сто друзей {132}
Ну что мне, сто раз надо повторять?! {132}
нужно учесть этот момент {135}
няня {136}
Один с сошкой, а семеро с ложкой {134}
оперативно {135}
От всей души поздравляю ... {136}
по сто пятьдесят {133}
полтинник {136}
После обеда {136}

Поспешишь, людей насмешишь {135}
пуд {133}
пятидесятилетие {136}
пятидесятники {137}
пятьдесят грамм {137}
пятьдесят на пятьдесят {137}
расходов на полтинник,
  а пользы на грош {137}
Семеро одного не ждут {133}
семи смертям не бывать, одной не миновать {134}
семибанкирщина {134}
семибоярщина {134}
Семичастный {134}
семь бед – один ответ {134}
Семь невест Ефрейтора Збруева {134}
Семь раз отмерь – один раз отрежь {133}
Семь стариков и одна девушка {134}
семь чудес света {134}
сию минуту {135}
созвониться {135}
сотки {133}
сотня, сотенная, сотняга {132}
сто лет он мне не нужен {132}
сто лет он мне не приснился {132}
Сто пудов! {133}
стольник {132}
стольничек {132}
стопудово, {133}
стопудовый хит {133}
У меня в кармане честная сотня... {132}
У семи нянек дитя без глазу {134}
уже седьмой час {136}
фифти-фифти {137}
фронтовые сто грамм {133}
часов в шесть {136}
Чёрная сотня {133}
черносотинцы {133}
Что? Где? Когда? {132}
шесть соток {133}
Я был на седьмом небе от счастья. {133}
Я об этом узнал на днях {136}

Music & Art

А вы, друзья, как ни садитесь,
  всё в музыканты не годитесь {141}
а осетрина-то с душком {143}
А судьи кто? {142}
акробатические трюки {145}
анималист {147}
Арлекины и пираты, циркачи и акробаты {145}
балдеть {146}
баталист {147}
без страховки {145}
бизнесмены {142}
близнецы-братья {149}
большое видится на расстоянии {150}
борзые щенки {143}
борзыми щенками {143}
братан {141}
в кустах случайно оказался рояль {141}
В ловких и натруженных руках {145}
в ритме вальса {141}
Важнейшим из всех искусств
  для нас является кино {144}
вечный бой {150}
вживую {147}
видак {147}
Волк и заяц, тигры в клетке –
  все они марионетки {145}
Вон из Москвы, сюда я больше не ездок {142}
Все счастливые семьи похожи
  друг на друга, каждая несчастливая
  семья несчастлива по-своему {143}
Вышел на Дворжак, кругом один Мусоргский,
  выпил Чайковского, в животе–Пучини. {140}
голая {148}
Горбушка {146}
Горе от ума {142}
Да, скифы мы. Да, азиаты мы... {150}
диски {146}
достойно кисти Айвазовского {147}
Жаль только жить в эту пору прекрасную
  уж не придётся ни мне, ни тебе {150}
живая музыка {146}
задавать тон {141}
задеть струну {141}
запилы {146}

И вечный бой! Покой нам только снится {150}
И невозможное возможно {150}
И факир,чей вид внушает страх {145}
игра свето-тени {147}
играл первую скрипку {141}
играть с листа {141}
играют мимо нот {142}
Из искры возгорится пламя {150}
Интересное кино! {144}
к топору зовите Русь {149}
Карету мне, карету! {142}
Кающаяся Магдалина {148}
Кина не будет – электричество кончилось! {144}
киношка {144}
копия всегда хуже оригинала {148}
краткость – сестра таланта {143}
Кто платит, тот и заказывает музыку {141}
культурный {142}
кустодиевские женщины {148}
лабал {147}
лабать на саксе {146}
лабух {147}
левитановская осень {148}
Ловкость рук – и никакого мошенничества! {145}
лубок {148}
лубочность {148}
мазня {147}
маниловщина {143}
маринист {147}
Машина Времени {145}
медленный {146}
медляк {146}
Мёртвые души {143}
металлисты {146}
Может, Чайковского {140}
Мужчиной можешь ты не быть,
  но джентльменом быть обязан {150}
музон {146}
Мы будем снимать кино или
  мы не будем снимать кино?! {145}
Мы любим людей за то добро,
  которое им делаем и ненавидим их
  за то зло, которое им причиняем {143}
на видеке/на видаке {144}
на мажорной ноте {141}
нагая {148}

настроен на минорный лад {141}
наступать на горло собственной песне {149}
натурщица / натурщик {147}
натюрморт {148}
Но дым отечества нам сладок и приятен {142}
Ну ты циркач! {145}
обнажённая {148}
он действует мне на нервы {141}
он играет у меня на нервах {141}
оркестрирована {141}
отрываться {146}
панорама, диорама {148}
пастельные тона {147}
пачкотня {147}
пейзажист {147}
пели под фанеру {146}
передвижники {148}
Перо вновь приравняли к штыку {149}
петь вживую {146}
под фанеру {147}
подбирать на слух {141}
покой нам только снится {150}
попса {146}
попсовик {147}
портретист {147}
постельные {148}
поэт в России, больше чем поэт {149}
поэтом можешь ты не быть,
    но гражданином быть обязан {149}
разыграна как по нотам {141}
Ревизор {143}
с корабля на бал {142}
с листа {141}
сакс {147}
сапожник {145}
сидюки {146}
сольник {146}
соляк {147}
Счастливые часы не наблюдают {142}
тащиться {146}
тащиться от Клинтона {147}
толстовщина, {143}
триптих {148}
у меня пучит живот, {140}
Умом Россию не понять {150}
Факир был пьян – фокус не удался {146}
факир на час {145}

фанера {146}
фанерщик {146}
фокусник {145}
фокус-покус {146}
Цирк – да и только {145}
Чай не водка–много не выпьешь. {140}
Чайковский {140}
Человек в футляре {143}
человек-оркестр {141}
Чем меньше женщину мы любим,
   тем легче нравимся мы ей {150}
Что за комиссия, Создатель,
   быть взрослой дочери отцом!? {142}
Что станет говорить княгиня
   Марья Алексеевна? {142}
чумовой {146}
чумовой медляк {146}
шедевр {147}
шишкинский лес {148}
Это полотно принадлежит {147}
этюд {148}
Я беру взятки, но борзыми щенками {143}
Я сегодня прямо с корабля на бал {142}
Я хочу, чтоб к штыку приравняли перо {149}

Food & Drink

А мне в чужом пиру похмелье {160}
алаверды {158}
бодать {157}
бодун {157}
Будет тебе там и ванна, и кофе,
   будет и какао с чаем! {153}
быть навеселе {152}
в доску {156}
в дугу {156}
в дым {152}
в дымину {156}
в лоскут {156}
в нетрезвом состоянии {159}
в пьянстве замечен не был,
   но по утрам пил холодную воду {160}
в сиську {152}
в сосиску {152}
в стельку {156}
В Тулу со своим самоваром не ездят. {155}

в хлам {152, 156}
вдрызг {156}
веселие Руси есть пити – не можем мы без того
  быти {152}
водка бывает хорошей и очень хорошей {159}
водочка {160}
Вы не будете чаёвничать? {154}
выпить / выпивать {155}
Выпьешь чайку – позабудешь тоску {154}
вытрезвитель {159}
галстук {156}
Глядя на пиво – хорошо и плясать {152}
голова как пивной котёл {153}
губит людей не пиво, губит людей вода {153}
дёрнуть {156}
дерябнуть {156}
джигит {158}
до белой горячки {152}
дразнить унитаз {159}
ёрш {153}
за знакомство {157}
За нас с Вами и за чёрт с ними! {158}
за перспективу {158}
загудеть {156}
закладывать за воротник {156}
залить глаза {152}
запить {156}
запой {156}
здоровенная/офигенная {153}
зюзя {156}
и ванна, и кофе, и какао с чаем {155}
И я там был, мёд-пиво пил,
  по усам текло, а в рот не попало {153}
квасить {156}
колдырнуть {156}
Кулик {155}
куликать {155}
между первой и второй пуля не полетела {157}
между первой и второй
  перерывчик небольшой {157}
меры в женщинах и в пиве
  он не знал и не хотел {153}
на бровях {152}
на брудершафт {158}
на посошок {159}
на ты {158}
набраться {155}

надраться {152, 156}
надринькаться {156}
надрызгаться {156}
нажраться {152, 155}
наесться {152}
назюзюкаться {152, 156}
Назюзюкался, Иван Романыч!
　　Молодец! In vino veritas, говорили древние. {156}
наканифолиться {156}
накачаться {155}
накваситься {155}
накероситься {156}
наклюкаться {155}
налакаться {155}
нализаться {152, 155}
налимониться {156}
напиться в дрезину, в лом, в дрибодан {152}
Напиться до положения риз {152}
Не угодно ли чаю откушать {154}
Ну, если только на чашку чаю. {154}
ну, клюкнул, мерзавец, маленько...
　　на гривенник, что ли, клюкнул? {155}
обезвоживание {160}
один удар по почкам заменяет кружку пива {153}
опохмелиться {153, 160}
ослиная моча {153}
от пива будешь писать криво {153}
пейте, люди, пиво пенное –
　　будет морда обалденная {153}
перепить любого {157}
пивка для рывка {152}
пить чай {154}
Плохо организованное
　　похмелье переходит в запой. {160}
поддать / поддавать {155}
полечиться {160}
политика кнута и пряника {155}
после первой не закусывают {157}
посох {159}
похмелье {157, 159}
похмелюга {157}
принять {155}
пряник {155}
пьяный {156}
рассол {160}
риза {152}
рывок {152}

с бодуна {157}
с пивом/под пиво сойдёт {153}
с похмелья {157}
самовар {155}
Сказал бы словцо – да уж выпито пивцо {152}
со свиданием {157}
сообразить на троих {156}
тамада {157}
тёща {154}
тостующий пьёт до дна {157}
требуйте долива после отстоя пены {153}
Третьим будешь? {156}
трубы горят {160}
Тульский пряник {155}
уйти в запой {156}
упился медами, опехмелялся слезами {159}
характеристика {160}
хобот {156}
чаёвничать {154}
чай гонять {154}
Чай пить – не дрова рубить {154}
Чрезмерное употребление алкоголя вредит вашему
  здоровью! {157}
Что-то стало холодать –
  не пора ли нам поддать? {155}
Что ты сияешь как самовар? {155}
Что, даже чаю не попьёте? {154}
я вчера перебрал {159}

Etiquette & Deceptions

А я, знаете ли, предпочитаю... {163}
авось {169}
Авось не бог, а полбога есть {170}
Авось, обойдётся {169}
Авось, пронесёт {169}
Авось, проскочу {169}
Авось, само пройдёт {169}
авоська {170}
Береги платье снову, а честь смолоду {167}
бесплатный сыр бывает только в мышеловке {166}
битва за урожай {164}
будем говорить {163}
ввёл меня в заблуждение {166}
видите ли {163}
Вот угодил-так угодил {162}

Даже не знаю {163}
дар Божий {162}
дарёное не дарят {163}
дарёному коню в зубы не смотрят {162}
дарственная надпись {162}
динамист {165}
дорог не подарок – дорого внимание {163}
дорого яичко к Христову дню {162}
дурак {168}
духи, цветы и разные безделушки {163}
Зачем мне совесть? Я не богатый. {167}
Звезда пленительного счастья {166}
Знаете ли? {163}
значит {164}
и смех, и грех {171}
Идите вы на фиг, я сам заблудился! {166}
Как меня угораздило! {169}
Как мне повезло! {169}
Как я мог так лохануться?! {166}
какие-нибудь часики {163}
Как-то не сложилось {169}
кидалово {165}
кидать / кинуть {165}
кинуть кого-то на деньги {165}
книга – лучший подарок {162}
короче {164}
Кошелёк потерялся {169}
кривая вывезет {170}
крутить динамо {165}
Куда ты привёл нас, Сусанин Иван? {166}
лентяи {168}
лопнуть от смеха {171}
лототрон {165}
лох {165}
лохотронщик {166}
лузер {168}
мне даже неудобно {163}
мошенник {166}
мошенничество {166}
на авось {170}
на всякий случай {170}
На дурака не нужен нож, ему с три
  короба соврёшь и делай с ним что хошь {165}
на халяву {166}
на халяву и уксус сладок {168}
Надо решить вопрос с бухгалтером {164}

Не во всякой туче гром; а и гром да не грянет;
  а и грянет, да не по нас;
  а и по нас – авось не убьёт. {170}
Не обещайте деве юной любови
  вечной на земле... {166}
не путать божий дар с яичницей {163}
непредсказуемый {169}
неудачник {168}
Но ты же обещал! {166}
обещания {166}
Обещанного три года ждут. {166}
обманутые ожидания {166}
Обошлось {170}
Ожидания – самый скучный повод. {166}
она меня продинамила {165}
Она подарила мне сына {163}
пальцем не пошевелит {168}
первоапрельская шутка {171}
Первого апреля никому не верь. {171}
по щучьему веленью, по моему хотенью {168}
Поавоськаем: авось,
  до чего-нибудь доавоськаемся {170}
Поле чудес в стране дураков {165}
Понадеялся на русский авось {170}
понимаешь {163}
Правда –хорошо, а счастье – лучше {167}
праздновать {169}
применять его на практике {166}
продинамить {165}
Пронесло {170}
процесс пошёл {164}
Работа не волк, в лес не убежит. {169}
рабочий день {169}
с хитрецой {165}
с хитринкой {165}
самая читающая нация в мире {162}
сверхъестественный {169}
сказки {168}
случай {169}
смех – лучшее лекарство {171}
смех без причины – признак дурачины {171}
смех сквозь слёзы {171}
смеха боится даже тот, кто ничего не боится {172}
смешинка в рот попала {171}
смеялись до упаду {171}
смеяться от всей души {171}

Смеяться, право, не грешно
 над всем, что кажется смешно. {171}
старик со старухой {168}
Так получилось {169}
так сказать {163}
трагикомедия {171}
Ты, ты-ты кинула, ты {165}
Тьмы низких истин нам
 дороже нас возвышающий обман {165}
у него рот до ушей {171}
У них не сложилось {169}
У тебя вообще совесть есть или нет? {167}
удача {169}
фатализм {169}
халтура / халтурить {169}
халтурщик {169}
халява / халявить {168}
халявный {168}
халявщик {168}
хаханьки {172}
хватит разводить хиханьки да хаханьки {171}
Хитрость – второй ум {165}
хитрый {165}
хиханьки {172}
хорошо смеется тот,
 кто смеётся без последствий {172}
хорошо смеется тот, кто смеется последним {171}
хохотун / хохотунья {171}
хуже нет, чем ждать и догонять {167}
что вижу, то и пою {166}
щука {168}
Этот вопрос решается. {164}
юмор – это когда страшно хочется смеяться;
 а сатира – это когда хочется
 смеяться, а страшно {172}
Я об этом мечтал всю свою жизнь,
 подарок моей мечты {162}
Я потерял кошелёк {169}
Я сам обманываться рад. {167}
Я собирался, но не получилось {169}

Linguistics & Ephemera

А вы и ухом не моргнули {174}
апплет {180}
аська {181}

ася {181}
Баба с возу – кобыле легче {174}
бабуля {176}
баннеры {180}
Без определённого места жительства {178}
Без пруда не выловишь и рыбку из него / рыбки из пруда {174}
безалаберный американец {180}
безалкогольное пиво {179}
бесплатное лечение {179}
блог {180}
бомж {178}
браузер {180}
Брежнев умер, но тело его живёт {175}
бутылка {175}
Бутылочку водочки и пару бутылочек пивка. {175}
варез {181}
век живи, век учись {183}
вешать лапшу на уши {174}
винчестер {182}
вирус {180}
вкусный гамбургер {179}
второгодник {182}
вычислительные машины {180}
ГАИ {178}
гаишники {178}
ГКЧП {177}
главная страница {181}
глюк {181}
горькая сладость {179}
Государственная автомобильная инспекция {178}
государственный деятель {179}
дайлап {181}
двадцаточку {176}
двоечники, {182}
двойка {182}
дедовщина {176}
деды {176}
деньжищи {177}
деревенщина {177}
дизайнер {180}
дневник {181}
добрая тёща {179}
доступ {181}
драйв {182}
единица {182}
ежовщина {176}

железный Феликс {179}
жёсткий диск {182}
загружать {181}
зачётная книжка/ зачётка {182}
звонилка {181}
зелёные {176}
И баба с возу, и волки сыты {174}
и глазом не моргнул {174}
И овцы целы, и волки сыты {174}
и ухом не повёл {174}
иностранщина {176}
Интернет-провайдер {181}
Как обычно, сынок. {176}
Камчатка {182}
качалка {181}
качать, скачивать, откачивать {181}
КГБ {178}
кол {182}
коллективное хозяйство {178}
колхоз {178}
коммунистический союз молодёжи {178}
комп {180}
комсомол {178}
КПСС {178}
культурная революция {179}
Ленин умер, но дело его живёт {175}
логин {180}
локальный {182}
лытдыбр {181}
Любишь кататься – люби и катайся {174}
Любишь кататься – люби и саночки возить {174}
мастер {180}
математическое обеспечение {180}
математичка {182}
менеджер {180}
милостивый государь {179}
Милые бранятся – только тешатся / чешутся. {175}
мне не нужны твои ЦУ {177}
модем {181}
Мы рождены, чтоб Кафку / сказку
    сделать былью {175}
Мыло {181}
Не боги / йоги горшки обжигают {174}
Не плюй в колодец, вылетит – не поймаешь {174}
Не по Сеньке шапка {175}
Не по Хуану сомбреро {175}
не учи учёного {183}

небольшая толпа {179}
негостеприимный русский {180}
неграмотный {175}
неопрятный француз {180}
неприкосновенный запас {177}
неуд {182}
неудовлетворительно {182}
НЗ {177}
НКВД {178}
общага {183}
общежитие {183}
оксюморон {179}
ОМОН {178}
он испытывал лёгкую тяжесть в ногах {179}
отличники {182}
отряд милиции особого назначения {178}
оффтопик {180}
пара {182}
пароль {180}
пассворд {180}
ПК – персональный компьютер {180}
ПМО {180}
повторенье – мать ученья {183}
подсказывать {182}
полезная пепси-кола {180}
Политбюро {178}
портвешок {175}
поставить/ влепить {182}
посты {180}
Почём Марльборо, бабуля? {176}
Почему мой друг – да потому, что я жизнь учил не
    по учебникам, просто я работаю
    волшебником {183}
провалиться на экзамене {183}
прога {180}
программное обеспечение {180}
программно-математическое обеспечение {180}
прогуливать уроки {182}
пятёрка {182}
Россия-Матушка {175}
Рунет {181}
русичка {182}
сайт {180}
Сдаёте зелёненькие? {176}
сдувать, содрать {182}
секрет полишинеля {179}

секретный сотрудник {177}
сексот {177}
сервер {181}
серфинг {180}
сеть {182}
Сигареточкой не угостите? {176}
Сказка о рыбаке и рыбке {177}
скрипт {181}
скрол {180}
Слово – не воробей, вылетит – не поймаешь {174}
совхоз {178}
софт {180}
спам {180}
СПИД {178}
списывать {182}
стипендия {182}
стипуха {182}
сын {176}
таксист {176}
тёмное освещение {179}
тешатся {175}
троечники {182}
тройка {182}
трояк {182}
тяжело в ученье – легко в бою {182}
У вас ещё лапша на ушах не обсохла {174}
у тебя ещё молоко на губах не обсохло {174}
УВИР – Управление виз и регистраций {178}
удовлетворительно {182}
ученье свет, а неученье тьма {182}
училка {182}
учительница {182}
учиться, учиться и учиться {182}
ушк {175}
уютный троллейбус {179}
файл {181}
форум {180}
хакер {180}
хард {182}
хомяк {181}
хорошая зависть {179}
хорошисты {182}
ценное указание {177}
ЦУ {177}
Чернуха {177}
четвёрка {182}
чешутся {175}

ЧК – Чрезвычайная комиссия {177}
ЧП – Чрезвычайное происшествие {177}
Что посеешь / посмеешь, то и пожнёшь {174}
шпаргалка {182}
штука {176}
штурмовщина {176}
штучка {176}
ЭВМ {180}
электронная вычислительная машина {180}
я не волшебник, я ещё только учусь {183}
Я тебе по-хорошему завидую {179}
яйца курицу не учат {183}

Word & Phrase Index

50-я годовщина, 136
А вы и ухом не моргнули, 174
а Вы что рекомендуете?, 33
А вы, друзья, как ни садитесь, всё в музыканты не годитесь, 141
а ля мужик, 63
А мне в чужом пиру похмелье, 160
А мы и не торопимся, 119
а осетрина-то с душком, 143
А потому обычай мой: с волками иначе не делать мировой, как снявши шкуру с них долой, 103
А сколько бы Вы мне дали?, 11
А судьи кто?, 142
А ты огурцом, 107
А я готовлюсь стать отцом, 36
А я, знаете ли, предпочитаю..., 163
абонентная книжечка, 37
аварийная ситуация {38}
Авось не бог, а полбога есть, 170
авось, 169
авоська, 40, 170
автолюбители {38}
ажиотажный спрос, 87, 89
аккуратная фигурка, 54
аккуратно, 54
акробатические трюки, 145
актуальный вопрос, 55
актуальный, 54
акулы пера, 46
аловерды, 158
Алло, 35
Алло, дорогой Леонид Ильич слушает..., 82
альковные страсти, 63
амикошонство, 64
амурные дела, 63
анималист, 147
Антошка-Антошка – пойдём копать картошку, 96
аортокоронарное шунтирование, 90
аппарат, 88
апплет, 180
аристократы, 112
Арлекины и пираты, циркачи и акробаты, 145
аська, 181
ася, 181
Ах война, война-война, дурная девка – стерва она, 71
Ах война, что ж ты, подлая, сделала, 71
Ах ты, поганка!, 99
Ах, вот где собака зарыта, 94
аэропорт, 61
Баба Катя, 177

баба моя, 128
Баба с возу – кобыле легче, 174
баба, 21, 25, 129, 175
бабанка, 25
бабка, 25
бабник, 25, 127
бабские разговоры, 24
бабульки, 25
бабуля, 25, 176
Бабушка надвое сказала, 26
бабушка, 24, 25, 175
бабы, 24
бабье лето, 25
баксы, 60
балдеть, 146
бандитский капитализм, 90
бандитская пуля, 117
баннеры, 180
бар, 61
барышня, 20, 23
баталист, 147
батлы, 62
башка болит, 116
Без определённого места жительства, 178
без очереди, 41
без пальта, 57
Без пруда не выловишь и рыбку из него, 174
без страховки, 145
Без труда не выловишь и рыбки из пруда, 174
без царя в голове, 84
Без этого хоккей потерял бы едва ли не половину своей зрелищной привлекательности, 72
безалаберный американец, 180
безалкогольное пиво, 179
безбилетник, 37
белая смерть, 100
белуга, 105
белые мухи, 76
белые пятна на карте, 45
белые страницы, 45
белый гриб, 98
белый пиар, 60
Береги платье снову, а честь смолоду, 167
бесит меня, 28
бесплатное лечение, 179
бесплатный сыр бывает только в мышеловке, 166
бесподобно, 11
бесполезняк, 29
беспредел, 91
беспроигрышную серию, 72
бессознательное, 40
Библиотека имени Ленина, 111
бизнес-вуман, 25
бизнесмены, 142
битва за урожай, 164

биться, как рыба об лёд, 105
бланманже, 64
бледная поганка, 99
блезир, 64
блестяще, 11
блеять, 102
близкая родственница по линии сына, 128
близнецы-братья, 149
Блин!, 48
блицкриг, 58
блог, 180
Бог подаст, 49
бодать, 157
бодун, 157
Боже мой!, 49
Боже царя храни, 84
большая деревня, 112
большое видится на расстоянии, 150
Болят мои раны {48}
бомбить {39}
бомж, 178
борзые щенки, 143
Борис, ты не прав!, 89
боровик, 98
борьба за выживание, 120
ботать по фени, 85
ботлы, 62
брак без брака, 127
брак по любви, 126
брак по расчёту, 126
брак, 127
братан, 141
братва, 14, 21
браток, 33
брать, 112
браузер, 180
Брежнев умер, но тело его живёт, 175
бренд, 92
бренди, 63
бриллианты, 23
бродячая, 93
брют, 63
будем говорить, 163
Будет и на нашей улице праздник, 111
Будет тебе там и ванна, и кофе, будет и какао с чаем!, 153
будет хлеб – будет и песня, 82
будировать, 64
будут в дауне, 62
Будьте добры, 33
бутылка, 175
Бутылочку водочки и пару бутылочек пивка, 175
бушизмы, 91
быстрее, 69
бытовая травма, 117
быть навеселе, 152

быть по жизни оптимистом, 120
бычок, 119
Бюро находок, 38
в гостях, 73
в доску, 156
в дугу, 156
в душном помещении, 116
в дым, 152
в дымину, 156
в итальянское посольство за визой, 40
в кайф, 29
В какой малинник ты попал!, 97
В какой ресторан пойдём?, 33
в кустах случайно оказался рояль, 141
В Ленинграде женихи, в Москве невесты, 112
В ловких и натруженных руках, 145
в лоскут, 156
В Москве играют, в Ленинграде пляшут, 112
В Москве чихнут, в Ленинграде аспирин принимают, 112
в нетрезвом состоянии, 159
В огороде бузина – а в Киеве дядька, 97
в осень и у воробья пиво, 80
В очередь, сукины дети, в очередь!, 41
в положении, 46
в принципе, да, 14
в пьянстве замечен не был, но по утрам пил холодную воду, 160
в ритме вальса, 141
в сиську, 152
в сорок пять баба ягодка опять, 11
в сортире террористов замочим, 90
в сосиску, 152
в стельку, 156
В Тулу со своим самоваром не ездят, 155
в хлам, 152, 156
в чулке, 87
в шесть часов, 136
Важнейшим из всех искусств для нас является кино, 144
важный момент в докладе, 135
варез, 181
Вас здесь не стояло, 41
Вас слушают, 35
ввёл меня в заблуждение, 166
вдрызг, 156
век воли не видать!, 85
век живи, век учись, 183
Велика Россия, а отступать некуда – позади Москва!, 58

Великая Октябрьская Социалистическая Революция, 2
Великая Отечественная Война, 59, 70
Венера, 129
верный ленинец, 82
Вертикаль не абсолют, 92
веселие Руси есть пити – не можем мы без того быти, 152
весеннее настроение, 78
Весна пришла – щепку на щепку падает, 78
вести себя как джентльмен, 130
вечеринка, 129
вечернее заседание, 136
вечерний сеанс, 136
вечный бой, 150
вешать лапшу на уши, 14, 174
вживую, 147
взять политический реванш, 87
видак, 147
видео, 61
видик, 62
видите ли, 163
винчестер, 182
виртуальные, 60
вирус, 180
вискарь, 62
вкусный гамбургер, 179
влепить, 182
вложить, 58
влюбиться, 126
вне игры, 73
во второй лиге, 72
во второй половине дня, 136
ВОВ, 59
водила {39}
водительские права {39}
водительское удостоверение {39}
Водка без пива – деньги на ветер, 153
водка бывает хорошей и очень хорошей, 159
водопроводчик, 25
водочка, 160
водяной, 99
военная выправка, 70
военные, 70
военный трибунал, 68
вождение в нетрезвом состоянии {39}
Война кровь любит, 71
Война не лечит, а калечит, 70
война, 70
волк в овечьей шкуре, 104
Волк и заяц, тигры в клетке – все они марионетки, 145
Волка ноги кормят, 103
волчий аппетит, 103
вольвушник, 62

Вон из Москвы, сюда я больше не ездок, 142
вопрос жизни или смерти, 120
воробей, 102
ворона, 101
Воры в законе, 86
восхитительно, 11
Восьмое марта, 129
восьмое чудо света, 134
Вот тебе, бабушка, и Юрьев день, 26
Вот угодил-так угодил, 162
вот это речь не мальчика, но мужа, 125
Воюй не числом, а уменьем, 70
впадали в детство, 28
времена царя-Гороха, 85
время приёма пищи, 68
время, 135
всё видит в розовом свете, 45
все средства хороши, 70
Все счастливые семьи похожи друг на друга..., 143
Всё, отвоевался, 70
Всевышний, 91
всенародный праздник единения партии и народа, 60
всмятку, 91
Вспомню я пехоту и родную роту, и тебя за то, что дал мне закурить, 118
Вставай, страна огромная..., 58
встать в очередь, 40
встреча без галстуков, 90
вступит в свои права, 77
всю малину испортил, 97
вторая мировая война, 59
вторая половина, 46
второгодник, 182
Второй срок, 92
второй хлеб, 96
втрескаться в кого-то, 126
втюриться в кого-то, 126
Вы выходите / сходите на следующей?, 37, 41
Вы не будете чаёвничать?, 154
Вы трое – оба ко мне, 69
Вы уже выбрали?, 33
выглядеть, как белая ворона, 45
выжить, 120
выносливость, 72
выпивать / выпить, 155
Выпьешь чайку – позабудешь тоску, 154
высадка союзников в Нормандии, 59
высокая мода, 64
высокая точность, 54
высоко держать планку, 75
высшая мера наказания, 87
вытрезвитель, 159
Выходи за меня замуж, 127

выходить замуж, 112
вычислительные машины, 180
Вышел на Дворжак..., 140
вышка, 87
гав-гав, 101
гадюка, 128
гаечный ключ, 121
ГАИ, 178
гаишник, 39, 178
галстук, 156
гамбургер, 61
гаупт-штурмбанфюрер, 59
Где огурцы, тут и пьяницы, 107
где раки зимуют, 80
генерал Зима, 79
Геракл, 88
геронтократии, 88
гиперинфляция, 87
ГКЧП, 177
главная страница, 181
Главное не победа – главное участие, 73
глюк, 181
Глядя на пиво – хорошо и плясать, 152
Говорите!, 35
Говорят, 'Если хочешь принять правильное решение...', 158
голая, 148
голова как пивной котёл, 153
головная боль, 116
гололёд, 77
Голосуй сердцем!, 90
Голосуй, а то проиграешь, 90
голубая мечта, 44
голубка, 128
голубой, 44
Гони инспектору бабки и двигай дальше!, 40
Горбушка, 146
Горе от ума, 142
город на семи холмах, 110
горькая сладость, 179
горько, 127, 157
господин, 21, 24
Господь с тобой, 50
госпожа, 21, 24
Госпожа, сержант Смирнов. Разрешите Ваши документы, 24
Государственная автомобильная инспекция, 178
Государственная Инспекция по Безопасности Дорожного Движения, 40
государственный деятель, 179
готовь сани летом, а телегу – зимой, 77, 79
гражданин, 20
Гражданин, Ваш билет!, 20
Гражданин, подвиньтесь!, 20
гражданка, 20
грамотей, 16
грибник, 98
грибница, 98

грибной дождь, 78, 98
грибные места, 98
грибы, 98
гром не грянет – мужик не перекрестится, 78
грубая игра, 73
грымза, 128
губа, 68
губит людей не пиво, губит людей вода, 153
гудит как улей, 100
гусарский насморк, 117
Да не посрамим земли Русские..., 70
Да, ребята..., 125
Да, скифы мы. Да, азиаты мы..., 150
Давай закурим, 119
Давай подарим ему книгу..., 162
Давай поженимся, 127
Давайте без сантиментов, 64
Давайте с Вами поменяемся, 37
Давайте..., 164
Даже не знаю, 163
Дай Бог, чтобы твоя страна тебя не пнула сапожищем..., 52
дайлап, 181
дайте пройти, 36
дали прикурить, 118
дама, 23
Дама, вы мне все ноги оттоптали, 23
Дамы и господа, 24
дар Божий, 162
дарёное не дарят, 163
дарёному коню в зубы не смотрят, 162
дарственная надпись, 162
дать по тыкве, 108
дают зелёный свет, 44
два раза по пятьдесят, 137
Два раза по сто пятьдесят!, 133
Два сапога – пара, 52
двадцатку, 39
двадцаточку, 39, 176
двадцать, 176
двоечники, 182
двойка, 182
двойные ошибки, невынужденные ошибки, 72
Двум смертям не бывать, а одной не миновать, 120
девушка, 20, 24, 130
Дед плачет, бабка плачет..., 101
дед, 91
дедовщина, 68, 176
дедушка, 24
деды, 68, 176
Дело – табак!, 119
дембель, 68
День Святого Валентина, 129

день чудесный, 79
деньги, 177
деньжищи, 177
деревенщина, 177
деревня, 177
держать удар, 72
дёрнуть, 156
дерябнуть, 156
десерт, 33
десятку / десяточку, 39
детей находят в капусте, 96
Дети – цветы жизни на могиле родителей, 27
Детская болезнь левизны в коммунизме, 27
дефицит, 40
дефолт, 88
Джентльмены удачи, 85, 107, 144
джигит, 158
джинсы, 62
дизайнер, 180
динамист, 165
диски, 146
Дискотека имени Леннона, 111
для блезиру, 64
Для милого дружка и семь вёрст не околица, 134
дневник, 181
до белой горячки, 152
до свадьбы заживёт, 117
до свидания, 36
до синевы выбрит, 45
до синевы пьян, слегка выбрит, 45
добить фашистскую гадину в её логове, 59
добрая тёща, 179
Доброе слово и кошке приятно, 11
договориться {39}
дождь стеной, 79
дойная корова, 91
докторское мы, 117
Долг платежом красен, 63
дом, 86
домашняя страница, 181
домохозяйка, 25
домушник, 86
дорог не подарок – дорого внимание, 163
дорогая, 128
дорого яичко к Христову дню, 136, 162
Дорогому Ивану Иванову..., 162
дорогуша, 128
достойно кисти Айвазовского, 147
доступ, 181
дразнилка, 12
дразнить унитаз, 159
драйв, 17
дринкануть, 62
Друг, оставь покурить, а в ответ – тишина, это он не вернулся из боя, 118

другая альтернатива, 57
Дружба дружбой, а табачок врозь, 119
думать так было бы ребячеством, 27
дурак любит красное, 44
дурак, 55, 168
духи, цветы и разные безделушки, 163
душа в душу, 129
Ё моё! {48}
Его голыми руками не возмёшь, 14
его заказали, 23
его как ветром сдуло, 77
Его нет и неизвестно, когда он будет, 36
Его послали …, 130
его ушли, 88
единица, 182
Её можно трясти, как грушу, 97
ежовщина, 176
ездят зайцем, 37
Емеля, 168
ему медведь на ухо наступил, 104
Ему про Фому, а он – про Ерёму, 13
ёрш, 153
Если бы да кабы…, 99
Если бы молодость знала, если бы старость могла, 89
Если мозги утекают, значит они есть, 92
Если не секрет, сколько Вы получаете?, 16
если смерти, то мгновенной, если раны – небольшой, 120
если ты мужчина, 124
есть и моя доля в бочке мёда, 100
Ешь пирог с грибами, а язык держи за зубами, 99
жалко у пчёлки знаешь где?, 101
жалко, 101
жало, 101
жалобная книга, 33
Жаль только жить в эту пору прекрасную уж не придётся ни мне, ни тебе, 150
Жареная рыбка…, 106
Жду ответа, как соловей лета, 79
Желаете что-нибудь на десерт?, 33
Желаю Вам иметь четырёх животных…, 159
железная леди, 125
железно, 133
железный Феликс, 179
желторотик, 44
жёлтый, 44

жена без мужа вдовы хуже, 125
жениться, 112
жёнушка, 128
женщина, 20, 24, 130
женщина за рулём – что фашист на танке {38}
Женщина, вы выходите на следующей?, 24
Женщина, вы кошелёк уронили, 24
женщины лёгкого поведения, 46
жёны, 112
жёсткий диск, 182
жетон, 37
Жив курилка?, 119
живая музыка, 146
живая сила, 68
живот, 120
Живу я, как поганка – а мне летать охота!, 99
жизненно важно, 120
жизни или смерти, 120
жизнь – не сахар, 100
жизнь бьёт ключом, 121
Жизнь как смертельная болезнь передающаяся половым путём, 120
жить, 120
за билетами на самолёт, 40
За большие заслуги…, 82
за грибами!, 98
За двумя зайцами погонишься, ни одного не поймаешь, 36
за знакомство, 157
За мной не заржавеет, 17
За нас с Вами и за чёрт с ними!, 158
за перспективу, 158
за плечами, 137
за семью морями, 134
За царя, за Родину, за веру, 84
За чем стоим?, 40
за чертой бедности, 87
За что купил – за то и продал, 17
забычковать, 119
Завтра в Москве ожидается один градус. В Петербурге – совершенно другой, 113
завязать, 87
загружать, 181
ЗАГС, 127
загудеть, 156
задавать тон, 141
задеть струну, 141
задрать планку до заоблачных высот, 75
заживает как на собаке, 93
заживать, 120
зажигалка, 119
зайка, 128
закадрить, 130
закладывать за воротник, 156
закончился ничьей, 72
Закурить не найдётся?, 119

закуски, 33
залить глаза, 152
замена водительских прав {38}
Замоскворечье, 111
заниматься любовью, 127
занять очередь, 40
запасть на кого-то, 126
запилы, 146
записки, 35
запить, 156
запой, 156
зарплата, 25
Зато мы делаем ракеты…, 83
Зачем мне совесть? Я не богатый, 167
зачётка, 182
зачётная книжка, 182
заяц, 37
Звезда пленительного счастья, 166
звонилка, 181
здоровенная, 153
здоровый образ жизни, 117
Здоровья в аптеке не купишь, 116
здравствует Москва и да погибнет Петербург!, 112
здравствуйте, 34
зелёные, 44, 176
зима настоящая, 80
Зима прошла, настало лето – спасибо партии за это, 77
зима-красна, 79
зимовать, 80
зимовье, 79
зимой и летом одним цветом, 76
зимой и летом одним цветом, 76
зимостойкий, 79
Зимушка-зима, 79
Зимы ждала, ждала природа! , 76
Зимы ждала, ждала природа!, 76
змея, 102
знаем, проходили!, 104
знает, где раки зимуют, 80
знаете ли, 163
знак качества, 60
знаток, 132
значит, 164
Золотая моя столица, дорогая моя Москва, 110
Золотко, 128
золотые дети, 27
зона, 86
зуб дёргает, 117
зуб ноет, 117
зюзя, 156
И баба с возу, и волки сыты, 174
и в зной, и в стужу, 77
и ванна, и кофе, и какао с чаем, 155
И вечный бой! Покой нам только снится, 150

и глазом не моргнул, 174
И к бабке / гадалке не ходи, 26
и лично, 82
И невозможное возможно, 150
и овцы целы – и волки сыты, 104, 174
И рады мы проказам матушки зимы, 79
И решил несчастный..., 106
и смех, и грех, 171
и ухом не повёл, 174
И факир, чей вид внушает страх, 145
И я там был, мёд-пиво пил, по усам текло, а в рот не попало, 153
Иван Иванов на месте?, 34
Иван, не помнящий родства, 12
и-го-го, 101
игра свето-тени, 147
играл первую скрипку, 141
играть в снежки, 77
играть с листа, 141
играют мимо нот, 142
Идите вы на фиг, я сам заблудился!, 166
идти замуж, 112
Из искры возгорится пламя, 150
извините, 25, 58
извинять, 58
извиняюсь, 58
изрубить в капусту, 108
имидж, 61
импичмент, 62
имплоймент брендинг, 61
иностранщина, 176
интеллигент, 58
интеллигентно, 55
интеллигентность, 54
интеллигентный, 54
Интеллигенция – , г**, а надо дело делать, 91
Интересное кино!, 144
Интернет, 180
Интернет-провайдер, 181
исполнять свои супружеские обязанности, 47
их деятельность несовместима с их официальным, 46
их кинули, 88
Их уровень смерти, это наш уровень жизни, 120
ихний / ихние, 58
ищи ветра в поле, 78
йога, 24
к топору зовите Русь, 149
кадр, 126
кадрить, 126, 130
кадровик, 61
кадровые, 61
кадры решают всё, 61, 126
каждая собака знает, 104
каждое лыко в строку, 51
Каждому овощу – свой срок, 96

Каждый охотник желает знать, где сидит фазан, 44
каждый платит за себя, 33
кайф, 29
Как гром среди ясного неба, 78
Как дела?, 14, 119
Как жизнь?, 121
как за каменной стеной, 127
как кот мартовский, 78
как медведь в берлоге, 100, 104
Как меня угораздило!, 169
Как мне повезло!, 169
как мы себя чувствуем, 117
как об стенку горох, 96
Как обычно, сынок, 176
как огурец, 10
как огурчик, 10, 96, 107
как пчёлы на мёд, 100
как рыба в воде, 105
как рыба об лёд, 76
как рыбке зонтик, 105
как сельди в бочке, 105
как сморщенный гриб, 99
как снег на голову, 77
как собака на сене, 93, 104
как собаке пятая нога, 94, 104
Как я мог так лохануться?!, 166
какие-нибудь часики, 163
Какой малинник, 97
Какой фрукт выискался, 96
Как-то не сложилось, 169
Камчатка, 182
кантри, 62
картрушник, 62
капуста зелёная, 107
капуста, 96, 107
карась, 106
Карету мне, карету!, 142
кар-кар, 101
каркать, 101
карманы Гусинского, 91
карт-бланш, 64
картофельное поле, 96
картофельные бунты, 96
картошка, 96, 107
Карту купи, лапоть!, 51
катавасия, 15
катенька, 132
катить бочку, 86
качалка, 181
качать, 181
Кающаяся Магдалина, 148
квартал, 57
квасить, 156
Квитанция нужна? {39}
КГБ, 178
кидала, 88
кидалово, 165
кидать, 165
километр, 57
Кина не будет – электричество кончилось!, 144
киношка, 144
кинуть, 88, 165

кинуть кого-то на деньги, 165
киса, 128
кисуль, 128
классный, 11
класть, 57
клеить, 126
клиент всегда неправ, 32
клише, 64
клубничка, 97
клюква, 97
ключ, 121
клюшка, 20, 128
книга – лучший подарок, 162
кобра, 128
коза, 102
козла, 92
козырнуть этими словами, 16
кокотки, 63
кол, 182
колдырнуть, 156
коллективное, 40
коллективное хозяйство, 178
колхоз, 21, 178
командир {39}
комильфо, 63
коммунистический союз молодёжи, 178
коммуняки, 22
комп, 180
комплименты, 129
компьютер, 62, 180
компьютеры спаму не имут, 70
комсомол, 178
Кому 'товарищ,' а тебе 'гражданин', 20
Кому война, а кому мать родна, 74
кондуит, 16
Конечно, это не моё дело..., 16
конкретно, 28
конкретный, 28
консенсус, 57
Конспект Маркса, 111
контролёр, 37
контролируемая эмиссия, 89
коньяк, 63
Копать от забора и до обеда, 69
копия всегда хуже оригинала, 148
кормилец, 46
Королева спорта, 74
короче, 164
корректно, 55
корректный, 54
кот, 128
котя, 128
кофе, 153
Кошелёк потерялся, 169
КПСС, 178
красная девица, 44
краснокоричневые, 22
Красный Пролетарий, 21
краткость – сестра таланта, 143
крейзануться, 62
крепкое слово, 91

Креста на тебе нет!, 50
Крещенские морозы, 79
кривая вывезет, 170
кровь-морковь, 96
крутить динамо, 165
круто, 28
крутой, 28
крякать, 102
кря-кря, 102
Кто его / её спрашивает?, 10, 35
кто не курит и не пьёт, тот здоровеньким помрёт, 116
Кто платит, тот и заказывает музыку, 141
Кто последний?, 40
кто-то теряет, кто-то находит, 38
куда Макар телят не гонял, 13
Куда ты привёл нас, Сусанин Иван?, 166
куда царь пешком ходил, 84
кудах-тах-тах, 101
кудахтать, 101
Кузькину мать, 12
ку-ка-ре-ку, 101
ку-ку, 102
кукарекать, 101
кукушка, 102
Кукушка-кукушка, сколько мне жить?, 102
кулаки, 21
Кулик, 155
куликать, 155
культ личности, 60
культурная революция, 179
культурный, 142
Куплю жене сапоги!, 52
курево закончилось, 119
Куренье – медленная смерть, 119
Куренье вред, а некурящих нет, 119
курилка, 119
курочка, 128
куртизанки, 63
кустодиевские женщины, 148
лабал, 147
лабать, 146
лабать на саксе, 146
лабух, 147
лает, 101
лапа – лапуля, 128
лапотная Россия, 51
лапоть / лапти, 51
Лапти, да лапти, да лапти мои!, 51
лаять на кого-то, 102
лаяться с кем-то, 102
левитановская осень, 148
левое плечо вперёд, 68
легавая собака, 86
легавый, 86
лёгкая атлетика, 74
Лёд тронулся, командовать парадом буду я, 76

лейбл, 62
ленд-лиз, 59
Ленин умер, но дело его живёт, 175
ленинец, 21
Леночка, Наташенька, Машуля, 129
лентяи, 55, 168
лепить горбатого, 86
лепить снежную бабу, 77
лето припаси-ка, а зима прибери-ка, 80
лето пролежишь, зимой с сумой побежишь, 79
лечиться даром – даром лечиться, 116
лимитчики, 110
личный состав, 68
лишение водительских прав сроком на год {39}
ловбургер, 61
Ловить рыбу в мутной воде, 105
Ловкость рук – и никакого мошенничества!, 145
логин, 180
ложить, 58
ложка дёгтя в бочке мёда, 100
локальный, 182
лопнуть от смеха, 171
лотофон, 165
лох, 29, 165
лох педальный, 29
лохотронщик, 166
лубок, 148
лубочность, 148
лужа, 111
лузер, 55, 168
луковица, 108
лучшая половина человечества, 47
лучше не бывает, 121
Лучше один раз увидеть, чем сто раз услышать, 132
лучше рубль в руке, чем два в банке, 87
лучший, 57
лыко, 51
лытдыбр, 181
ль рады мы, 79
льёт, как из ведра, 78
лэнд-лиз, 59
любезнейший, 20
Любишь кататься – люби и катайся / саночки возить, 174
Люблю грозу в начале мая..., 78
любовник, 127, 130
любовница, 127, 130
Любовь зла – полюбишь и козла, 128
любовь с первого взгляда, 126, 130
Люди простят все, кроме вранья, 92

люди, 68
людские ресурсы, 61
мазня, 147
Май холодный – год хлебородный, 78
Маленькая рыбка лучше большого таракана, 105
маленькая собачка – до старости, 93
маленькие детки – маленькие бедки, а вырастут велики – будут большие, 27
малина, 97
мальчик для битья, 125
мальчишник, 125
маниловщина, 143
манкировал своими супружескими обязанностями, 64
маньяки и шпионы, 91
маринист, 147
Марс, 129
мартышка, 20
маршрутка, 28
масло масляное, 57
мастер, 180
мастер на все руки, 127
математическое обеспечение, 180
математичка, 182
матершинники, 91
махорка, 118
Машина Времени, 145
маэстро, 33
мегера, 128
медведь на ухо наступил, 100
медвежатник, 86
медвежья болезнь, 100
медвежья услуга, 103
медленный, 146
медляк, 146
медовый месяц, 99, 127
м-е-е, 102
между нами, девочками, говоря, 124
между первой и второй перерывчик небольшой, 157
между первой и второй пуля не пролетела 157
Мели Емеля – твоя неделя, 12
мелкий политический деятель эпохи Аллы Пугачёвой, 82
менеджер, 180
менты, 87
меньшевик, 21
меню, 33, 64
мерс, 62
Мёртвые души, 143
мёртвые срама не имут, 70
меры в женщинах и в пиве он не знал и не хотел, 153
места весьма отдалённые, 47
места не столь отдалённые, 47
Место встречи изменить нельзя, 86

месяц, 127
металлисты, 146
метаться, 29
метель, 77
метель, снежная буря, 77
метро, 57, 61
милостивый государь, 20, 84, 179
Милые бранятся – только чешутся, 175
Минздрав СССР предупреждает..., 119
минуточку, 135
Михаил коров доил, 13
Мишка-Мишка, где твоя улыбка?, 13
младогегельянцы, 88
младореформаторы, 87
мне даже неудобно, 163
Мне кажется, ты похудела, 11
Мне не нужна квитанция {39}
мне не нужны твои ЦУ, 177
мне нездоровится..., 116
мне то же самое, 33
мобильные телефоны, 34
моветон, 63
модем, 181
Может так договоримся?, 17
Может, Чайковского, 140
Можно Вас на минуточку, 33
можно, 21
Мои пэрэнтцы сегодня домой не придут..., 62
мой сладкий, 128
мокрое дело, 86
мокрушник, 86
молодо – зелено, 88
молодой человек, 20, 24
Молодой человек, как Вам не стыдно..., 36
Молодые, поздравьте друг друга!, 127
молодым везде у нас дорога, старикам везде у нас почёт, 88
молоко, 117
Момент – сейчас приду, 135
момент в жизни, 135
момент, 135
моргать, 85
мороз и солнце, 79
Мороз и солнце, день чудесный, 80
москаль, 113
Москва – третий Рим, а четвёртого не будет, 110
Москва выросла, Петербург выращен, 111
Москва не сразу строилась, 110
Москва слезам не верит, 110
Москва создана веками, Питер миллионами, 111
Московская прописка, 110
мотор {39}
мочалка, 20
мочи нет терпеть, 117

мочить, 86
мочить в сортире, 91
мошенник, 166
мошенничество, 166
мужеподобная, 125
мужественное лицо, 124
мужественность, 124
мужик, 21, 25, 125, 128
мужик в юбке, 125
мужская профессия, 125
мужской разговор, 124
мужчина, 20, 130
Мужчиной можешь ты не быть, но джентльменом быть обязан, 150
музон, 146
мундштук, 118
му-у-у, 101
мусор, 86
Мы будем снимать кино или мы не будем снимать кино?!, 145
мы встречаемся, 130
Мы ещё повоюем, 70
Мы идём в аут, 129
Мы любим людей за то добро, которое им делаем и ненавидим их за то зло, которое им причиняем, 143
Мы рождены, чтоб сказку / Кафку сделать былью, 175
Мы с Наташей решили пожениться, 127
Мы собрались здесь, чтобы выпить, так давайте же выпьем за то, что мы здесь собрались!, 158
Мы старый мир разрушим до основанья, а затем, / зачем..., 21
Мыло, 181
мычать, 101
мэн, 21
мяу-мяу, 101
мяукать, 101
на авось, 170
На бедного Макара все шишки валятся, 13
на безрыбье и рак рыба, 105
на блюдечке с голубой каёмочкой, 44
на бровях, 152
на брудершафт, 59, 158
на видеке / видаке, 144
На войне, как на войне, 70
на всякий случай, 170
на выставку, 40
На дворе марток, надевай трое порток, 77
на днях, 136
На днях он Вам даст ответ, 136
На дурака не нужен нож, ему с три короба соврёшь и делай с ним что хошь, 165
на мажорной ноте, 141
На нём, как на собаке, всё заживает, 104

На поезд посадки нет, 37
на посошок, 159
на приём к ветеринару, 40
на самом деле, 28, 54
на своём любимом покрытии, 72
на своём поле, 73
на семи холмах, 134
на скамейке запасных, 72
на ты, 158
на халяву, 56, 166, 168
на халяву и уксус сладок, 56, 100, 168
На хрен мне это, 108
на что жалуемся, 117
на чужом поле, 73
набраться, 152, 155
нагая, 148
наградил по-царски, 84
Надежда Надюша, 129
Надо решить вопрос с бухгалтером, 164
надо сегодня оторваться не по-детски, 29
надраться, 152, 156
надринькаться, 156
надрызгаться, 156
нажраться / наесться, 152, 155
назвался груздем – полезай в кузов, 98
назло бабушке отморозить / отрезать себе уши, 26
назюзюкаться, 152, 156
найти, 92
наканифолиться, 156
накаркать, 102
накачаться, 155
накваситься, 155
накеросиниться, 156
наклюкаться, 155
налакаться, 155
нализаться, 152, 155
налимониться, 156
нам так по кайфу, 29
нам хорошо за сорок, 137
напиться в дрезину, в лом, в дрибодан, 152
Напиться до положения риз, 152
народ, 68
народное хозяйство, 60
нарушения правил, 73
нарушили правила дорожного движения {39}
Нас не объегоришь и нас не подкузьмишь, 12
насморк, 116
настоящий мужик, 63, 124, 125
настоящий русский язык, 125
настроен на минорный лад, 141
наступать на горло собственной песне, 149
Наступил на землю русскую, да оступился, 70
натуральный, 54

натурщица / натурщик, 147
натюрморт, 148
нахал, 130
начать, 57
начать набело, 45
начать спуртовать, 74
начистить репу, 108
наши дети будут жить при коммунизме, 28
не бабье это дело, 24
Не боги горшки обжигают, 174
Не в службу, а в дружбу, 16
Не во всякой туче гром..., 170
не дай Бог, 49
Не дал Бог ста рублей, а пятьдесят не деньги, 137
Не делаете умное лицо – Вы же офицер, 69
Не ела душа чесноку, так и не воняет, 107
Не жизнь, а существование, 120
Не знаю, как там в Лондоне..., 93
Не имей сто рублей, а имей сто друзей, 132
Не йоги горшки обжигают, 174
не каркай, 102
Не лаптем щи хлебаем, 51
Не мешок картошки, 107
не на жизнь, а на смерть, 120
Не обещайте деве юной любови вечной на земле..., 166
не парься, 28
не пихайтесь, 36
Не плюй в колодец, 175
Не плюй в колодец, вылетит – не поймаешь, 174
не по образцам зима и лето бывает, по воле божьей, 80
Не по Сеньке шапка, 175
Не по Хуану сомбреро, 175
не по-детски, 28
не путать божий дар с яичницей, 163
Не сочтите за труд, 16
Не так страшен чёрт, как его малюют, 50
не толкайтесь, 36
Не угодно ли чаю откушать, 154
Не упоминай имя Господа своего всуе, 49
не учи учёного, 183
не царское это дело, 84
не щадя живота своего, 120
небольшая толпа, 179
Небось картошку все мы уважаем, если намять её с сольцой?, 96
невежда, 16
негостеприимный русский, 180
неграмотный, 175
недовешивать, 32
незнакомый человек, 23
некорректное поведение, 54

неопрятный француз, 180
непереводимая игра слов, 91
непредсказуемый, 169
неприкосновенный запас, 177
нести свой крест, 50
нет мест, 32
Нет такого мужа, который не мечтал бы хоть на час стать холостяком, 125
неуд, 182
неудачник, 55, 168
неудовлетворительно, 182
неуставные отношения, 68
нечист на руку, 47
НЗ, 177
ни рыба, не мясо, 105
Никто не водится со мной, 99
Нихт Шиссен!, 59
Ничего, как-нибудь перезимуем, 80
НКВД, 178
Но дым Отечества нам сладок и приятен, 118, 142
Но мы то не лошади!, 119
Но ты же обещал!, 166
новарищи, 23
новобранец, 68
Новые Русские, 34
нокаутировал, 71
нормально, 14, 121
нос картошкой, 96
ночные бабочки {48}
Ну спасибо тебе, бабанька!, 25
Ну ты циркач!, 145
Ну что мне, сто раз надо повторять?!, 132
Ну, вообще, 125
Ну, если только на чашку чаю, 154
ну, клюкнул, мерзавец..., 155
нужно учесть этот момент, 135
няня, 136
О спорт! Ты мир!, 71
О! Мальчик, 125
О, наши русские коалы!, 103
обезвоживание, 160
обещания, 166
Обещанного три года ждут, 166
обживать новое жильё, 120
Обижаешь, начальник! Мокрое дело шьёшь, 87
обманутые ожидания, 166
обнажённая, 148
обойтись народными / домашними рецептами / средствами, 116
Обошлось, 170
обсчитать, 32
общага, 183
общежитие, 183
объегорить, 12
обыкновенная царапина, 117
обязательная программа, 71
огород, 97
огурец, 10, 107

Один с сошкой, а семеро с ложкой, 134
один удар по почкам заменяет кружку пива, 153
Одна капля никотина убивает лошадь, 119
Одну минуточку / минуту / секунду, 35
Ожидания – самый скучный повод, 166
ожидания, 166
оказать медвежью услугу, 100
оказывать знаки внимания, 129
оксюморон, 179
октябрь, 22
октябрята, 21
оленина по-царски, 84
олигархи, 91
олигархический капитализм, 88
ОМОН, 178
Он / она / я у телефона, 35
Он Вам перезвонит, 35
он Вас не понял, 33
он вообще такой по жизни, 121
Он говорит по другому телефону..., 35
он действует мне на нервы, 141
он завязал, 87
он играет у меня на нервах, 141
он испытывал лёгкую тяжесть в ногах, 179
Он к ней пристаёт, 130
Он лыка не вяжет, 51
он меня продинамил, 165
Он настоящий мужик, 25
он нашёл себе новую бабу, 24
Он не лыком шит,
он по жизни, 121
Он положил на неё глаз, 130
он ушёл, 88
Она в ауте, 129
она всех щучит, 105
она готовится стать матерью, 36
Она его закадрила, 130
она какая-то Маша, 12
она меня продинамила, 165
Она подарила мне сына, 163
Она сводит меня с ума, 126
Она строит ему глазки, 130
оперативно, 135
опохмелиться, 153, 160
определить победителя по системе "гол+пас", 72
оранжевые мами..., 44
Организм не приемлет никакого положения..., 159
оркестрирована, 141
освистаны, 73
осень, 80
осетрина, 105
ослиная моча, 153

оставить записку, 35
остался только сороковой размер, 40
От всей души поздравляю ..., 136
от всех болезней нам полезней солнце, воздух и вода, 116
от Ильича до Ильича, 82
От копеечной свечи Москва сгорела, 111
от кутюр, 64
от пива будешь писать криво, 153
отдел кадров, 61
откачивать, 181
открытие второго фронта, 59
отличники, 182
отлично, 182
Отогрелся в Москве, да замёрз на Березине, 70
оторваться, 29
отпущения, 92
отрываться, 146
отряд милиции особого назначения, 178
отшили, 130
офигенная, 153
официант, 32
оффтопик, 180
охренеть, 108
очередь, 40
па-де-де, 64
пальто, 57
пальцем не пошевелит, 55, 168
паника в магазинах, 87
панкующая редиска, 107
панорама, диорама, 148
пара, 182
параша, 86
парень, 130
париться, 28
пароль, 180
паршивая овца в стаде, 45
пассворд, 180
пастельные, 148
пастельные тона, 147
Пасть порву! Моргалы выколю!, 85
пачкотня, 147
Паша с Уралмаша, 12
пейджер, 34
пейзажист, 147
пейте, люди, пиво пенное – будет морда обалденная, 153
пелетон, 64
пели под фанеру, 146
пенсионный возраст, 120
первая страница, 181
первоапрельская шутка, 171
Первого апреля никому не верь, 171
первое свидание, 130
первый президент России, 89
Первый срок, 91
первым делом – самолёты, ну а девушки – потом , 69

Передайте ему, пожалуйста, трубку, 34
Передайте пожалуйста, что..., 35
Передайте, пожалуйста, на книжечку, 37
передать эстафетную палочку, 75
передвижники, 148
Пережить это смутное время, 120
Перезвоню, 14
перезимовать, 80
перекур, 119
перепить любого, 157
Перефразируя Марка Твена..., 92
перловая каша, 68
Перо вновь приравняли к штыку, 149
перо, 86
персональные, 180
персональный компьютер, 180
Петербургу суждено окончить свои дни, уйдя в финское болото, 111
петух, 101
петь вживую, 146
Петя, Петя-петушок, 101
печь, 168
пиар, 60
пиариться, 61
пиаровская статья, 60
пиаровский, 61
пиарщик, 61
пивка для рывка, 152
писюк, 62
Питер женится, Москва замуж идёт / берёт, 112
Питер строился рублями, Москва – веками, 111
пить как сапожник, 105
пить чай, 154
ПК, 180
план Барбаросса, 58
пленум, 61
пломбировать канал, 117
плотник, 25
плох тот солдат, который не мечтает стать генералом, 69
Плохо организованное похмелье переходит в запой, 160
ПМО, 180
по бумажке, 82
по голове, 121
По грибы!, 98
по кайфу, 29
по лэнд-лизу, 59
по очкам, 71
По семейным обстоятельствам, 105
по Сеньке и шапка, 13
по сто пятьдесят, 133
по телефону, 34

по щучьему веленью, по моему хотенью, 55, 168
Поавоськаем: авось, до чего-нибудь доавоськаемся, 170
побаливает, 117
победитель социалистического соревнования, 60
побелеть от страха, 45
поблагодарить..., 82
Повоевали – и будет, 71
по-военному чётко, 71
повторенье – мать ученья, 183
поганка, 99
под матрацем, 87
под пиво сойдёт, 153
под фанеру, 147
подарки, 129
подберёзовик, 98
подбирать на слух, 141
поддавать / поддать, 155
подкаблучник, 128
подкаблучный муж, 128
подкатывать / подкатить к кому-нибудь, 126, 130
подкузьмить, 12
Подмосковные вечера, 110
поднять планку, 75
Подождите, пожалуйста, 35
подосиновик, 98
подрезать {38}
подсказывать, 182
подсластить пилюлю, 100
подснежники {38}
подъехать, 130
Поезд дальше не идёт, просьба освободить вагоны, 37
пожалуйста, 16, 37
Пожалуйста, господина Смита, 34
позвонит, 57
поздно, 29
поздняк, 29
Пойдём куда-нибудь сегодня вечером?, 129
поймать второе дыхание, 74
пока, 36
пока уляжется пыль, 87
показали себя настоящими мужиками, 125
Показать Кузькину мать, 12
показать, где раки зимуют, 80
покой нам только снится, 150
покраснел, как помидор, 96
покраснеть от злости / стыда, 44
Поле чудес в стране дураков, 165
полезная пепси-кола, 180
полечиться, 160
Политбюро, 178
политика выкручивания рук, 73
политика кнута и пряника, 155
половина сахар – половина мёд, 100
половой человек, 32
положить, 58

полтинник, 39, 136
поменять пепельницу, 33
по-мужски, 124
Понадеялся на русский авось, 170
понимаешь, 163
понос, 116
понтово, 28
Попросите, пожалуйста / Позовите Ивана Иванова, 34
попса, 146
попсовик, 147
поражать живую силу противника, 68
портвешок, 175
портретист, 147
порядок в танковых войсках, 69
послать его к чёртовой матери / бабушке, 50
после дождичка в четверг, 79
после обеда, 136
после первой не закусывают, 157
Посмотрим, как ты обязательную откатаешь, 71
посох, 159
Поспешишь, людей насмешишь, 135
поставить, 182
поставить на счётчик, 23
Поставьте меня на лист ожидания, 41
постельные, 148
посты, 180
посуда, 25
Посчитайте нам пожалуйста, 33
посылать на хрен, 108
Потанцуем?, 130
потенциальные возможности, 57
поторопись, 69
поужинать в ресторане, 129
похмелье, 116, 157, 159, 160
похмелюга, 157
Почём Марльборо, бабуля?, 176
Почему мой друг – да потому, что я жизнь учил не по учебникам, просто я работаю волшебником, 183
пощёчина, 130
поэт в России, больше чем поэт, 149
поэтом можешь ты не быть, но гражданином быть обязан, 149
Правда, – хорошо, а счастье – лучше, 167
правильно, 55
правое плечо вперёд, 68
праздновать, 56, 169
превышение скорости {39}
предложить руку и сердце, 126

представительницы древнейшей профессии, 46
предъявите Ваш билет, 37
преемник, 90
Президент работает с документами, 89
президентский марафон, 74
презренный металл, 46
прекрасный пол, 24
преступная халатность, 83
преступный мир, 14
приватизация, 22
приказ о демобилизации, 68
приказал долго жить, 46
прикольно, 28
применять его на практике, 166
принимают пищу, 68
принтер, 62
принципиальную оценку, 83
принять, 155
приставания, 130
приставать, 130
прихватизация, 22
прихватить, 22
приятного аппетита, 33
провалиться на экзамене, 183
прога, 180
программа, 180
программное обеспечение, 180
программно-математическое обеспечение, 180
прогуливать уроки, 182
продавщица, 24
продинамить, 165
проезд на красный сигнал светофора {39}
Прожиточный минимум, 120
производственная травма, 117
произвольная программа, 71
Пройдёмте в милицию, 37
пройти отборочный турнир, 72
пролетарии, 112
Пронесло, 170
проныра, 32
пропустить много мячей, 72
просвещённый чекист, 91
Проси больше, дадут, сколько нужно, 92
Проспект Маркса, 111
Прости Господи! {48}
проститутка {48}
Прости, дяденька, 103
простите, 25
Простите меня, 90
просторечие, 58
противоположный пол, 129
противотанковые ежи, 58
прохиндей, 15, 32
Прохиндиада, 15
процесс пошёл, 164
прочный, 54
проще пареной репы, 107
пряник, 155
пуанты, 64
пуд, 133
пускаться во все тяжкие, 46

Пусть нас лапотной Россией называет Вашингтон..., 51
Путинки, 92
путь к сердцу мужчины лежит через желудок, 130
пушка, 86, 111
Пушкинская площадь, 111
пьяницы и материнщики, 91
пьяный, 156
пэрентцы, 62
пюре, 64
пятая нога, 94
пятёрка, 182
пятидесятилетие, 136
пятилетка, 127
пять с плюсом, 11
пять тысяч рублей, 62
пятьдесят грамм, 137
пятьдесят на пятьдесят, 137
Работа не волк, в лес не убежит, 56, 169
рабочий день, 56, 169
ради Бога, 49
ради Христа, 49
разбавить водой, 32
Разбег, толчок... И – стыдно подыматься..., 75
разбираться, 14
разборка, 14, 85
Разве это жизнь?!, 121
развлечься, 129
разгильдяй, 15
Разрешите вас пригласить, 129
Разрешите за вами поухаживать?, 129
Разрешите прикурить?, 119
разыграна как по нотам, 141
расколоться, 86
раскрученный бренд, 92
раскудахталась!, 102
раскулачивание, 21
расслабься, 28
рассол, 160
расстройство желудка, 116
растает как первый снег, 77
расти, как грибы после дождя, 78, 98
расходов на полтинник, а пользы на грош, 137
реально, реальный, 28, 54
реальный шёлк, 54
ребята, 22
реветь белугой, 105
Ревизор, 143
Революция пожирает своих детей, 22
революция, 21, 136
редиска, 85, 96, 107
рейганомика должна быть рейганомной, 83
рейтинг, 61
ремонт, 63
репа, 107
рецидивист, 87
ржать, 101
риза, 152
розовый, 45, 87

рокировочка, 90
российская экономика, 179
российские законы, 179
Россия-Матушка, 175
рубль упал, 88
рукопожатие, 91
рулет, 64
Рунет, 181
русичка, 182
русская кость тепло любит, 79
русский городовой {48}
Рыба она так себе..., 105
рыба, 105
рыбка, 128
рыбонька, 128
рывок, 152
рыцари плаща и кинжала, 46
с бодуна, 157
с волками жить – по-волчьи выть, 103
с корабля на бал, 142
с листа, 141
с мёдом, 117
с младых ногтей, 27
с пивом сойдёт, 153
с похмелья, 157
с утра до ночи судачит, 105
с хитрецой, 165
с хитринкой, 165
сайт, 180
сакс, 147
салабон, 68
салага, 68
салфетки, 33
самая читающая нация в мире, 162
самовар, 61, 155
самоволка, 68
самопиар, 61
сантименты, 64
сапоги, 52
сапожник, 145
Сапожник без сапог, 52
сбить дыхалку, 74
сбросить рубли, 87
сбрось мне на пейджер, 34
свадьба, 117
сверхъестественный, 169
свести счёты с жизнью, 47
свидание, 129
свинья, 102
Своевременно и правильно оплачивайте проезд, 37
связи, 32
свят-свят, 49
Сдаёте зелёненькие?, 176
сделать обрезание, 91
сделать предложение, 126
сдувать, 182
Сейчас я ему покажу, где раки зимуют, 80
сейчас, 135
секрет полишинеля, 179
секретный сотрудник, 177
секретный, 54
сексистское общество, 130
сексот, 177

селёдка, 105
сёмга, 105
Семеро одного не ждут, 133
семи смертям не бывать, одной не миновать, 134
семибанкирщина, 23, 134
семибоярщина, 134
Семичастный, 134
семь бед – один ответ, 134
Семь невест Ефрейтора Збруева, 134
Семь раз отмерь – один раз отрежь, 133
Семь стариков и одна девушка, 134
семь чудес света, 134
семья, 90
сервер, 181
серфинг, 180
серые кардиналы, 45
серый, 45
сеть, 182
Сигареточкой не угостите?, 176
Сиди – не кукарекай!, 102
сидюк, 62, 146
сильные мира сего, 47
сильный, 47
синий от холода, 45
синяк, 117
синяк под глазом, 117
сию минуту, 135
Сказал бы словцо – да уж выпито пивцо, 152
Сказка о рыбаке и рыбке, 129, 177
сказки, 55, 168
скачивать, 181
скинь мне на пейджер, 34
Сколько лет, сколько зим!, 76
сколько мёд ни говори, – во рту слаще не станет, 99
Сколько ты зарабатываешь?, 10
Сколько ты получаешь?, 10
Сколько у тебя выходит..., 10
скрипт, 181
скрол, 180
слава Богу, 49
слегка пьян, до синевы выбрит, 45
сливки, 40
словечки, 16
Слово – не воробей, вылетит – не поймаешь, 54, 174
случай, 169
Слушай, что тебе царь говорит, 84
смех – лучшее лекарство, 171
смех без причины – признак дурачины, 171
смех сквозь слёзы, 171
смеха боится даже тот, кто ничего не боится, 172
смешинка в рот попала, 171
смеялись до упаду, 171
смеяться от всей души, 171

Смеяться, право, не грешно над всем, что кажется смешно, 171
смотрит на мир сквозь розовые очки, 45
снегоуборочная машина, 77
снежная буря, 77
сногсшибательно, 11
со всей пролетарской ненавистью, 22
со свиданием, 157
со смаком, 16
Собака – друг человека, 93, 104
собака лает – ветер носит, 78, 104
Собаке – собачья смерть, 104
Собачье Сердце, 22
собачья жизнь, 93, 104
собачье сердце, 22
советская экономика, 179
советский человек, 40
советы, 21
совхоз, 178
согласие, 57
содрать, 182
созвонимся, 14, 35
созвониться, 135
сойти с дистанции, 74
солдат спит, а служба идёт, 69
солидно, 54
солидный, 23, 54
солнышко моё, 128
сольник, 146
соляк, 146
сообразить на троих, 156
сосиски сраные, 83
сотки, 133
сотня, сотенная, сотняга, 132
сотовые телефоны, 34
софт, 180
сохранить нынешний статус-кво, 57
социалистические страны, 83
спам, 180
спелый персик, 96
специалист по эйчар, 61
СПИД, 178
списывать, 182
справочная, 35
спросите чего полегче, 125
средняя продолжительность жизни, 120
срок мотать, 87
старик со старухой, 55, 168
Старик, ты сегодня в ударе, 10
Старики-разбойники, 117
Старичок Судачок, 105
старперы, 29
старый гриб, 99
стать мужчиной, 125
стейтсовый, 62
стипендия, 182
стипуха, 182
сто лет он мне не нужен / не приснился, 132
Сто пудов!, 133

Word & Phrase Index

сто, 132
столетие, 136
стольник, 39, 132
стольничек, 132
стопроцентный, 54
стопудово, 133
стопудовый хит, 133
стоять в очереди, 40
стоять на шухере, 86
стражи порядка, 46
стукачи, 86
сугробы, 77
судак, 105
сударыни, 24
Сударыни, больше растяните подмышечные впадины!, 24
сударыня, 20, 23
сударь, 20
судачить, 105
судьба, 135, 169
счастливые часов не наблюдают, 129, 142
Счёт, пожалуйста, 33
съедает рублёвые сбережения, 87
сын, 176
Так получилось, 169
так сказать, 163
Так шуми же мутная..., 106
Такой хоккей нам не нужен, 72
такси, 61
таксист, 39, 176
тамада, 157
Тамбовский волк тебе товарищ, 20
Таракан сидит в стакане..., 106
таракан, 106
тачка, 39
тащиться, 146
тащиться от Клинтона, 147
твёрдый, 54
твоими устами да мёд пить, 100
телефонное право, 34
телик, 62
тёмное освещение, 179
тен, 62
терпеть можно, 117
техосмотр {38}
тешатся, 175
тёща, 129, 154
То ли дождь – то ли снег, то ли будет – то ли нет, 76
товарищ, 20
товарка, 20
Тоже мне девушку нашёл?, 20
толстовщина, 143
толчковая нога, 75
тостующий пьёт до дна, 157
точно, 133
трагикомедия, 171
трактир, 32
требуйте долива после отстоя пены, 153
треска, 105
Третий Рейх, 59
Третьим будешь?, 156

трещать, 105
тридцатник {39}
триптих, 148
троечники, 182
тройка, 182
трояк, 182
трубы горят, 116, 160
трудятся как пчёлки, 99
трузера шузы, 62
Тульский пряник, 155
тусоваться, 129
тусовка, 129
туше, 64
тушёнка, 59
Ты мне друг или картошка?, 107
Ты настоящий мужик / парень, 10
ты не мужик, а тряпка, 125
Ты пойдёшь со мной на вечеринку?, 129
ты поправилась, 11
Ты сегодня выглядишь..., 10
Ты сегодня превзошёл самого себя, 10
Ты уже не мальчик, юный барабанщик, 125
Ты, ты-ты кинула, ты, 165
тыква, 108
Тьмы низких истин нам дороже нас возвышающий обман, 165
Тяжела ты, шапка Мономаха!, 85
тяжёлая атлетика, 74
тяжело в ученье – легко в бою, 85
тяжеловес, 88
тянуть время, 73
тянуть на себя одеяло, 85
У Вас не найдётся огоньку?, 119
У вас ещё лапша на ушах не обсохла, 174
У Вас сигареточки не будет?, 119
У вас тут такая катавасия!, 15
У кого толчковая – левая, а у меня толчковая – правая!, 75
У меня в кармане честная сотня..., 132
у меня голова раскалывается, 116
У меня голова трещит, 105
У меня есть девушка, 130
у меня пучит живот,, 140
У нас господ нет!, 24
У нас есть старинная русская забава – поиск виновных, 92
У нас такой умный пёсик..., 94
у него зимой снега не выпросишь, 76
у него рот до ушей, 171
У них не сложилось, 169

у президента крепкое рукопожатие, 89
У семи нянек дитя без глазу, 27, 134
У тебя вообще совесть есть или нет?, 167
У тебя есть девушка / молодой человек?, 130
у тебя ещё молоко на губах не обсохло, 174
убивать людей, 68
уборка, 25
Уважаемые пассажиры, не забывайте свой вещи, 38
уверенность в завтрашнем дне, 102
УВИР, 178
удалён с поля, 72
удаление, 72
удар ниже пейджера, 34
удар ниже пояса, 34, 71, 73
удача, 169
удовлетворительно, 182
уже седьмой час, 136
уживаться с, 120
узнать, где раки зимуют, 80
уйти в запой, 156
уйти, 88
укутан как капуста, 96
умно, 55
Умом Россию не понять, 150
упился медами, опохмелялся слезами, 159
Управление виз и регистраций, 178
устав, 68
уступите место женщине, 36
утка, 102
ухаживать за кем-то, 126, 129
участки, 99
ученье свет, а неученье тьма, 182
училка, 182
учительница, 182
Учиться военному делу настоящим образом, 70
учиться, учиться и учиться, 182
ушк, 175
уютный троллейбус, 179
файл, 181
файлец, 62
файфушник, 62
Факир был пьян – фокус не удался, 146
факир на час, 145
факс, 62
фактически, 54
факультативный, 65
фальстарт, 74
фанера, 146
фанерщик, 146
фатализм, 169
Федот – да не тот, 13
Федя-Бредя съел медведя, 12
феминистки, 25
Фефочка, скажи: ыыба, 105

фигурное катание, 71
фингал, 117
финишный рывок, 74
фиолетовый, 44
фирменное блюдо, 33
фифти-фифти, 137
фокусник, 145
фокус-покус, 146
форель, 105
форс-мажор, 65
форсмажорные
  обстоятельства, 64
форум, 180
фронтовые сто грамм, 133
фрицы, 59
фуэте, 64
фэйс, 62
хакер, 180
халатность, 83
халдей, 15
халтура, халтурить,
  халтурщик, 56, 169
халява, халявить, халявный,
  халявщик, 56, 168
хамство, 32
характеристика, 51, 160
хард, 182
хаханьки, 172
хватит разводить хиханьки да
  хаханьки, 171
Хенде Хох, 59
Хитрость – второй ум, 165
хитрость, 165
хитрый, 165
хиханьки, 172
хмырь, 15
хобот, 156
ходить за грибами, 98
ходить по бабам, 127
хозяин, 93
хозяйка, 25
холостяк, 125
Холостякуешь, 125
хомяк, 181
хороша Маша – да не наша, 12
хорошая зависть, 179
хороший, 57
хорошисты, 182
хорошо смеется тот, кто
  смеётся без последствий,
  172
хорошо смеется тот, кто
  смеется последним, 171
хорошо, 182
хотели как лучше, а
  получилось как всегда, 22
Хоть горшком назови, только
  в печку не ставь, 20
хоть на стенку лезь, 117
хохотун / хохотунья, 171
хочу – казню, хочу – милую,
  84
хрен редьки не слаще, 108
хрен с ним, 108
хрен, хреновина, хреновый,
  108

хренотень, 108
Христа ради, 49
хрюкать, 102
хрю-хрю, 102
хуже нет, чем ждать и
  догонять, 167
царапина, 117
Царская охота, 84
ценное указание, 177
Цирк – да и только, 145
цокать, 101
цок-цок, 101
ЦУ, 177
цыплёнок, 102
цып-цып-цып, 102
чаёвничать, 154
чаевые, 33
чай гонять, 154
Чай не водка – много не
  выпьешь, 140
Чай пить – не дрова рубить,
  154
чай с малиной, 117
Чайковский, 140
чайник, 38
часов в..., 136
частники, 39
Чего желаете?, 33
человек, 130
Человек в футляре, 143
человек-оркестр, 141
чем бы дитя не тешилось,
  лишь бы не плакало, 27
Чем меньше женщину мы
  любим, тем легче нравимся
  мы ей, 150
чёрная зависть, 45
Чёрная сотня, 133
черносотинцы, 133
Чернуха, 177
чёрные дни в истории, 45
чёрный, 45, 177
чёрный пиар, 60
чёрный юмор, 45
черпак, 68
черпать, 68
чёрт побери, 50
чёрта лысого ты получишь
  вместо денег, 50
чёртовой бабушке, 26
чертовски хороша, 50
чертяка, 50
чеснок, 107
Чеснок семь недугов изводит,
  107
Чеснок толчёный, да таракан
  печёный, 107
честный вор, 107
четвёрка, 182
четыре рулона в одни руки, 40
чешутся, 175
чик-чирик, 102
чирикать, 102
чифирь, 86
ЧК (Чрезвычайная комиссия),
  177

ЧП (чрезвычайное
  происшествие), 177
Чрезмерное употребление
  алкоголя вредит вашему
  здоровью!, 157
что вижу, то и пою, 166
Что дают?, 40
Что ему передать?, 35
Что за комиссия, Создатель,
  быть взрослой дочери
  отцом!?, 142
Что за петербуржство?, 112
Что ни город – то норов, 110
Что посеешь / посмеешь, то и
  пожнёшь, 174
Что станет говорить княгиня
  Марья Алексеевна?, 142
Что ты ворчишь, как старая
  бабка, 25
Что ты сияешь как самовар?,
  155
Что я тебе, мальчик?!, 125
Что, даже чаю не попьёте?,
  154
что, трубы горят?, 116
Что? Где? Когда?, 132
чтобы жизнь мёдом не
  казалась, 100
Что-нибудь из косметики, 163
что-нибудь из напитков, 33
Что-нибудь из одежды, 163
Что-то стало холодать – не
  пора ли нам поддать?, 155
чубайсизация страны, 22
чубайсята, 22
чувак, 21, 29
чувства, 64
чумовой медляк, 146
Шайбу! Шайбу!, 72
шампанское, 63
Шарик, 93
Шариков, 93
шариковщина, 93
швабра, 128
швейцар, 32
шедевр, 147
шёлк, 54
шерамыжник, 65
шерочка с машерочкой, 65
шестёрка, 86
шесть соток, 133
шеф {39}
шипеть, 102
шипучее вино, 63
шире шаг, 69
шить дело, 86
шишкинский лес, 148
шнапс, 59
Шнеллер!, 59
шоу, 61
шпаргалка, 182
шрамы украшают мужчину,
  117
шрапнель, 68
штраф, 37, 39
штука, 176

штурмовщина, 176
штучка, 176
шуба, 23
шут гороховый, 96
ш-ш-ш, 102
щенок на охоту ехать, – собак кормить, 93
Щепка, 78
щука, 55, 105, 168
щучить, 105
ЭВМ, 180
эйчаровец, 61
экономика должна быть экономной, 83
электронная вычислительная машина, 180
эскапады, 64
эстафета поколений, 75
Это актуальный вопрос, 54
Это всё ерунда / фигня по сравнению с мировой революцией, 21
это камень в мой огород?, 97
это не картошка, 107
Это не телефонный разговор, 10, 34
Это платье на тебе сидит, как влитое, 11
Это платье тебе очень идёт, 11
Это полная чушь, несуразица, сапоги всмятку, 91
Это полотно принадлежит, 147
Это чёрт знает что!, 50
Этот вопрос решается, 164
этюд, 148
эффект снежного кома, 77
Эх, жизнь моя жестянка – ну её в болото, 99
юмор – это когда страшно хочется смеяться..., 172
Я беру взятки, но борзыми щенками, 143
Я бы Вам столько не дал, 11
Я бы с ним в разведку пошёл, 10
Я был на седьмом небе от счастья, 133
Я Вам сам позвоню, 14
Я Вас выпущу, 37
Я Вас отблагодарю, 17
Я водяной – я водяной, 99
Я вообще не знаю, что там можно написать..., 92
я вчера перебрал, 159
Я ему, значит, говорю., 164
Я за вами, 40
Я клею её, 126
я лягу на рельсы, 89
Я могу это убрать / унести?, 33
Я на десять тыщ рванул, как на пятьсот, и спёкся, 74
я не волшебник, я ещё только учусь, 183
Я об этом мечтал всю свою жизнь, подарок моей мечты, 162
Я об этом узнал на днях, 136
Я отойду на минутку, 41
Я плачу, 33
я полагаюсь на Ваш вкус, 33
Я потерял кошелёк, 169
Я приглашаю Вас в ресторан, 33
Я прошу руки Вашей дочери, 127
Я с ребёнком, 17
Я сам обманываться рад, 167
я себя неважно чувствую, 116
я себя паршиво чувствую, 116
я себя погано чувствую, 116
Я сегодня гуляю, 33
Я сегодня прямо с корабля на бал, 142
я сильно извиняюсь, 58
Я собирался, но не получилось, 169
Я тебе в матери гожусь!, 20
Я тебе по-хорошему завидую, 179
Я хотел / хотела пригласить тебя в кино, 129
Я хочу, чтоб к штыку приравняли перо, 149
Я угощаю, 33
яблоко от яблочка недалеко падает, 27, 96
яйца курицу не учат, 183
яйцо всмятку, 91
Японский Бог {48}
Японский городовой! {48}

SUBJECT INDEX

1991 coup attempt, 177
A Man in a Case, 143
accents, 57
acronyms, 177
adjectival endings, 175
Aivazovsky, Ivan, 147
Alice in Wonderland, 105
Andropov, Yuri, 46
Animal Farm, 103
animals, 99, 101, 128
Anna Karenina, 143
anniversaries, 136
aphorisms, 174
apologies, 58
April Fool's Day, 171
arguments, 97
army, 68
art, 147
babushka, 25
bachelors, 125
backwardness, 51
bears, 99
beer, 152
bees, 100
Bender, Ostap, 44
Berezovsky, Boris, 72, 135, 141
birch, 51
Blackmore, Richie, 146
Blok, Alexander, 150
Bolsheviks, 21
Brezhnev, Leonid, 45, 46, 72, 82, 175
bribes, 17
Bulgakov, Mikhail, 22, 93
Buratino, 165
Bush, George H.W., 89
Bush, George W., 91, 155
Butov, Mikhail, 102
Carroll, Lewis, 105
cars, 38
Cartland, Barbara, 177
cats, 78
Chatsky, Alexander, 142
Chechnya, 89
Chekhov, Anton, 143, 156
Chernomyrdin, Viktor, 22, 88
Children of the Arbat, 177
children, 27, 132, 136, 182
Chubais, Anatoly, 22, 72
Churbanov, Yuri, 47
Cinderella, 183
cinema, 144
Circus, The, 145
Clinton, Bill, 48, 64, 146
cockroaches, 105
Cold War, 46, 54
cold, 79
colors, 44, 147
compliments, 10, 20, 54
computers, 180
con artists, 165
conjugation, 175
crayfish, 79
dachas, 98-9

Dal, Vladimir, 80, 107, 111, 137, 152
dating, 32, 97, 129
deception, 165
devil, 50
Diamond Arm, 50, 93, 104, 153
diminutives, 175
dining out, 32
doctors, 116
dogs, 93, 103, 104, 143
Don't Change the Meeting Place, 86
Dostoyevsky, Fyodor, 155
Double, The, 155
drinking, 133, 152, 155, 157, 159
drinking, 46, 62
driving, 38
Druz, Alexander, 132
Due to Family Circumstances, 105
Dylan, Bob, 78
Dzerzhinsky, Felix, 179
eating out, 32
economics, 87, 120
El Greco, 148
elections, 90
endearments, 99, 128
English, 61
etiquette, 162
euphemisms, 44, 60, 156
Evenings Near Moscow, 110
expletives, 48, 91
fairy tales & fables, 55, 103, 168
false friends, 54, 61
Family, The, 90
fatalism, 169
favors, 16
fifty, 136
fights, 14
filler words, 163
film, 144
firings, 88
fish, 105, 128
flattery, 10
flirting, 130
forms of address, 20, 23
freebies, 56, 168
French, 63
fruit, 96
Gaidar, Yegor, 120
gardening, 96
garlic, 107
Gentlemen of Fortune, 51, 85, 107, 144
Gerashchenko, Victor, 88
German, 58
gifts, 162
God, 49
Godunov, Boris, 84
Gogol, Nikolai, 143
Gorbachev, Mikhail, 13, 49, 57, 164, 177
Gorky, Maxim, 27, 167
gossip, 17
Grachev, Pavel, 14, 72

grades, 182
grammar, 57
greetings, 35
Griboyedov, Alexander, 142
Guns & Roses, 146
Gusinsky, Vladimir, 135, 149
hangovers, 157, 159
Harrison, George, 146
hazing, 68
health, 89, 116, 140
Heart of a Dog, 93
Hitler, Adolph, 58, 79
hockey, 72
honey, 100
horseradish, 108
human resources, 61
hundred, 132
idioms, 174
Inspector General, The, 143
insults, 15, 20
Internet, 180
invitations, 33
Itinerants, 148
Izmaylov, Leon, 154
jazz, 146
jokes, 171
Kafelnikov, Yevgeny, 96
Kamchatka, 182
Karamzin, Nikolai, 171
Khrushchev, Nikita, 12
Kiriyenko, Sergei, 88, 145
Kolyma, 85
Korzhakov, Alexander, 23
Kovalyov, Sergei, 63
Krylov, Ivan, 103, 141
Kustodiev, Boris, 148
Kutuzov, 79
labor camps, 85
laughter, 171
lazy people, 168
Lenin, Vladimir, 27, 82, 149, 175
Lermontov, Mikhail, 25
Lewinsky, Monica, 147
life expectancy, 120
Ligachyov, Yegor, 12, 89
lines, 40
lip synching, 146
literary allusions, 142
literature, 142
love, 126, 130, 174
Lower Depths, The, 167
Luzhkov, Yuri, 71, 110, 141
lying, 165
Lyube, 71
Makarevich, Sergei, 145
males, 124
marriage, 126, 129
Marx, Karl, 111
Mayakovsky, Vladimir, 149
medical care, 116
men, 25, 64, 124
metro, 37
Mikhalkov, Nikita, 148

Subject Index

military, 68, 70
minute, 135
mobile phones, 34
money, 39, 46, 87, 132, 176
Monomakh, Vladimir, 85
Moscow Does Not Believe in Tears, 51, 110
Moscow, 110, 111
Motyl, Vladimir, 166
movies, 144
mushrooms, 78, 98
music, 140, 146
Mussorgsky, Modest, 140
names, 12
Napoleon, 79
Nekrasov, Nikolai, 149
Nemtsov, Boris, 72
New Russians, 34, 162
nonsense phrases, 163
Okudzhava, Bulat, 71
Oleynikov, Nikolai, 106
oligarchs, 88, 72, 135, 141, 149
olympics, 71, 74, 82
Orlova, Lyubov, 145
Orwell, George, 103
Ostrovsky, Nikolai, 167
oxymorons, 179
Page, Jimmy, 146
pagers, 34
painting, 147
parents, 27, 132
payment, 39
pejoratives, 15
Peter the Great, 112
phone etiquette, 34
poets, 149
pogroms, 133
poor Russian, 14
popsa, 146
presidency, 89
prices, 120
Primakov, Yevgeny, 88, 104
Prince Vladimir, 152
prison, 85
privatization, 22
promises, 85, 166
propaganda, 149
prostitution, 46
proverbs, 174
public relations, 60
public transport, 36
Pugachyova, Alla, 82
Pushkin, Alexander, 25, 84, 126, 150, 165, 167, 177
Putin, Vladimir, 90, 91, 93, 133, 136, 155
putinisms, 91
queues, 40
rain, 78
reformers, 88, 134
restaurants, 32
revolution, 21
Robber Lads, 117
ruble, 87
running, 73
Rybakov, Anatoly, 177
Safin, Marat, 26

salaries, 10, 16
salespeople, 15
samovar, 153
school, 182
Scythians, The, 150
settling of accounts, 14
Seven Brides of Private First Class Zbruyev, The, 134
Seven Old Men and One Young Girl, 134
seven, 133
sex, 130
Shifrin, Efim, 148
Shishkin, Ivan, 148
Shostakovich, Dmitry, 106
Siberian Barber, 148
sickness, 140
skating, 71
slang, 28, 91
Sleeping Beauty, 140
smoking, 118
snow, 76
Sobchak, Anatoly, 22, 144
software, 180
soldiers, 68, 120
Solovki, 85
sounds, 102
sovietisms, 21, 27, 77, 82, 136, 153, 176, 177
Specific Traits of Russian National Hunting, 153
spies, 46
sports, 71, 73
spring, 77
St. Petersburg, 111
Stalin, Josef, 85, 99, 103, 144, 172
Star of Tempting Happiness, The, 166
Stepashin, Sergei, 141
stress, 57
sugar, 100
summits, 90
Susanin, Ivan, 166
Suslov, Mikhail, 45
Suvorov, Alexander, 70
Swan Lake, 140
swearing, 48-9
taxis, 39
Tchaikovsky, Pyotr, 140
tea, 140, 154
teases, 12
technology, 62, 180
teenagers, 28
telephone, 34
terms of endearment, 99, 128
tests, 183
thieves, 86
threats, 85
Three Sisters, 156
thunder, 78
Tikhonov, Vyacheslav, 82
Time Machine, 145
time, 135
toasts, 157
tobacco, 119
Tolstoy, Alexei, 165

Tolstoy, Leo, 143
track and field, 73
traffic police, 38, 178
trains, 37
translators, 54
tsars, 84
Tula, 153
Tyutchev, Fyodor, 78, 150
Van Gogh, Vincent, 26
vegetables, 96, 98, 107
vegetarianism, 107
verbs, 175
vodka, 159
voting, 90
Vyshinsky, Andrei, 103
Vysotsky, Vladimir, 73, 96, 118, 153
wages, 10
waiters, 15, 32
War of 1812, 65, 79
war, 70
weather, 76
winter, 76, 79
Woe from Wit, 142
wolves, 103-4
women, 10, 24, 32, 38, 47, 64, 97, 125, 129, 163
wordplay, 174
work, 56, 61
World War II, 58, 70, 73
writers, 149
Yastrzhembsky, Sergei, 89
Yeltsin, Boris, 12, 14, 49, 62, 71, 84, 89, 104, 134, 141, 145, 163
yeltsinisms, 89
Yevtushenko, Yevgeny, 52, 103, 149
Yezhov, Nikolai, 176
Zemfira, 166
Zhvanetsky, Mikhail, 120, 159
Zyuganov, Gennady, 49, 61

publications for
Russophiles

R.I.S. Publications

since 1990

Business Russian

A practical guide to learning the Russian you need for doing business in Russia! This essential text for the intermediate to advanced student is appropriate for either classroom or individual use. It is intensely practical, which means you'll not only learn important business vocabulary and usage, but also become knowledgeable about business operations, customs and behavior. Full of examples of documentation and contemporary conversations, this book includes chapters on important subjects like business travel, correspondence, exhibitions, negotiations, agreements and contracts, and formation of businesses. Includes a complete Russian-English business dictionary as well!

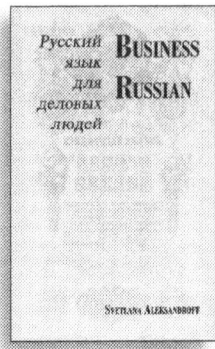

[**L501** • 182 pp. • softcover • **$16**]

Bilingual Wall Map

The first-ever map of Russia and the FSU using the latest in GIS mapping technology. Now in its second printing, this popular map is a highly accurate, crisp, clean and colorful guide to one-sixth of the Earth's surface. A unique feature of this map is that it is really two identical maps – on one side it is entirely in Russian, on the other entirely in English. It shows all population centers over 50,000 inhabitants (and most over 10,000), geographic features and administrative regions. Cities are indexed right on the map and there is an enlarged Moscow region map.

[**M660** • 3 ft. x 4 ft. (folds to 5" x 8.5") • **$10**]

To order, phone 800-639-4301 or visit www.russianlife.net

A Taste of Russia Cookbook

The definitive modern cookbook on Russian cuisine, layering superbly researched recipes with informative essays on the dishes' rich historical and cultural context. With over 200 recipes on everything from *borshch* to *blini*, from Salmon Coulibiac to Beef Stew with Rum, from Marinated Mushrooms to Walnut-Honey Filled Pies, *A Taste of Russia* shows off the best that Russian cooking has to offer. Full of great quotes from Russian literature about Russian food and designed in a convenient wide format that stays open during use.

[GB570 • 224 pages • $17.50]

"This is simply the best and most complete book on Russian cooking in English."
Suzanne Massie

22 Russian Crosswords

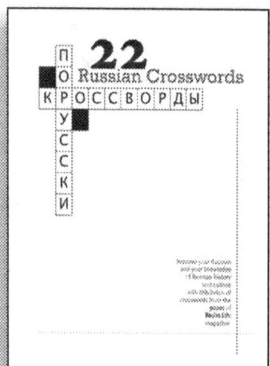

Test your knowledge of Russian as well as Russian history, culture and life with these 22 challenging crossword puzzles taken from the pages of *Russian Life*. All the clues are in English, but you must fill in your answers in Russian. If you get stumped, of course all of the puzzles have answers printed at the back of the book.

[RC07 • 26 pp. • spiral-bound, 8½ x 11 • $10]

R.I.S. Publications • PO Box 567, Montpelier, VT 05601
802-223-4955 • fax 802-223-6105

Russian Life
SINCE 1956

Russian Life is a bimonthly trip into the heart of Russian reality. It is a colorful, informative trip to the land of tsars and commisars. A balanced, thoughtful look at life as it is being lived in Russia today – the Russia you won't read about in your local or national paper or newsmagazine!

Enjoying a 50-year publication history, Russian Life offers a unique view on the life, history and society of Russia – as seen from Russia.

It is some of the best writing about Russia – the world's largest country – available today!

History... Art... Travel... Politics... Business... Culture... Music...

And more!

Subscribe to Russian Life for just $33 – 30% off the normal newsstand price! Plus, mention this ad and get a FREE 3' x 4' Bilingual Wall Map of Russia

To get your first taste of Russian Life, use the order form below, or call or visit our secure website. We look forward to having you join the discriminating readership of Russian Life!

BIMONTHLY.
FULL COLOR.
INDEPENDENT.

Three ways to subscribe today risk free:
- ❑ rip out this ad and **mail** it with your $33 payment ($38 for delivery outside the US) to: Russian Life, PO Box 567, Montpelier, VT 05601.
- ❑ **phone** 800-639-4301 (802-223-4955 outside North America)
- ❑ visit our **website**: www.russianlife.net

SUBSCRIBE

Name..
Address...
City........................... State .... Zip/Postal Code ....
Country ....
Email..
SR2

www.ingramcontent.com/pod-product-compliance
Lightning Source LLC
Chambersburg PA
CBHW071227080526
44587CB00013BA/1529